Information Systems Project Management

Pearson Education

We work with leading authors to develop the
strongest educational materials in management information systems,
bringing cutting-edge thinking and best learning
practice to a global market.

Under a range of well-known imprints, including
Financial Times Prentice Hall, we craft high quality
print and electronic publications which help
readers to understand and apply their content,
whether studying or at work.

To find out more about the complete range of our
publishing, please visit us on the World Wide Web at:
www.pearsoneduc.com

Information Systems Project Management

Methods, Tools and Techniques

John McManus

and

Trevor Wood-Harper

 Prentice Hall

FINANCIAL TIMES

An imprint of **Pearson Education**

Harlow, England • London • New York • Boston • San Francisco • Toronto • Sydney • Singapore • Hong Kong
Tokyo • Seoul • Taipei • New Delhi • Cape Town • Madrid • Mexico City • Amsterdam • Munich • Paris • Milan

Pearson Education Limited
Edinburgh Gate
Harlow
Essex CM20 2JE

and Associated Companies throughout the world

Visit us on the World Wide Web at:
www.pearsoneduc.com

First published 2003

ISBN: 0 273 64699 0

British Library Cataloguing-in-Publication Data
A catalogue record for this book is available from the British Library

Typeset in 9.25/13 Stone Serif by 68
Printed and bound by Bell & Bain Limited, Glasgow

CONTENTS

PREFACE

It is a statement of fact that project management has gone through a major culture change, as fundamental as the introduction of the first software management method-ologies in the 1970s. So what does information systems project management mean to professionals and students where project management is seen as mission critical? According to the Association of Project Managers (APM) more and more organizations are employing project management, either as they adopt a management-by-project's approach or because they are already performing mainstream project management activities. They are looking for project management standards and seeking confirm-ation that individuals working in project management are competent in this field. In writing this book the authors were motivated by the need for a book which bridged the gap between what is project management and how project management relates to the world of information systems. To this end the book endeavours to balance both the theory of project management and how this theory actually relates to those working in the professional field delivering software projects.

The authors intended this book either as a tutorial and reference source for the pro-fessional, or as a one- or two-term postgraduate reading book in colleges or univers-ities for those working in the field of information systems but also studying project management. In presenting the core subject matter consideration was given to the APM model as a basis for writing the material. The four key areas defined within the model are:

1. Project management
2. Organization and people
3. Techniques and procedures
4. General management

Table P.1 highlights chapter dependencies against the subject matter. Not all subjects within a key area have been covered in this book, specifically those topics concerned with General management. The authors believe that with the exception of Quality those subjects are outside the scope of this book.

Table P.1 *Information Systems Project Management* – chapter dependencies for APM's subject matter

UK Project Management Body of Knowledge	What's covered in this book (chapter guide)	Notes
Project Management		
1.1 Systems Management	Chapters 3 and 4	Ethos of book runs through
1.2 Programme Management		Not covered in this book
1.3 Project Management	Chapters 1 and 2	Ethos of book runs through
1.4 Project Life Cycle	Chapter 3	
1.5 Project Environment	Chapter 1	
1.6 Project Strategy	Chapter 4	
1.7 Project Appraisal		Implicitly covered in Chapter 1
1.8 Project Success/Failure Criteria	Chapter 1	
1.9 Integration		Not covered in this book
1.10 Systems and Procedures	Chapter 1	See section Written description of procedures
1.11 Close-out	Chapter 4	See section on PRINCE – project closure
1.12 Post Project Appraisal	Chapter 1	Refer to section on Lessons learned
Organization and People		
2.1 Organization Design	Chapter1	
2.2 Control and Coordination		
2.3 Communication	Chapter 2	
2.4 Leadership	Chapter 2	
2.5 Delegation	Chapter 2	Refer to section on Project organization
2.6 Team Building	Chapter 2	
2.7 Conflict Management	Chapter 1	
2.8 Negotiation		Not covered in this book
2.9 Management Development		Not covered in this book
Techniques and Procedures		
3.1 Work Definition	Chapter 4	See Methods of planning
3.2 Planning	Chapter 4	See Methods of planning
3.3 Scheduling	Chapter 4	See Project scheduling
3.4 Estimating	Chapter 5	
3.5 Cost Control	Chapter 5	
3.6 Performance Measurement	Chapter 5	
3.7 Risk Analysis and Management	Chapter 5	
3.8 Value Management		Not covered in this book
3.9 Change Control	Chapter 4	
3.10 Mobilisation	Chapter 4	See section on PRINCE

Table P.1   Continued

General Management

4.1	Operations/Technical Management	Not covered in this book
4.2	Marketing and Sales	Not covered in this book
4.3	Finance	Not covered in this book
4.4	Information Technology	Not covered in this book
4.5	Law	Not covered in this book
4.6	Procurement	Not covered in this book
4.7	Quality	Chapter 6
4.8	Safety	Not covered in this book
4.9	Industrial Relations	Not covered in this book

ABOUT THE AUTHORS

John McManus is a practising manager, speaker, teacher and consultant and author in the fields of strategy, project management, software development, business reengineering, total quality management, and change management. A senior manager, John has 15 years' front-line software, project, and general management experience. He has managed the development of a variety of software projects, utilizing Rapid Application Development, Structured Software Analysis Design Method, PRINCE and other software led project methodologies. He has managed large project teams and is responsible for providing independent assessments on numerous software projects. He is a Fellow of the Royal Society, a professional member of the British Computer Society, a Chartered Software Engineer and holds degrees from Manchester and London Universities. His books include *Competitive Strategies for Service Organisations*, *How to Reengineer Your Business*, *The Role of the Project Manager and Resisting Change*. In addition to his books he has authored numerous journal papers which have been translated into French, German and Japanese.

Trevor Wood-Harper is Professor of Information Systems and Director of the Information Systems Research Centre (ISRC) at the Information Systems Institute, in the faculty of Business and Informatics, University of Salford, Manchester, UK. He is also Visiting Professor of Management Information Systems at the University of South Australia, Adelaide and held visiting chairs at the University of Oslo, Copenhagen Business School and Georgia State University. Trevor has co-authored 11 books and monographs and over 140 research articles on a wide range of topics including the multiview methodology, software maintenance, electronic commerce, action research, business process reengineering, ethics in systems development, fundamentals of information systems and doctoral education. Currently he is researching into information systems methodologies for business process reengineering and total quality management.

AUTHORS'
ACKNOWLEDGEMENTS

The authors would like to acknowledge the help of many people who gave suggestions, material and assistance in producing this book. The most prominent amongst these were Sid Holmes, Ellen Teague, Russ Finney, Nigel Murkitt, David Watson, Karl E. Wiegers, Johanna Rothman, Gen F. Hoffnagle and Peggy Cargiulo. We are also grateful for the contribution and help received from Paul Bocij and the editorial staff at Pearson Education, especially Jacqueline Senior. Several colleagues of John McManus also provided valuable comments: they include Stuart Smith, John Starkie, Dan Trindell, Mark Wright, Pero Kalugerovich, Lee Foster, Sally Wilson, Neville Jennings, Peter Cummings, Don Carver, Jenny Patient and Neil Flinn.

John McManus
Trevor Wood-Harper

INTRODUCTION

Although a large number of texts deal with project management as a whole, few – if any – focus on the management of information systems (IS) projects. Whilst many of the functions served by an IS project manager are comparable with those served by project managers in other fields, few texts acknowledge the subtle – and sometimes not so subtle – differences that make the IS project manager's role unique. This book attempts to redress the balance by focusing on the role of a person appointed to manage an IS project.

As practitioners in the field will agree, the management of an information technology project brings with it a range of problems and challenges. In other fields, a sound knowledge of project management techniques and the ability to deal with people is often sufficient to bring most projects to a successful conclusion. In the world of information systems, however, project managers require a far broader range of skills. In addition to displaying a high degree of technical competence, managers must also display a wide range of social skills, such as an ability to motivate staff, handle group conflict and communicate with users at all levels in the organization. An ability to handle administrative functions is also required, from producing cost estimates, to taking part in quality audits.

The overall theme of the book is the question of what makes a 'good' project manager. The book examines this question from a number of different perspectives. Early chapters, for example, focus on the skills, knowledge and personal qualities needed to become an effective project manager. Later chapters look at how managers should handle individual aspects of a development project, such as scheduling and quality.

An important element of the text is its focus on many of the practical issues associated with the management of projects. In addition to providing the theoretical knowledge needed by students and practitioners, the text also provides a wealth of practical advice and guidance. Some of this guidance is provided in the form of checklists that can be used to monitor tasks as they are carried out. Additional guidance and advice is drawn directly from the experience of the authors and other practitioners.

Much of the research in the area of IS project management has been carried out in the United States. Whilst the text acknowledges the contribution of American academics and practitioners in this field, the content of the book is presented in a form suited to UK and European readers. This means that traditional approaches and methods are presented in parallel with those techniques used across the European Union. As an example, in discussing quality procedures, the text looks at three major models: the Capability Maturity Model, TickIT and the ISO 9000 framework. Of these, the first is popular in the United States, the second is unique to the United Kingdom, and the third is used across the whole of Europe.

Students and practitioners should find that the content of the text follows a natural progression and has a logical structure. The following list provides an overview of the content of the book.

- Chapter 1 provides an introduction to IS project management by examining how changes in global markets have caused organizations to adopt new structures. One of the structures to emerge as a result of these changes is the project organization, a structure intended to encourage and support small project groups. The chapter also considers some of the factors that contribute to the success or failure of a project, such as unresolved group conflict and poor planning.
- Chapter 2 poses the question: what makes a *good* project manager? The material examines the role of a project manager in terms of tasks, knowledge, competencies and personal skills. Some of the topics covered include approaches to decision making, managerial styles, leadership skills, the nature of power and the importance of staff motivation.
- Chapter 3 looks at common approaches to software development. The material discusses a range of approaches and techniques, including the waterfall method, the spiral method, Rapid Applications Development, Joint Applications Development, Dynamic Systems Development Method and Soft Systems Methodology. An emphasis is placed on object oriented development since this offers a large number of benefits. The concept of a tool set model is also introduced as a technique for selecting development tools.
- Chapter 4 builds on the material presented in Chapter 3 by looking at the management of large software development projects. The material concentrates on the typical life cycle of a project, examining each stage in detail. Approaches towards planning, scheduling and reporting are discussed in depth. The PRINCE approach to project management is used to highlight examples of good practice and illustrate many of the points discussed. The final part of the chapter introduces the concept of configuration management as a means of controlling the assets that belong to a project.
- Chapter 5 is concerned with estimating cost and managing risk. Techniques for estimating cost are examined in depth and a number of examples are provided. The COCOMO model is introduced as a technique for estimating cost and Function Point Analysis is introduced as a technique for estimating the size and complexity of projects. The final part of the chapter looks at risk management and describes approaches towards dealing with problems that arise during the life of a project.
- Chapter 6 is devoted to an examination of issues related to quality. An introductory section defines the concept of quality and discusses the major

characteristics associated with software quality. Three major quality frameworks are discussed in depth: the Capability Maturity Model, the ISO 9000 framework and the TickIT scheme.

The text is appropriate for several groups of readers:

- Practitioners will gain a sound understanding of the approaches and techniques used in the management of information systems projects.
- Postgraduate students will find that the text provides much of the background information needed to follow courses such as those offered by the IPM. In addition, they will find that the text serves as an invaluable source of reference.
- Undergraduate students will gain an understanding of the role of the project manager and the complexity involved in managing large projects.

A number of student features have been incorporated into the text in order to make the material covered more accessible to readers. Each chapter begins with a brief introduction and a set of specific learning objectives. Similarly, each chapter ends with a summary of the key points that have been discussed. All chapters are accompanied by a variety of self-assessment tasks, including short answer questions and discussion questions. A comprehensive case study, together with appropriate questions, is also included at the end of each chapter. In addition, as mentioned earlier, a number of checklists appear throughout each chapter. These checklists provide practical advice and highlight important points for readers to consider.

General and useful information sources

http://www.pmi.org/publictn/pmjournal/
The *International Journal of Project Management* is the professional journal of the Project Management Institute. It is published quarterly and available to all members.

http://www.projectnet.co.uk/pm/pmt/pmt.htm
Project Manager Today is the leading project magazine seen each month by some 15,000 managers. It provides monthly news and views about project management together with case studies, in-depth articles and software reviews.

http://www.geocities.com/Athens/Delphi/8390/
Project Management Help Desk
The PMHD was founded to provide assistance to the international project management community and promote PM fundamentals.

CHAPTER 1

The challenge within information systems project management

Introduction

This introductory chapter considers the modern business environment and its impact on organizations involved in the information technology industry. Changes in global markets have caused many organizations to adopt new structures so that they can compete more effectively and achieve more consistent success with the projects they undertake.

One of the issues covered by the material is the emergence of project-based organizational structures that support the efforts of small project groups. However, whilst such structures offer many benefits, they require the support of the entire organization in order to be truly effective. In addition, project managers are required to employ their knowledge and skills to the full in order to deal with potential problems, such as internal conflict.

Although the chapter covers a great deal of ground, the material is linked together by an underlying theme. The central purpose of the chapter is to highlight the wide range of factors that contribute to the success of a project. Perhaps more importantly, attention is also given to why some projects fail.

Learning objectives

Some of the topics covered include:

- The changing nature of the global marketplace and how organizations have adapted to these changes.
- The nature of the project organization.
- How organizational structure influences approaches to project management.
- How conflict arises within groups and how to deal with it.

At the end of this chapter, students will be able to:

- Explain the changes that have taken place within the global marketplace and how these have affected organizations.
- Identify and explain common factors likely to improve the way in which projects are managed.
- Identify and explain common factors associated with the failure of information systems projects.
- Identify and explain common factors associated with the successful completion of information systems projects.
- Explain how conflict may arise within project groups and identify approaches that can be used to resolve such conflicts.
- Examine the structure of an organization, identifying some of the strengths and weaknesses apparent in that structure.
- Apply the concept of a project organization in terms of how such a structure can improve the way in which projects are managed.

Observations on project management

In the early 1990s, the global and domestic markets for software and related information technology markets were seen as relatively stable and predictable. Today's markets are characterized by rapid change, increased competition and faster response and greater flexibility in terms of meeting differing customer requirements. In order to meet the challenges of these new markets, many organizations have begun to redefine themselves. Such redefinition is characterized by the language of down-sizing, reengineering and process management, where classic vertical structures with emphasis on task and functional planning are being superseded by new customer-focused, people-based 'Management by Projects'. Each year, US businesses manage approximately 175,000 information technology projects for developing and maintaining applications and systems. These projects have an estimated cost of more than $250 billion each year. Consequently, delivering value-for-money software projects is a *key challenge* for many organizations.

Management by projects is responsive to customer requirements, and as such is focused on gaining competitive advantage through people. Unlike other industries, competitive advantage is not generated through products or services since it has been recognized that these can be easily copied, substituted or superseded. Instead, an emphasis is placed on *people, skills, knowledge* and the ability to manage relationships with colleagues, customers and suppliers. Underpinning this culture is a strong emphasis on:

- strong information systems project managers, with superior systems and commercial skills;
- effective project management teams;
- good project management procedures and practices;
- rigorous project control methodologies; and
- administrative systems that support the project organization.

It is a fact that project management in most information technology organizations currently ranges from undisciplined to chaotic. Few organizations have the infrastructure, education, training, or management discipline to bring projects to successful completion. Research indicates that more than half of all information technology projects become runaways – overshooting their budgets and timetables while failing to deliver on their goals. Approximately 25 per cent end up so out of control that the project is killed outright before completion. This level of inefficiency is costing pan-European business billions of pounds each year. Some evidence to support this view comes from a survey undertaken by KPMG in the United Kingdom in 1997. The survey covered 120 organizations and included sectors such as manufacturing, distribution, retail, oil and gas. The results of the survey suggested that 62 per cent of the organizations questioned had experienced at least one runaway project. A runaway project was defined as a major project that had not achieved original objectives or one which had exceeded original budgets by at least 30 per cent. When asked about the response the company had made or was making to the problem of runaway projects, 84 per cent of the respondents said the company was resolved to improve project management in the future, with 55 per cent looking externally for improved project management. This goes some way to explaining recent growth in project outsourcing, estimated as being worth some $2.2 billion in 1998 (source: ITNet 1997).

Table 1.1 summarizes some of the causes of runaway projects. The values given show the percentage of organizations that cited a given factor as contributing to the project becoming a runaway. As can be seen, the majority of the problems experienced can be attributed to poor project management.

Table 1.1 Six top causes of runaway projects

	Percentage
1. Project objectives not properly specified	52
2. Bad planning and estimating	49
3. Technology new to organization	45
4. Inadequate project management methodology	42
5. Insufficient senior staff on team	42
6. Poor performance by hardware/software suppliers	42

The price of failure

In traditional software projects self-deception is a prominent characteristic of system failure. In other words, understanding what the customer wants is crucial to any successful system development project. Put simply, everyone's efforts are wasted if the product produced is not what the customer needs.

In the last decade a significant number of project failures have been reported. Some examples include the £125 million CONFIRM Travel reservation system, the £45 million failure of the Californian department of motor vehicles project and Florida's bungled attempt to automate its state benefits system. In the United Kingdom similar failures include the following:

- A £16.5 million project to computerize the Inland Revenue returns process.
- In 1993 the London Stock Exchange terminated its automated share settlement system at a cost of £75 million. Taking into consideration the Taurus debacle, this figure grows to £500 million.
- The 17-year project to automate the Department of Social Security in 1997 was deemed to be over budget by 400 per cent.

Research indicates, for projects that fail, there is a tendency to jump to the implementation phase as quickly as possible and put through a Return On Investment (ROI) validation.[1] This is due to project sponsors and information technology management believing that due diligence and planning represent unwarranted delays and wanting to see concrete progress as soon as possible. Over the next few years, organizations will increasingly implement a pre-launch phase, designed to shape the loosely stated ideas of project sponsors into a clear articulation of the real business problem and a comprehensive definition of the project's objectives, cost/benefits, and agreed-upon roles and responsibilities.

The pre-launch phase should include the production of a project-based, service-level agreement which includes the business justification, an outline for the overall approach, rough-cut resource estimates (skills/personnel, cash), a summary of risks and the approach to managing risk. The Meta Group believes that many organizations will equate project size with risk and only develop service-level agreements for larger (say more than 20-person month) projects.

Ewusi-Mensan and Przasnyski, from the College of Business Administration at Loyola Management University in Los Angeles, observed that few organizations seem to learn from their mistakes. They discovered that 60 per cent of organizations surveyed in the United States had terminated more than one project for the same reasons. Perhaps more disturbing is that 70 per cent of these organizations failed to keep any records of their failed projects. Research carried out in 1984 by Professor Albert Lederer of Oakland University in the US highlights a number of key symptoms in the failure to deliver information technology systems.

In the authors' experience such symptoms are characteristic of projects with centralized structures and vertical command chains – where business and technology are moving twice as fast as information systems developments. Add to this the actuality that some managers are afraid to grapple with the great unknown that information technology represents and it is not too difficult to appreciate why projects fail. When a project goes wrong it is all too easy to hide behind the old 'information technology strategy wasn't aligned with the business' excuse. True, this can be a problem but it is rarely the only reason as Lederer has pointed out. Table 1.2 draws on Lederer's work to summarize some of the symptoms associated with the delivery of a poor information system.

Since Table 1.2 highlights a number of interesting and important factors, it is worth examining the items listed in more detail.

1. Frequent requests for changes by users

The undermining and failure of many projects is associated with development scope creep. Project managers need to rigorously monitor requests for changes. Each request should be logged (who, what, when, why and what is affected) and assessed for impact on time and cost. It is important to remember who the sponsor is and what his objectives are – managers should check with the sponsor first before changing anything significant. It is perhaps worth pointing out that the complexity of change increases as:

- the number of parallel baselines to be supported increases;
- the number and geographical distribution of development teams expand;

Table 1.2   Symptoms of poor information systems delivery

1. Frequent requests for changes by users
2. Users' lack of understanding of their own requirements
3. Overlooked tasks
4. Insufficient communication
5. Poor or imprecise requirements definition
6. Lack of adequate methodology and guidelines for estimating
7. Lack of coordinating of systems development
8. Changes in information systems development personnel
9. Insufficient time for testing
10. Lack of preparation
11. Poor business strategy alignment

- the volume of code increases;
- the number of change requests rises;

These factors lead to a range of additional problems, including:

- problems in propagating changes across baselines;
- high communication overhead;
- uneven levels of skill against development teams; and
- loss of control and visibility into the change cycle.

At least some of these problems can be resolved through the provision of high quality training. In a general sense, all organizations benefit from access to a highly trained and skilled workforce. However, ensuring that staff keep existing skills up to date and are encouraged to acquire new skills is of particular importance in the context of development projects. As an example, if a key member of a development team becomes unavailable (perhaps through illness), a project might suffer a series of awkward and expensive delays. However, if some of that person's duties can be performed by other members of the team, then at least some of the delay can be avoided.

2. Users' lack of understanding of their own requirements

Using staff with pure information technology knowledge is fine if such personnel have an in-depth understanding of the business process, However, many projects have a strategic angle which is not always understood by users. This can result in poor business definitions.

3. Overlooked tasks

If project personnel do not keep careful records of previous projects, they tend to forget about the less visible tasks. Unfortunately, those tasks add up in terms of time and cash. Omitted effort often adds about 25 per cent to a development project.

4. Insufficient communication

Project delivery requires cooperative effort, good communications and early warning systems. Project managers need to keep users aware of what is going on at all times. They should also be the person who tells users first of any changes in the schedule or plan. The project sponsor should be consulted before things are put into action. Project managers who 'blindside' their sponsors will be treated in kind and will lose their integrity.

Some information systems project managers take a very clear approach; people should know what information is required of them, and if they fail to give it accurately, they are punished. One way of making this happen is by cross-checking the information that is given. This is necessary at times, but it can be counter-productive. If someone knows that their work is being cross-checked, they may not put a great deal of effort into providing accurate answers to the questions asked of them. The person may also feel angered at an apparent lack of trust and may even go out of their way to be untrustworthy.

Another favoured approach is to ask for information in writing. This has the same drawbacks as cross-checking, with the added one that people will not usually be willing to give as much information in writing as they would verbally. It is more productive, after being given some information, to send the giver a memo, which summarizes what was said. This serves to check the accuracy of communication and to remind them of any commitments they have given. In general, managers tend to agree that the most important part of handling information as an information systems project manager involves keeping minutes for everything. If a meeting is not worth minuting, it was not worth having. The use of informal minutes for meetings prevents confusion.

5. Poor or imprecise requirements definition

Some projects have more requirements than they need, right from the very start. For example, performance is stated as a requirement more often than it needs to be and can unnecessarily increase a project's time horizon. Many of the time and cost over-runs in systems development can often be traced to what is known as the semantic gap (or rework cycle). Excessive undiscovered rework might take many forms in the case of a development project, including redesign, re-negotiation of user requirements and, in extreme cases, closedown of the project. Its undisputed affect is a loss of productivity, which makes it difficult to predict project costs. Figure 1.1 shows the relationship between planned and non-planned work.

6. Lack of adequate methodology and guidelines for estimating

Many projects overrun because of poor estimates. Obtaining good estimates is a prerequisite – estimates will not lower costs but will improve the chances of winning business. There is evidence to suggest that a tried and tested estimating process aids business reputation. Research leads us to believe that project negotiations are significantly enhanced when estimates are easily understood, developed via a demonstrable process and their basis is well founded. For accomplished information systems project managers, estimates will become the basis for scope negotiation. In the absence of solid support for project estimates, we believe most information systems project managers will have few alternatives aside from acquiescing to unattainable expectations. From a

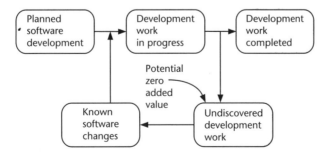

Figure 1.1 Inference diagram planned v non-planned work

cultural perspective, organizations must be prepared to walk away from a project rather than commit to unrealistic dates or budgets.

7. Lack of coordinating of systems development

Some developers think that fast and loose development is a route to quick delivery. This is incorrect since development accounts for a significant percentage of the project pie. Careful control of development is essential. A lot of the answers that are given to project managers attempting to monitor and control the projects they are responsible for amount to little more than playing for time (Sims, 1993, p. 19). We believe that at some future point we will have either the time or the knowledge that we now lack. Meanwhile we may put off the problem by giving an answer that is designed to distract the manager with some other issue. This can be thought of as more misdirection than misinformation. Sometimes, an answer may be designed to show that a particular part of a project is not worth proceeding with for the present. Putting off the problem may be very sensible since the problem may go away. It is common to be hassled for information about something, which the information systems project manager then forgets, without any apparent consequences. Project managers can save an enormous amount of time and energy by building up expertise in recognizing which problems are going to go away and which ones will not.

8. Changes in information systems development personnel

A common source of aggravation in software projects arises from people, but this is rarely admitted. Project managers should always try to negotiate resources up-front. Personnel changes (for whatever reason) part way through a project are clearly not desirable.

9. Insufficient time for testing

Failure to leave enough time for testing exposes the project to unnecessary risk. Applications development projects typically overrun their schedules, so it is common for testing to be squeezed into a few days instead of weeks. Roll-out depends on testing. Knowing something will work never takes the place of proving that it will.

10. Lack of preparation

Many project management implementations focus on teams and devote little time and few resources to preparing the project sponsors and business partners for their part in the project. It is assumed that they will know their roles and understand the required project management techniques. By providing some education and training that orientates management, a higher level of understanding and commitment can be achieved. This approach also helps solve the dilemma of what level of senior management involvement is required – the answer is very little if they understand the information that is generated and the purpose of the techniques being used. Following their orientation, formal management commitment must be gained and communicated throughout all levels of organization. One approach is formally to sign off all implementation documents and have management give presentations on what they have signed off.

11. Poor business strategy alignment

It is usual for projects to show a return on their investment before being sponsored and investment is usually linked to shareholder returns. Business benefits will usually not be realized without strategic alignment of projects. There should be a demonstrable connection from the strategic plan, through the investment plan, to the projects that are undertaken. The focus or priority of the strategic plan will provide the direction for the investment plan and the basis for the definition of strategic objectives. The process of assessment will establish whether each project that is undertaken should be mapped to one or more strategic objectives. It should be remembered that projects with poor strategic alignment have a history of being abandoned sooner or later.

Lessons learned

Our heroes have always been cowboys – many organizations still deliver successful software projects but product delivery and success depend on star programmers, fire fighters and heroics. In other words, project performance is predicted by individual capability, not organizational capability. A recent paper argued that few lessons had been learnt by organizations engaged in project management development activities (Vowler, 1995, p. 14). Quoting Professor Manny Lehman of Imperial College, London:

> Development is neither easy nor certain. There's been a lot of progress in software process improvement and we can develop systems that are up to twice an order of magnitude larger and more complex than we could 20 years ago. Yet we still see a trail of disasters and overruns.

Lehman has identified a number of agencies that participate in the delivery of software projects including the corporate head office, quality control, user support, marketing and project management. All of these agencies have an impact on the process of delivering projects. One of the key lessons that needs to be passed on is the importance of continuous feedback to each of the participating agencies. In particular, details of any mistakes made should be shared early on. There is a view that mistakes are acceptable but failure is not. Failure is considered a mistake that cannot be recovered from. It is therefore important to create contingency plans and alternate approaches for products that have high risk.

The important thing to remember, whether a project succeeds or fails, is to carry out project reviews. Valuable information and insights can be gained from an effective review process and these will help improve control of future projects. Such reviews do not have to be complex: a few simple, pointed questions can reveal areas of weakness. Table 1.3 lists some general questions that might be asked when reviewing a project.

It should be noted that the fact that one project is deemed a success and another is not may not mean that the first project was better managed. As an example, in the case

Table 1.3 Some practical project review questions

Was the purpose of the project (or end product) clearly defined?
Were success criteria defined?
Was management commitment gained at the outset?
Were procedures for control established and followed?
Did those involved support the project team?
Was a project management team in charge?
Did they have the right skills and sufficient experience?
Did they have the right authority?
Were they given enough time for managing?
Were plans produced?
Were they at the right level?
Were they updated and used as working documents?
Were they realistic?
Was reality documented?
Were planned deadlines/effort/budget met?
Were appropriate tools used?

of an apparent project failure, it might be found that the information systems project manager had an impossible task and that by exercise of a high level of management skills the delays and over-expenditure were minimized. Alternatively, in an apparently successful project, it might be found that the time and cost targets may have had contingency and could be achieved with a very low level of managerial input. Comparisons of relative project performance must therefore not be made simply on the achievement or non-achievement of their time and cost targets or profiles. It is the perceived success or failure by all the parties concerned that is important, and it must be viewed in the light of the circumstances affecting each project.

Factors affecting project success

Baker, Murphy and Fisher studied 650 projects in the US and highlighted a number of factors which contributed to the success of a project (Baker, Murphy and Fisher, 1983). The factors identified are:

1. Project commitment to:
   – established schedules;
   – established budgets; and
   – technical performance goals.
2. Frequent feedback from parent organization.
3. Frequent feedback from client.
4. Client commitment to:
   – established schedules;
   – established budgets; and
   – technical performance goals.

5. Organization structure suited to project team.
6. Project team participation in determining schedules and budgets.
7. Parent commitment to:
   – established schedules;
   – established budgets; and
   – technical performance goals.
8. Parent enthusiasm.
9. Parent desire to build up internal capabilities.
10. Adequate control procedures, especially for dealing with changes.
11. Judicious use of networking techniques.
12. Minimal number of public/government agencies involved.
13. Lack of excessive government red tape.
14. Enthusiastic public support.
15. Lack of legal encumbrances.

Clearly the successful completion of a software project requires input from a variety of groups including the client, the project team, the parent organization, the producer and the end user. Each party has a role in defining and determining success. Each has specific tasks and responsibilities that must be fulfilled in order to achieve success. The client, for example, is expected to be concerned primarily about the success of the project in the long term. In most cases, the project is instigated at the request of the client, and the financial and other rewards for the client hinge on its successful implementation. The client cannot expect to abdicate responsibility by passing all duties to the project team. It has already been intimated that the team will be oriented towards objectives, which are only a subset of the overall aims of the project. The client must ensure that an emphasis on the subset does not threaten the achievement of the wider aims from which it is drawn. Facilitating the team is important for the client but, in the final analysis, the project is not instigated to facilitate the team. The project originates from a requirement to meet a need that exists for the client. That initial need must be kept in focus by all those involved in the project.

Contrasting the old and new organization

Organizational structures, decision-making processes and leadership practices are undergoing a transformation. This transformation comes in response to growing international competition and the impact on new technology. In addition, there is growing recognition that giving managers responsibility and the freedom to exercise initiative increases their motivation and energy. Organizations are starting to think of themselves not as a hierarchy of static roles, but as an interrelated portfolio of dynamic processes and projects, with small teams or units grown from bottom up. With this approach, the project team becomes the core of the business, leading and reinforcing the new way to work. For example, when the United States Postal Service Information Systems Service

Centers initiated a series of project management initiatives, it was because they faced extensive challenges in terms of their ability to meet clients' demands for performance and cycle time (Pritchard, 1998). Throughout Postal, there was an acute sense of the need to improve performance. An important factor in the efforts of the Postal Services was the awareness of management at a variety of the levels. From the Vice President for Information Systems, to the centre Directors, to the team members and their leaders, everyone knew there was an organizational need to conduct projects in a more cohesive, organized fashion. At the various levels within the agency, there were different interpretations of the need, but the need was universally recognized.

In one of the Regional Bell Operating Companies (RBOCs) in the US, a similar situation existed, but because of the nature and culture of the organization, the need was not universally recognized. To overcome that shortcoming, the project management champions in the organization arranged for a series of management briefings to explain the value of project management, both internally, and as a customer service and sales tool. Just as important as explaining the nature of project management, the briefings highlighted the need for consistent practices and the need for customer satisfaction. For many of the upper managers at the briefings, the insight on the needs was just as enlightening as the insight on project management practices (Pritchard, 1998).

These new-style project organizations have a much higher chance of succeeding in today's business environment of ferocious competition, rapid change, instability and global scope. The new organization totally differs in structure, form, processes and vitality. Figure 1.2 shows some of the contrasts between old-style and new-style organizations.

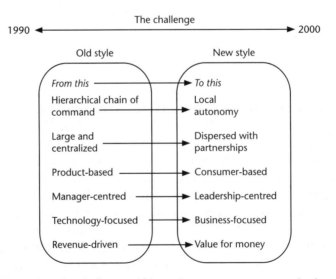

Figure 1.2 The challenge within project management organizations

Old-style organizations depended for success on a durable competitive advantage in a defined market, or localized and restricted competition. In contrast, new project organizations acknowledge that their product or service superiority will be short-term due to global competition and rapid technological change. Constant innovation and renewal are essential in maintaining uniqueness.

Old-style project organizations had well-defined boxes on an organization chart, and everybody knew exactly what each box meant. These organizations did not like people to do things outside of their boxes, because when people marched out of step it upset others trying to march in step (Abell, 1990). Consequently, these organizations enforced discipline through hierarchy and top-down management. Senior management set the rules, and the rest obeyed. The result, all too often, was a not-too-subtle interdiction of both initiative and personal responsibility. People did what they were supposed to do within the safety of their boxes, but not much more. Punishments for unsuccessful initiatives tended to outweigh rewards for successful ones, so initiatives were rare, and successful initiatives tended to become someone else's property. Responsibility was either collectivized, laid on the doorstep of a committee or shifted onto another department or individual.

In contrast, since the late 1990s, organizations have started to recognize the crucial importance of flatter structures and learning for competitive advantage, and are transforming themselves into project 'learning' organizations. IBM, for example, recognized early that large computer systems required a different business approach to small systems, and organized along product lines. But they didn't stop there. They decentralized responsibility by end-use market and geography as well. Separate organizational sub-units develop strategies and marketing to banks, local government, education and manufacturing, while other sub-units deal with marketing, sales and project delivery in each geographical region, each supported by their own project teams. The realization by organizations such as IBM is that most managers now need project management skills. Managing projects is no longer just for specialists in new flat organizations; it is a core skill.

A serious aspect of changing to a flatter and more participative project environment is the role of information systems project manager as perceived by themselves and others. This area is discussed in more detail in Chapter 2. If information systems project managers see themselves as only directing traffic, they may not be supportive of participative management initiatives. If they are expected to be involved in the process, it is vitally important that they have the support of their senior managers. Good information systems project managers are as important now as they have ever been, but the nature of their contribution has changed, and it will continue to change. Dr Myron Tribus (1989) offers the following opinion: 'that all personnel work within a system and that the job of any manager is to work on the system to improve it, continuously with the help of its staff.'

Project managers of today understand that people, their environment and the systems and processes that they work together with, are just as much a part of the product as the design, materials and service which the customer sees. Sometimes information systems project managers forget that the majority of business problems are more sociological then technical. Because projects are delivered through people, knowledge of how traditional management affects the motivation of system personnel is essential. Project managers must foster cooperation and teamwork, not conflict and competition. Conflict is a zero sum gain strategy; there is a winner and a loser. In broad terms the winner gains what the loser loses. With cooperation, however, we have a positive sum gain; a win-win strategy.

Structures and the project environment

Bureaucratic management, as illustrated in Figure 1.3, characterizes functional organizations, where decisions are made at the centre. Such structures are based on task specialization (one person – one job) which usually results in a low adaptive response both within the organization and within its environment. Authority is based on the manager–subordinate concept where subordinate management (level 4) authority is limited. Figure 1.3 is based upon a pyramid with four chains of command. In actuality there may, of course, be other functions and levels depending on the size of the organization and the complexity of the product(s) and technology employed. Structures such as this tend to be heavily centralized, i.e. major decisions are taken at the top either by the board or by the directors. In such circumstances senior management alone (i.e. level one and level two) are responsible for achieving the economic objectives of the organization. As functional organizations increase in size and complexity, problems arise: strain on the control and internal communication systems create physical and non-physical barriers which eventually lead to loss of performance and efficiency. Some of these barriers are listed in Table 1.4.

Functional organizations adhere too closely to the principles of specialization and such emphasis can become a weakness where technology, work roles and market

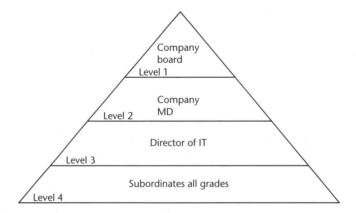

Figure 1.3 Example of a functional organization structure

Table 1.4   Physical and non-physical barriers in organizations

Poor internal communications (verbal and written)
Senior management – no feeling of mutual trust
No emphasis on team building
Poor employee morale – lack of employee motivation
Lack of information sharing ('need to know' mentality)
Lack of social responsibility
Lack of empathy with customers (internal and external)
Lack of employee empowerment
Quality and competence of decision makers
Lack of coherent infrastructure for employee development

requirements interact. What is needed is an organizational structure which exploits individual competency-based skills so that the organisation can deliver efficient, economic products and services of world class quality.

Research by Gobeli and Larson (1987) into project structures in the late 1980s found that, in between the functional organization and the dedicated project team, project organizations could be grouped into three versions of a matrix. Two versions of the matrix have variations of bias in the relative power and authority of the functional management and project management elements. Gobeli and Larson called these two variations a function matrix and a secondment matrix.

The significance of these structures is of great importance. Simply, incorrect project structures lead to frustration, low morale and poor motivation. It is essential to get the choice of structure as near to correct as possible. There is a tendency, once the need for formal project management is recognized, to rush into dedicated task teams. Although this provides several advantages, it also provides a number of disadvantages. Some of the advantages include singleness of purpose, a reduction in conflicting calls on resources, and improved security within the team of any confidential or secret information (Payne, 1993).

With regard to disadvantages, it is important to consider the composition of project teams. If a team is too small, specialist areas will have very little representation on the team. One resource alone is risky, since, if that person is sick or on leave, who will carry out his or her role? If approaches are made to the functional head for help, the new resource will have a long learning curve, which may even exceed the period of the requirement for the replacement. Should the specialist leave the organization, nobody will understand what he or she was doing, and the position is worse. In dedicated task teams, there is a tendency for the specialists to lose touch with their counterparts on other projects. This causes the loss of cross-fertilization of ideas, which normally occurs within a functional department. Specialists may fall behind with regard to the latest ideas that are not used on their project. This compounds the specialist's fears with respect to their career progression. They could also needlessly duplicate work on different projects.

If a project team is established as a dedicated task force, there are traditional problems that are related to the temporary nature of projects. Teams are characterized by short-term relationships, which are not the most conducive to quality performance. Writers such as Gilbreath (1988) write of the need to create networks of people who work together regularly, but not necessarily all on the same projects at the same time. However, he points out the following:

> The formation of ongoing networks that help to transcend artificial organizational barriers requires time and patience. Neither is bountiful in a project setting.

Another problem with the establishment of dedicated project task teams is the insecurity that exists within the project team as the project draws to a close. There is an inclination to continue the project, sometimes by looking for extra *loose ends* to complete as a way of maintaining employment because the future is uncertain. In this way, the project may overrun in both time and cost. When a dedicated team is disbanded, the question arises of who will be available to answer queries in relation to problems with a project that arise after its supposed completion. This is a particular problem when the projects are small and of short duration.

The matrix structural form shown by Figure 1.4 preserves the benefits of the functional department structure (such as information sharing and continuity), whilst enabling cross-functional coordination on a project basis. The matrix, however, is inherently unstable. The project-team member has two masters: his or her functional manager, and the information systems project manager. There is a tendency for a power struggle to develop between the functional manager and the information systems project manager for control of the staff member. Entrenched differences can be established between the two arms of a matrix, which can only be resolved by senior management intervention. This places an extra workload on senior management, making the adoption of a matrix structure bothersome.

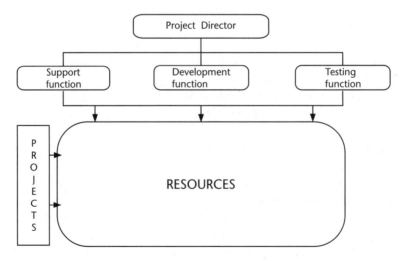

Figure 1.4 Example of a project matrix structure

The successful adoption of a matrix structure requires a mature approach from all participants. It does not matter now much monitoring is done by senior management; if the participants are unwilling, the change will fail. The need for change has to be recognized and encouraged by visible, credible early success, which can be held up as an example of the validity of thought behind the planned change (Carnall, 1990).

The project organization

In the early 1990s the functional and matrix structures for delivering information systems projects proved to be inefficient and poorly adapted for delivering client needs. The 'two boss' system of a matrix organization in which most project teams operate increases the potential for conflict as members receive incompatible demands and priorities from their different managers. Matrix management can be described as a system based upon deliberate conflict between the project and functional managers, who must continually negotiate the use of organizational resources.

In the last five years a new project model has emerged. This new model, called the project organization, is shown in Figure 1.5. We can learn more of this model by considering how it differs from functional and matrix organizations.

In essence project organizations seek to remove many of the barriers identified earlier (see Table 1.4) by creating an environment which supports, encourages and rewards staff at all levels. Research undertaken by Peters and Waterman (1982) identified eight attributes which high performance companies share. Interestingly, at least four of these attributes are to be found within project organizations. They are:

1. Staying close to the customer (learning his or her preferences and catering for them).
2. Productivity through people (creating in all employees the awareness that their best efforts are essential and that they will share in the rewards of the organization's success).

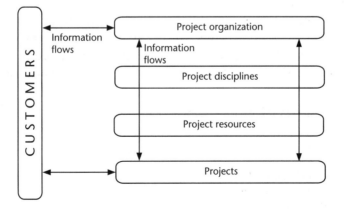

Figure 1.5 Example of a project organization (source: McManus, 1997)

3. Simple form, lean staff (few administration layers, few people at the upper levels).
4. Hands-on, value-driven (insisting that management keep in touch with the organization's essential business and promote a strong company culture).

Such organizations are characterized by those elements outlined in Table 1.5. The aim being to:

- refocus senior management on strategic decision making;
- reduce the implementation role of central services;
- distribute and commit resources to projects by placing them under the authority of the information systems project manager; and
- open direct lines of communication between the project and the customer/user, thereby directly relating the dynamics of the project to the dynamics of customer/user's objectives.

Each of the elements listed within Table 1.5 might benefit from further discussion.

Project management autonomy

The information systems project manager, assisted by his personnel, determines the objectives, policies, organization, resources and operational and managerial procedures of the project. He devotes his entire activity to the project. He defines relations with suppliers and subcontracts and permanent services of the organization. He or she chooses his staff. The information systems project manager receives a very broad delegation of power from the firm's senior management. He or she will set the general objectives of the project in cooperation with senior management. They report period-ically on the management of the project.

Dynamic segmentation

An information technology project can be described as an open, changing system. The organization of the project must therefore be adaptive and flexible, and allow for evaluation. In addition, the reduction of complexity and the absorption of fluctuations imply the need for increased variety in the organization system. This is best achieved by breaking it down into autonomous sub-systems with broad decision-making cap-abilities. The project is segmented into operational units on a human scale, into which

Table 1.5   Characteristics of project organizations

Project management autonomy
Dynamic segmentation
Resource control
Explicit objective, policies and rules
Written description of procedures
Management principles

the various functions are incorporated whenever possible. Each member is responsible for a physical portion of the project, both in its technical aspects and with respect to costs and time frames.

The information systems project manager coordinates the activities with other members; sets his or her own objectives, so as to be consistent with the general objectives of the project; defines his or her organization and management rules; and establishes the inter-unit rules in conformity with the principle of subsidiary. The project organization evolves through cell division, (or segmentation of responsibility) during the growth phase of the project, and then by cell absorption during the contraction phase. This method makes it possible to vary staffing quickly and facilitates good integration of new personnel. Whenever possible cellular division is also adopted as a means of defining the contractual responsibilities existing between the various external organizations that may or may not participate in the project.

Resource control

Whenever possible, the duration, scope and economy of the project and the resources of the firm which are required for implementing the project should be assembled and placed under the authority of the information systems project manager. Those resources, which cannot be handled in this way, are subject to a customer–supplier relationship. The permanent services of the firm can be placed in competition with organizations outside the firm.

Explicit objectives, policies and rules

The objectives, policies and organizational and managerial principles are set down in writing and distributed as a manual and project plan. These documents are revised whenever necessary.

Written description of procedures

Procedures define inter-unit rules. Procedures may also define the operational procedures of the activity, if they are repetitive in character or have a major impact on the success of the project. The procedures are submitted to the persons who will have to apply them for them to comment on. Anyone may request a revision. The procedures specific to a unit are laid down by the unit itself. An activity can be initiated without the procedures being in place since they can be laid down as the project progresses, on the basis of the experience required.

Management principles

The management of resources rests on strong communication and a policy based on transparency, trust, the right to make mistakes and the example set by the leaders. The climate in which the project is to develop is impregnated with the example set by the leaders, a concern with facts, pragmatism, a liking for action, rigor and a positive vision of people and of the present. The choice of information systems project manager often raises the problem of looking for the heaven-sent man or woman. In reality, the project creates the men who create the project. The exercise of responsibility, the demands of self-organization and autonomy, the effort to overcome obstacles and adversity do, in fact, teach a great deal. In particular, the segmentation of responsibilities into units provides an outstanding training ground for future information systems project managers. The determination to face new responsibilities becomes the driving force behind the learning process. The choice of leaders, then, is dictated by a few essential criteria: determination, the desire to learn and the will to over-achieve.

It follows that the competence of individuals, realistic objectives, and the mastery of techniques are no longer sufficient to ensure success of systems projects. Organization, segmentation of responsibilities and the methods of management determine, in large measure, the project's success. Each project can be considered unique and must be managed by a unique, specific combination of methods, systems and organizational processes, the detailed content of which is derived from a limited number of guidelines.

Advantages

There are many advantages to be found in project management based on the rules of discipline and self-organization. It is an effective solution to the problem of avoiding the double hazards of bureaucracy and anarchy. In addition, project management through self-organization makes it possible to have:

- overall optimization of the project;
- better allowance for complexity;
- quick decisions, integrating technology, costs, time frames and human parameters;
- good upstream–downstream integration (feasibility studies, implementation, roll out);
- speedy adjustment to the evolution of the environment and needs of the customer;
- enrichment of knowledge and managerial capacity, due to the concept of cellular organization; and
- economic use of resources and shortened completion times (times may range from those associated with traditional methods to half that time if the project is unusual or complex).

Project conflict

We touched briefly on conflict within project structures in an earlier section. It is widely known that the expectations of management are based on a 'unitary view' which carries with it the expectations that everyone in the organization has the same objectives (project or other wise) and will work together as a team, acknowledges the legitimacy of structural differences and respects superior authority. Anything which appears to interface with this view, is regarded as base behaviour and dealt with according to rules, procedures, customs and conventions, which exist within the particular organization. This view acknowledges the existence of management logic but ignores the existence of other views on what constitutes rational response. Given the nature of system development projects and their interdependence on teamwork, conflict is an inevitable occurrence. Conflict, defined distinctly from cooperation and competition, exists when incompatible activities occur, that is, where one person's actions harm, interfere, resist, oppose, or in some other way make another's action and position less active. Conflict occurs in both cooperative and competitive contexts.

Shared and limited resources, interdependent projects, dynamic life cycles, pressures to meet market demands and global competitive demands are factors that increase the potential conflict, especially when they occur simultaneously. Conflict in its worst form leads to a lack of respect and trust between groups, a lack of harmony and cooperation, and a breakdown in communication, with information being distorted, censored or withheld. Each group will tend to reject ideas, opinions and suggestions arising from other groups and feelings or emotions will run high. As emotions run high, there is a greater chance of mistakes being made by people whose judgement is clouded by stress. Groups will tend to have unspoken objectives that are different from those of the organization, such as to get the other group, block anything they propose, achieve dominance over them and show them in poor light to senior management. Organizational objectives will be subordinated to the group goals, which concentrate on achieving dominance or victory over the other groups. This accelerates the breakdown of communication between groups, and creates unfavourable attitudes and images of other groups. This sometimes contributes to inferior technical performance and schedule slippage with the result that the project is abandoned.

Management styles

Project managers have over the years adopted various styles (or modes) for managing conflict situations. These actions are conceptualized as falling into one of five styles for handling conflicts. They are:

1. Collaborating: sometimes referred to as confrontation or problem-solving – involves an approach where all affected parties are involved and work toward an optimal solution to their disagreements. Style traits:
    - the information systems project manager encourages a 'we are in it together' attitude;
    - the information systems project manager seeks a solution that will be good for all; and

– the information systems project manager tries to understand the others' views and positions.

2. Compromising: is characterized by a 'give and take' approach where bargaining is used to find solutions that bring some sense of satisfaction to the affected parties. Style traits:

   – when disagreeing with others, the information systems project manager is careful to communicate respect for them as people; and

   – the information systems project manager encourages a lot of give and take.

3. Avoiding: sometimes known as withdrawal, finds solutions to conflicts by one or both of the affected parties retreating, postponing, or ignoring the potential or actual disagreement. Style traits:

   – the information systems project manager tries to keep anger and frustration from being expressed; and

   – the information systems project manager tries to keep differences of opinion quiet.

4. Accommodating: involves 'going-along' perspective where areas of conflict are not emphasized and differences are resolved when one party adjusts to the other's desires. Style traits:

   – the information systems project manager ensures that the people working on the project understand a problem before seeking a solution.

5. Dominating: involves a competitive (win or lose orientation) where one party's position is exerted at the potential expense of the other. Style traits:

   – the information systems project manager treats issues in a conflict as a win-lose contest;

   – the information systems project manager sticks to his position to get others to compromise; and

   – the information systems project manager demands that others agree to his position.

Some writers (see, for example, Harrison, 1988) have argued that such modes of resolving conflict are more applicable to the resolution of disagreements than to the resolution of conflict. This is because their use and success in resolving disagreements is dependent on the nature of the existing relationships between individuals and groups. In addition they tackle only the symptoms of the conflict disease and not the underlying sources of conflict. Table 1.6 outlines possible sources of project conflict.

Dealing with conflict over the project life cycle

Project managers need to understand when in the project's life cycle conflicts are most likely to rise. Armed with such foresight, information systems project managers are likely to be more effective at dealing with inevitable conflicts. Most conflicts in the formative phase of the project occur over schedules, costs, priorities, and

Table 1.6   Sources of project conflict

Communication: Conflict resulting from poor information exchanges between groups within and external to the project. Such elements as misunderstanding of project-related goals and the strategic mission of the organization and the flow of information between technical and non-technical staff.

Costs: Conflict that arises from lack of funding or who gets to control the budget.

Interpersonal relationships: Conflict that centres on interpersonal differences rather than the job in hand. This would include conflict that is caused by prejudice and stereotyping.

Leadership: Conflict that arises from a need for senior management to take key strategic decisions or from a lack of decision making at the project level.

Managerial: Conflict that develops over how the project will be managed; reporting relationships and responsibilities, group relationships, project scope, project plans, work agreements and procedures.

Politics: Conflict that centres on issues of power and control, or hidden agendas.

Resources: Conflict resulting from competition for resources among information systems project managers and projects, or from competing sister organizations.

Technical: Conflict that arises out of technical opinion – such issues include design specifications, and technology employed within the project.

staffing. These four areas create turmoil because information systems project managers typically have only limited control over other areas likely to impact these issues, particularly with functional support departments. To minimize conflict, intensive planning prior to launching a project is required. Keeping the project goal clearly in mind goes a long way towards minimizing disruptive conflicts. Involving all of the parties affected by the project can help managers to anticipate potential sources of conflict and can help to start building the *esprit de corps* necessary to resolve the differences that will occur.

As a project enters the early programme phase, conflicts arise primarily over scheduling, priorities, staffing and technical issues. It is critical to provide feedback on how the project is progressing and to celebrate and reward early accomplishments. Frequent meetings and status review sessions help to develop interpersonal relationships that may be called upon in later, more stressful stages of the project. Research indicates that the greater the uncertainty about the correct way to do the task, the more problem-solving techniques that bring people face to face, rather than impersonal processes like rules and regulations, are required (Posner, 1995). Every effort should be made to integrate as early as possible the various functional groups affected by the project.

The main phase of the project finds more conflicts arising over scheduling issues. Resolving these conflicts requires continual efforts to keep people posted and to monitor work in progress. Technical issues should be resolved early in the process with an emphasis on early technical testing by all involved. Forecasting, thinking ahead, and communicating staffing requirements and changes can make life somewhat less hectic and anxiety prone.

As the project reaches the end, conflicts will still emerge around costs and schedules. It is important to keep project team members focused on these issues. If they feel a sense of ownership toward the project, then they will naturally identify with the project's success and contribute to it. Focusing on the eventual accomplishment and its significance can also tap into people's sense of pride.

The nature of software projects

Project management is concerned with managing the entity called 'project'. There is no single universal definition of a software project, although some definitions do have similar structures. Common to many project definitions are:

1. Projects consume a variety of resources.
2. Projects have a specific start and end point (or life cycle).
3. Projects have an owner (i.e. a customer).
4. Projects have a specific budget.
5. Projects have a clear method.
6. Projects have finite objectives.

If we rearrange these points, we can arrive at a more coherent definition:

> A unique undertaking with a concise life cycle, start and end dates, a finite budget, resource allocation and defined outcome or objective.

The assumption that the objectives and methods of a project can be clearly defined leads to a belief that the project's design can be confined within limits at an early stage. Bounded objectives become part of the Project Initiation Document (PID) and information systems project managers are deemed to be successful if they deliver on time and to budget, regardless of whether or not the product is useful or beneficial to the customer (or owner) and users. In the real world of information systems the development is only successful if it produces a worthwhile product that can be used profitably for some time after implementation to repay its investment. This is a key challenge within project management systems delivery.

Project life cycle

Although discussed in detail in Chapter 3, writers on project management tend to define a project life cycle first, and then subdivide it into phases. A more practical way is to consider the project life cycle as a collection of phases. Each project phase is marked by the completion of one or more deliverables. A deliverable is a tangible, verifiable work product such as a feasibility study, a detailed design, or a working prototype. The deliverables (within software projects), and hence the phases, are part of a generally sequential logic designed to ensure proper definition of the product of the project. Each project phase normally includes a set of pre-defined work products designed to establish the desired level of management control. The majority of these work products are related to the primary phase deliverable, and the phase typically takes its name from this item (requirements, design, build, test, etc.).

The phase sequence defined by most project life cycles generally involves some form of technology transfer or hand-off (for example, requirements to design, design to build and build to operations). Deliverables from the preceding phase are usually approved before work starts on the next phase. However, a later phase is sometimes begun prior to approval of the earlier phase deliverables when the risks involved are deemed acceptable. Most life cycles also share a common staffing and cost pattern: low at the start, higher towards the end, and dropping rapidly as the project draws to a conclusion. This pattern is illustrated in Figure 1.6.

Although many software project life cycles are similar, few are identical. Most have four or five phases, but some have nine or more (Duncan, 1995). Even within a single application area, there can be significant variations: one organization's software development life cycle may have a single design phase, whilst another's may have separate phases for functional and detail design.

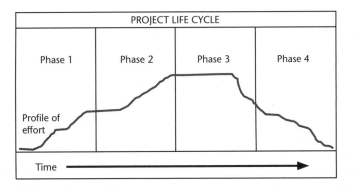

Figure 1.6 Generic life cycle of a project

Summary

■ Changes in global markets over the past decade have forced organizations to alter their structures so that they can remain competitive.

■ The characteristics of traditional and new organizations and organizational structures have evolved to cope with modern, fast-paced markets.

■ The nature of the 'new' project organizations. The characteristics associated with project organizations.

■ Some common reasons for project failure, and the lessons that can be learned from such failures.

■ The importance of communication at all levels within the organization and the project team.

■ Important factors that affect the success of a project.

■ The importance of the client and the importance of involving the client in every part of the project.

■ How the composition of project teams may influence the success of a project. The importance of adopting a correct structure in order to gain various benefits, such as developing the expertise of team members.

■ Some of the characteristics shared by successful organizations. How these characteristics can be mapped to project organizations.

■ How conflict arises within groups. Sources of conflict. How management style affects responses to conflict. Dealing with conflict over the project life cycle.

■ The life cycle of a project.

Bibliography

Abell D., 1990, *Perspectives for Managers*, IMD, Switzerland.

Baker B., Murphy D. and Fisher D., 1983, 'Factors Affecting Project Success', in Cleland D. and King W. (eds), *Project Management Handbook*, Van Nostrand Reinhold.

Carnall C., 1990, *Managing Change in Organisations*, Prentice-Hall, UK.

Duncan W., 1995, 'Developing a Project Management Body of Knowledge Document', *International Journal of Project Management*, Vol. 13, p. 91.

Gilbreath R., 1988, 'Working with Pulses not Streams: Using Projects to Capture Opportunity', in Cleland D. and King W. (eds), *Project Management Handbook*, Van Nostrand Reinhold.

Gobeli D. and Larson E., 1987, 'Project Structures versus Project Performance', in Proc. 11th Internet International Conference.

Harrison F., 1988, *Conflict, Power and Politics in Project Management, from Conception to Completion*, 9th World Congress On Project Management.

Kouzes J.M. and Posner B.Z., 1996, *The Leadership Challenge*, 2nd edn, Jossey Bass Wiley, USA.

McManus J., 1997, *The Role of the Project Manager*, Pitman Publications, UK.

Payne J., 1993, 'Introducing Formal Project Management into a Traditional, Functionally Structured Organisation', *International Journal of Project Management*, November 1993, p. 240.

Peters T. and Waterman R., 1982, *In Search of Excellence*, Harper and Row, USA.

Pritchard C., 1998, 'Organizational Need', *Project Manager Today*, October 1998, p. 17.

Sims D., 1993, 'Coping with Misinformation', *Management Decision*, No. 5, p. 19.

Tribus M., 1989, 'The Germ Theory of Management', *Selected Papers in Quality Improvement*, British Deming Association.

Vowler J., 1995, 'A Feast for Developers', *Computer Weekly*, January 1995, p. 14.

Further reading

Cleland D. and Gareis R., 1993, *Global Project Management*, McGraw-Hill.

Cleland D. and King W., 1993, *Project Management Handbook*, 3rd edn, McGraw-Hill.

Morris P., 1997, *The Management of Projects*, 2nd edn, Thomas Telford Publications.

Turner J., 1996, *The Project Manager as Change Agent*, McGraw-Hill.

Useful websites

http://web.mit.edu/pm/

The MIT web Information Systems site is committed to educating practitioners in IS and within the greater MIT community about project management tools and practices. These web pages are not intended as an exhaustive source of project management knowledge. Instead, they are a starting point to explore the field of project management and to encourage the use of project management methodology at the Institute.

http://www.4pm.com

Project Manager's Control Tower Project management articles, templates, training and techniques for project managers.

http://www.pmforum.org

The Project Management Forum – A global project management portal providing access to worldwide project management information.

Self-assessment exercises

1. The text puts forward a definition of a project. What is this definition?

2. Define a runaway project.

3. Which of the following is *not* a common characteristic of a runaway project?

   (a) Project's objectives not properly specified.
   (b) Bad planning and estimating.
   (c) Insufficient developers on team.
   (d) Technology new to organization.
   (e) Inadequate project management methodology.

4. In the US, research has found that 30 per cent of organizations have terminated more than one project for the same reasons. True or false?

5. List at least five symptoms of poor information sytems delivery.

6. What fundamental problem is associated with project or organizational structures based on a matrix model?

7. Research has shown that successful organizations tend to share eight characteristics. Four of these characteristics are also found within project organizations. List these characteristics.

8. What problems can be caused when conflict occurs within groups?

9. List at least four sources of conflict.

Case study

Looking back, looking ahead

Karl E. Wiegers and Johanna Rothman

Pat, a vice-president in an internet start-up company, was proud of her team's previous product release but concerned about why it had shipped a few weeks later than planned. At the project's retrospective, Pat was astonished to hear several team members say, 'It might have been done earlier, but I didn't know exactly what "done" meant. If I had known when my part was really finished, we might have been able to ship earlier.' It was a valuable comment, and Pat used the information on her next project to define clear release criteria, which helped improve her team's schedule performance.

Retrospectives provide a structured opportunity to look back at the project or phase you have just completed. You might see practices that worked well that you want to sustain, but you might also see what didn't go so well and gain insights on how to improve. The retrospective helps you identify the lessons you've learned from often-painful experience.

The astute project manager will begin each new project by reviewing the lessons learned from previous projects for ideas that will save time and avoid sleepless nights. You might not be able to quantify the value of learning from past experiences. Nonetheless, the small investment you make in a retrospective will almost certainly save you more time than it costs. In today's speed-driven and bottom-line conscious development world, you can't afford to repeat past mistakes and encounter the same surprises on project after project.

Retrospective defined

A retrospective is a gathering of knowledge, insights, and possibly metrics and artefacts from a completed project or project phase. Metrics might include actual results for schedule, effort, cost and quality, which you can use to improve your future estimates. You can archive key project documents, plans and specifications to serve as examples for future projects. A retrospective provides closure, a way for the participants to share their observations away from the day-to-day pressures. Even if the project was a colossal failure, the lessons you learn from evaluating it can produce something positive from the experience and point to useful improvement opportunities.

It may seem silly to talk about what a retrospective is named, but names have powerful associations. When someone calls a retrospective a post-mortem, we wonder who died; sometimes projects are successful! Naming a retrospective a post-partum suggests that the new baby product may grow up someday, but is far from mature. 'Retrospective' and 'post-project review' are neutral terms that suggest a contemplative reflection on previous experience to gain practical wisdom.

Hold a retrospective whenever you want to gather information about your project or evaluate how the work is going. Many projects iterate through a series of development cycles, so you should gather lessons after each cycle to help you with those that remain. Reflecting on past experience is especially worthwhile any time something went particularly well or particularly wrong. It's easy to forget what happened early in a project that lasts longer than a few months, so hold a short retrospective after reaching each major milestone on a long project. The healing effects of time and the exhilaration of recent success can ease the pain you suffered some time ago, but those painful memories contain the seeds of future improvements.

The retrospective process

An effective retrospective follows the simple process of planning, kick-off, data gathering, issue prioritization and analysis. The key players are the manager who sponsors the retrospective, the project team members and a facilitator.

Planning. Planning begins when the management sponsor who requested the retrospective works with the facilitator to determine the scope of the retrospective (the entire project or just a portion), the activities to examine and any specific issues to probe. During planning, you also need to identify who should be invited, choose an appropriate facility (preferably off-site and away from distractions), select the facilitation techniques you will use, and define an agenda.

We've had different results with splitting participants into groups. In one retrospective, Karl and another facilitator led two separate discussion groups in parallel. One group consisted of six managers, while the other group was made up of 15 software practitioners. The facilitators and the sponsoring manager believed that the practitioners would be reluctant to raise certain issues if their managers were in the room. Splitting the participants worked well in this situation, although we had to carefully merge and prioritize the issues from both groups. In another case, however, separating the participants proved unwarranted. The two groups involved were a software development team and a visual design team who had worked together on a major website development project. Karl underestimated the participants' collaborative mindset, and realized that, despite some points of friction between the groups, it would have been better to keep the entire team in the same room to discuss their joint issues.

Johanna has never separated participant groups, because she believes that separating the groups placates the people with the perceived power. It's important to prepare the managers by telling them that the retrospective may uncover issues that are uncomfortable for them. As Jerry Weinberg points out, 'No matter what it looks like, it's always a people problem,' and sometimes the people problems are management-generated. Consider requesting permission from the managers to ask them to leave the room if they seem to be inhibiting the discussion.

Kickoff. During a short kickoff session with all participants, the sponsoring manager introduces the facilitator and any other unfamiliar faces. The manager also identifies his objectives for the retrospective and thanks the participants in advance for their time and their honest contributions. The manager should clearly state his commitment to taking concrete actions based on the retrospective outcomes. The facilitator then outlines the agenda of events. To establish the appropriate constructive environment, the facilitator defines some ground rules, including:

- Allow everyone to be heard.
- Respect the other person's experience and perspective.
- Avoid criticizing input and ideas from other participants.
- Avoid blaming people for past events.
- Identify root causes, not just symptoms.
- Focus on understanding, learning and looking ahead.

Data gathering. While some retrospectives collect hard data and project artefacts, the core activity is gathering issues, observations, and concerns from the participants. We explore three basic questions in a retrospective: What went well? (We want to repeat it in the future.) What could have gone better? (We might want to change it.) What happened that surprised us? (These might be risks to watch for on future projects.)

An experienced facilitator has numerous techniques for eliciting information from different kinds of participant groups. The traditional approach is to have a facilitator stand by a flipchart in front of the group and ask the participants to suggest issues. The facilitator marks what went well with plus signs and less favourable experiences with minus signs. A variation is to use a round-robin approach, asking each participant in turn to raise one issue and cycling through the audience until everyone passes. This approach to issue generation typically takes 60 to 90 minutes. After issue generation is completed, the facilitator (or a scribe) records each issue raised on a separate index card. The participants then group the cards into related categories (affinity groups) and name the issue groups.

This traditional facilitation approach has several drawbacks.

- Sequential issue-generation is slow.
- It's easy for a few outspoken participants to dominate the input.
- It's easy to slip into an extended discussion of a single hot-button topic, instead of identifying additional issues.
- Some participants may be uncomfortable raising issues in a public forum.
- Influential or strong-willed participants might render others unwilling to speak up.

If you're concerned about any of these factors, consider using alternative facilitation approaches. Silent techniques that let participants generate issues in parallel can be more efficient and comprehensive than the public, sequential method. In one such approach, the facilitator and the retrospective sponsor identify several categories in which issues are likely to arise prior to the retrospective meeting. Common categories for software development projects include communication, organization, teamwork, management, requirements, design, construction, testing, subcontractors, business issues and processes. You probably won't need all of these categories for every retrospective. There is a risk that defining the category names in advance will limit what comes out of the group, so you might prefer to group issues and name the groups after issue generation is completed.

Write each category name on a separate flipchart page, and divide each page into labelled sections for what went well, what could have gone better, and what lessons were learned. During the meeting, have the participants write each of their issues on a separate 3×5 sticky note, indicating the pertinent category. The facilitator places these in the right section of the appropriate flipchart page. Spend about 20 minutes clarifying the things that went well, then move on to what could have gone better for another 20 or 30 minutes. Participants can walk around the room and see what other people wrote on the flipcharts to stimulate their own thinking.

This approach addresses most of the shortcomings of the traditional facilitator-at-the-flipchart method. Participants working concurrently can generate more issues in a given amount of time. There is little chance of being distracted by discussions as each issue is raised. And people who might be reluctant to state their opinions aloud willingly contribute them silently and anonymously. However, the facilitator will have to read all the sticky notes on the flipcharts aloud to share them with the entire group, make sure each issue is clearly stated and properly classified, and group related or duplicate issues.

To close the data-gathering portion of a retrospective, you might ask each team member two questions: What one aspect of this project would you want to keep the same on a future project? and: What one aspect of this project would you want to change on a future project?

Issue prioritization. A successful retrospective will generate far more issues than the team can realistically address. You must identify those items that the participants agree would be the most valuable to pursue. Some high-priority issues might point to effective practices you want to institutionalize on future projects. Others will reflect shortcomings in current practices that you need to address promptly.

A classic prioritization technique is Pareto voting. Each participant gets a limited number of votes, usually about 20 per cent of the total number of issues being prioritized. To simplify the data collection with a large group, some facilitators give each participant just three to five votes. Coloured adhesive dots work well for this voting process. The participants walk around the room, examine the flipcharts and place their dots on the sticky notes with the issues they believe are most important to address. Those issues that gather the most dots are most ripe for early action. However, seeing the dots on the sticky notes can bias participants who might not want to 'waste' votes on issues that clearly are not favoured by the earlier voters. To avoid that problem, you can have the participants place their voting dots on the backs of the sticky notes.

Analysis. If you have time during the retrospective, spend 15 or 20 minutes discussing each of the top priority items. Otherwise, assemble a small group to explore those topics after the retrospective meeting. For items noted as going particularly well, determine why they succeeded and what benefits they provided. Find ways to ensure that each of those aspects of the project will go well again in the future. For high-priority 'could have gone better' items, determine why each item didn't turn out as intended, the consequences of each and recommendations for doing it better the next time.

Retrospective success factors

A retrospective can succeed only in a neutral, non-accusatory environment. Honest and open communication is essential. If a project has been difficult or unsuccessful, some venting is to be expected; however, the facilitator must limit that venting and channel it in a constructive direction. Make sure your retrospectives don't turn into witch-hunts. The retrospective must emphasize guilt-free learning from the shared project experience. Let's look at some retrospective critical success factors.

Define your objectives. As the sponsoring manager, you should identify your objectives for the retrospective and the specific project aspects on which it should focus, along with identifying the potential beneficiaries of the activity: who will come out ahead if the information gathered during the retrospective guides some constructive process changes? Also, think about who might look bad if the root causes of problems are revealed. Remember, you're not looking for scapegoats, but you need to understand what really happened and why.

Use a skilled and impartial facilitator. It isn't realistic to expect the project manager to objectively facilitate a retrospective. The manager might have a particular axe to grind or want to protect his own reputation. Some project managers might unconsciously impede participation despite their good intentions. Other participants can be intimidated into silence on important points, or the manager might put his own spin on certain issues. To avoid these problems, invite an experienced, neutral facilitator from outside the project team to lead the retrospective. The facilitator's prime objective is to make the retrospective succeed by surfacing the critical issues in a constructive, learning environment. Consider having someone who is not an active participant in the retrospective act as scribe to record the issues generated.

Engage the right participants. Of course, the essential participants are all of the project team members. Management representatives are invited to the retrospective only if they were actually members of the project team. However, you should provide a summary of lessons learned to senior management or to other managers in the company who could benefit from the information.

Some teams might be too busy, too large or too geographically separated for all team members to participate in a retrospective concurrently. In such a case, select representatives of the various functional areas that were involved in the project. If a large project was subdivided into multiple subprojects, each one should perform its own retrospective. Delegates from each subproject can then participate in a higher-level retrospective at the overall project level.

When people who we believe have key insights claim they're too busy to participate, we ask them if they think everything went well on the project. Generally, they have some important observations and constructive suggestions. We then help those people balance their current time demands against the need to hear their input on the previous project.

If the project involved multiple groups who blame each other for the project's problems or who refuse to sit down together to explore their common issues, you might begin by discussing the friction points between the groups. Chances are good that you'll uncover important project issues. If the groups can't get along in the retrospective, they probably clashed during the project, too. The retrospective might address what needs to change for those groups to collaborate more effectively next time.

Prepare the participants. If the participants aren't accustomed to retrospectives, and if the project being studied had serious problems, an invitation to a retrospective can stimulate fear, confusion or resistance. Some participants might be sick with anxiety, while others will be eager to let the accusations fly. Provide information and reassurance to the participants through the invitation material and during 'sales calls' made on team leaders and key participants. Describe the process in advance, and establish an appropriately constructive mindset, by emphasizing that this is a future-oriented and process-improvement activity.

Focus on the facts. A retrospective should address the processes and outcomes of the project, not the participants' personalities or mistakes. The facilitator has to ensure the participants don't blame or placate others by concentrating on what actually happened. However, people often experience events in different ways. Understanding the different interpretations can release hard feelings and provide the opportunity for new insights.

Identify the action plan owner. Identify the person who will write and take ownership of an improvement action plan and see that it leads to tangible benefits. Assign each action item in the plan to an individual who will implement it and report progress to the action plan owner. This owner must carry enough weight in the organization to steer these individuals toward completing their action items.

Retrospective action planning

After the retrospective, don't try to tackle all of the identified issues immediately. Choose up to three issues initially from the top priority list; the rest will still be there for future treatment. Write an action plan that describes your improvement goals, identifies steps to address them, states who will take responsibility for each activity and lists any deliverables that will be created. At your next retrospective, check whether these actions resulted in the desired outcomes. Remember, an action plan that doesn't lead to concrete actions is useless. Karl once facilitated retrospectives for the same internet development group two years apart. Some issues that came up in the later event were the same as those identified two years earlier. Failing to learn from the past practically guarantees that you will repeat it, and nothing kills an organization's attempt to hold retrospectives faster than recommendations which aren't implemented.

Lessons learned

For the maximum organizational benefits, accumulate lessons learned from your retrospectives. We prefer to write lessons learned in a neutral way, so it isn't obvious whether we learned each one because something was done well or because the team made a mistake.

The information in your lessons-learned database could include:

- Statement of the lesson.
- Lesson-learned subject category.
- Date the lesson was entered into repository.
- Project name.
- Risks of ignoring the lesson.
- Recommendations for implementing the lesson.
- Work product involved.
- Pertinent life cycle phase.

The people side

Because we're human, our personalities influence how we react to situations. During one retrospective that Johanna facilitated, a management participant had tears in his eyes when he described a particular concern. Johanna spoke to him at a break and the words flooded out of him. He said he felt that his management didn't trust him, yet he didn't feel comfortable saying so. He agreed to have Johanna bring up this sensitive topic.

When the group reconvened, Johanna said that one participant did not feel trusted by management because of three points that she wrote on the flipchart. The room was silent for a minute. Then someone else said, 'Me, too.' Several others chimed in, and then they looked at the senior manager. Johanna reminded the group we weren't judging individuals, but rather airing our concerns so we could address them. The senior manager then asked, 'Does anyone here trust me?' No one responded. It was a very telling moment. The senior manager then listed that lack of trust as a problem.

The project team is the best source of information about how a recently completed project or development phase really went. Use a retrospective to help the team assemble a whole picture of the project, so the project leader can use that information to create a more effective environment the next time. But remember that all organizational change takes time, patience and commitment from all stakeholders. If people don't want to change, they won't.

This paper was originally published in *Software Development*, February 2001. Copyright © 2001 *Software Development*, CMP Media LLC. Reprinted with permission.

Questions

1. Discuss the symptoms of poor system delivery and describe ways to overcome them.
2. Define what is meant by scope creep and how it can be prevented.
3. With respect to dealing with project issues, what facilitation techniques would you use and why?
4. Describe the characteristics of a new wave project management organization.
5. Explain why people are important to the success of a project.

Note

1. *Source*: Reengineering Fact File, Meta Group, USA (1997).

CHAPTER 2

The role of the information systems project manager

Introduction

This chapter examines the role of the project manager in depth. The discussion begins by exploring what makes a 'good' project manager. The first part of the discussion looks at the characteristics of the project manager's role, describing the tasks he is expected to carry out and the knowledge he is required to have. The second part of the discussion examines the personal qualities expected of a competent project manager. These qualities include highly developed problem solving skills and the ability to motivate others.

Each of the key skills required by an effective project manager is examined in depth. The ability to motivate others, for example, is viewed from several perspectives. A theoretical view of motivation leads to a discussion of the problems that can occur if the members of a project team feel undervalued. Problem solving and decision making are dealt with in a similar manner. General models of decision making and problem solving are introduced so that the material can move on to examine these areas in the context of IS project management.

A number of topics are emphasized throughout the chapter. These include issues related to power and leadership, the importance of effective communications and approaches to management.

Learning objectives

Some of the topics covered include:

- The role of the information systems project manager.
- The body of knowledge required by information systems project managers.
- The importance of motivation.
- Management styles and their impact on interpersonal relationships.
- The concept of power and its role in managing people, projects and relationships.
- Approaches to making decisions and solving problems.
- The importance of communication.

At the end of this chapter, students will be able to:

- Define the role of the project manager with reference to required personal qualities and professional knowledge.
- Explain the importance of motivation and develop strategies to increase the motivation of team members.
- Explain approaches to management with reference to power, motivation and decision making.
- Apply models of decision making and problem solving to a variety of situations.
- Develop strategies for managing communications within a project.

Introducing the information systems project manager

Information systems project managers are concerned with optimizing and coordinating resources in project management. Project management has a culture all of its own, which requires a high degree of flexibility and involves dealing with uncertainty, complexity, indefinite or inadequate authority, temporary situations and employee relationships. The authority of an information systems project manager can vary from that of executive responsibility in a line management sense to that of a coordinator by persuasion. The span of control over personnel, budgets, etc., may also vary from project to project. In addition, his responsibility may also be divided up geographically between locations. Put simply, the information systems project manager is responsible for the success of the project in terms of time, cost, quality and technical performance. For the information systems project manager the key project processes include:

- visioning, developing goals and objectives;
- planning the project and optimizing effectiveness;
- monitoring, analysing, estimating and forecasting future states up to the conclusion of the project; and
- leading, directing, commanding or controlling the course of the project.

The term management derives from the idea of handling (from the Latin *manus* meaning *hand*) and therefore controlling things. The term leadership derives from the Anglo-Saxon word for *path*, and incorporates the concepts of movement, direction, and change, in addition to the traditional people-oriented concepts of following, team membership and example. In the context of a project, where something new is to be developed, both terms have relevance. We chose to use the words *manager* and *management* because of their wide acceptance, but recognize that, in the project environment, the words *leader* and *leadership* are also synonymous.

The information systems project manager must provide the leadership necessary to secure the people and groups from different departments, companies and ethnic cultures and form them into a single, coherent team. The manager must then provide the drive needed to ensure that the project is completed on time and within budget.

Managers must accept the personal accountability and responsibility for any one project, since this is a prerequisite for the success of such undertakings. The implication for the individual information systems project manager is that a project gives exposure to many areas of the business, for example, funding, investment appraisal, design and execution, planning and control. A wide range of experience can be condensed into a relatively short time period. Dawson (1988) writing in *Analysing Organisations* identified a number of generic attributes that could be identified with managers. Table 2.1 lists Dawson's criteria in an adapted form. These criteria can be used to construct a profile of the information systems project manager.

In attempting to determine what makes a 'good' project manager, a traditional response has been to list a series of personal qualities, such as *intelligence, experience, knowledge, decisiveness, integrity, initiative, communication* and *administrative skills*. In UK companies, these qualities are frequently used as key measures to identify key project personnel. The problem with this approach is that people who are well endowed with all these equalities are not easily found. Moreover, even if managers are found with a large number of these attributes, the skills that are lacking may be difficult to instil through training (for example, integrity or a sense of humour). The implication is that a good information systems project manager will have some of these qualities, but no particular mixture stands out as the minimum requirement.

Table 2.1   Information systems project manager – basic job components

1. Task	Manage project resources
2. Method	Direct and controlling
3. Technology	Computer software project tools
4. Variety	Moderate to high
5. Sequencing	Substantial latitude
6. Timing	Open (project-dependent)
7. Pace	Self-determined and motivated
8. Quality	Usually predetermined (e.g. UK ENISO 9000)
9. Specialization	Moderate to low
10. Interdependence	High
11. Partialness	Whole project
12. Performance	To time and within budget
13. Monitoring	Project board/committee
14. Accountability	Project reporting and interview

Checklist 2.1 illustrates some of the tasks and decisions that need to be dealt with as a project enters its initial stages. The checklist illustrates many of the practical skills, knowledge and characteristics that we associate with a competent project manager.

Competencies within project management

From an organization and client perspective, selecting the right information systems project manager is critical. When executive management selects an information systems project manager for a project, several factors should be considered. As an example, project managers working within information technology must possess a high level of technical expertise. Required skills and knowledge include an understanding of the technology of software engineering, awareness of programming tools and techniques used in software development, knowledge of current analysis methods and knowledge of project management techniques. However, they need not necessarily be technical experts in all aspects of a project. Of course, the information systems project manager should also have above average-managerial abilities.

Whilst all this seems obvious, according to research most information systems project managers are perceived to be average or below average in the areas of leadership skills, interpersonal relationships and administration (planning etc.). Since there is a high correlation between the quality level of these attributes of project managers and the use of best practices, careful analysis of the project manager's managerial experience and capability on projects should be made prior to selection or appointment.

In the software services industry managerial shortcomings are often overcome by using assistant project managers with skills in one or more areas where an information systems project manager may have weaknesses, such as in administration activities like project planning.

One important characteristic a project manager must possess is the ability to see the total (or big) picture. Effective project managers recognize that many factors affect the outcome of a project. They must consider not only the technical aspects but also others like the economic, personnel and legal aspects. Their perspective is broad, seeing the whole picture, and requires taking a systems approach. It is argued that many project managers lack this characteristic. They often fall into the trap of emphasizing the technical side while neglecting other important areas. As a result, relations with the client or sponsor may deteriorate. This may lead to legal complications arising due to lack of compliance with the contract and the project team may suffer from high staff turnover. Reliance solely on the technical aspects often results in a project riddled with problems beyond schedule slippage and overruns.

As explained in Chapter 1, information system project managers and other systems personnel must be educated so that they can carry out their responsibilities in a devolved environment. In particular, they must learn to focus less on technology and become more attuned to some of the softer skill sets. Table 2.2 shows the body of knowledge and accompanying skills expected of project managers. The table also shows a comparison between knowledge required by UK and US project managers.

Changing methods of delivering software projects have major implications for the skills required of all systems professionals. Many of them still have to make a determined effort to shake off their traditional image, which is often perceived by the clients and sponsors as alien and obstructive. In the past, skills were learned through apprenticeships or even through the experience of making mistakes. However, this approach is considered slow and inefficient when compared to a program of specific learning, especially where complexity is involved. Information systems project managers come from many disparate backgrounds and often bring a broad range of skills to the job.

At this point it is worth pointing out that there is a difference between a skill and a competency. The primary difference between a competency and a skill is that a skill will be made up from a number of competencies. Both the Association for Project Management (APM) in the UK, and the Project Management Institute (PMI) in the US, have highly developed project management curriculums based on key competencies. The curricula used in the UK and the US are outlined in Table 2.2. The value of such curricula lies in knowledge transfer and marketability. Students of project management will want to have a tangible record of their studies because qualifications represent value in the job market. This value is a reflection of the quality of the qualification, of course, but it is also highly desirable in itself. It provides the pull for an increasingly rapid transfer and consequent advance of knowledge.

Checklist 2.2 can be used to support the business review process but also illustrates the very wide body of skills and knowledge needed by a project manager. As can be seen, managers require knowledge of areas that include costing, purchasing, systems analysis, risk management, work flow planning and quality assurance.

Table 2.2   Comparisons of UK and US body of knowledge in project management

APM *Body of Knowledge*	PMI *Guide to the Project Management Body of Knowledge* (PMBOK)
1.1 Systems Management	Chapter 1 – Introduction
1.2 Programme Management	Chapter 1 – Introduction
1.3 Project Management	Chapter 1 – Introduction
1.4 Project Life Cycle	Chapter 1 – Introduction
1.5 Project Environment	Chapter 2 – The Project Management Context
1.6 Project Strategy	Not addressed in depth in PMBOK
1.7 Project Appraisal	Chapter 5 – Scope Management Chapter 11 – Risk Management
1.8 Project Success/Failure Criteria	Not addressed in depth in PMBOK
1.9 Integration	Chapter 4 – Integration Management*
1.10 Systems and Procedures	Chapter 3 – Project Management Processes
1.11 Close-out	Chapter 3 – Project Management Processes
1.12 Post Project Appraisal	Chapter 3 – Project Management Processes
2.1 Organization Design	Chapter 9 – Human Resources Management
2.2 Control and Coordination	Chapter 3 – Project Management Processes
2.3 Communication	Chapter 10 – Communication Management*
2.4 Leadership	Chapter 2 – The Project Management Context Chapter 9 – Human Resources Management
2.5 Delegation	Chapter 9 – Human Resources Management
2.6 Team Building	Chapter 9 – Human Resources Management
2.7 Conflict Management	Chapter 9 – Human Resources Management
2.8 Negotiation	Chapter 12 – Contract/Procurement Management
2.9 Management Development	Chapter 2 – The Project Management Context
3.1 Work Definition	Chapter 5 – Scope Management
3.2 Planning	Chapter 5 – Scope Management
3.3 Scheduling	Chapter 6 – Time Management*
3.4 Estimating	Chapter 7– Cost Management
3.5 Cost Control	Chapter 7 – Cost Management
3.6 Performance Measurement	Chapter 7 – Cost Management
3.7 Risk Analysis and Management	Chapter 11 – Risk Management*
3.8 Value Management	Not addressed in depth in PMBOK
3.9 Change Control	Chapter 4 – Integration Management
3.10 Mobilization	Chapter 5 – Scope Management
4.1 Operations/Technical Management	Chapter 9 – Human Resources Management
4.2 Marketing and Sales	Not addressed in depth in PMBOK
4.3 Finance	Chapter 11 – Risk Management Chapter 7 – Cost Management
4.4 Information Technology	Chapter 10 – Communication Management
4.5 Law	Chapter 12 – Contract/Procurement Management
4.6 Procurement	Chapter 12 – Contract/Procurement Management

Table 2.2 Continued	
4.7 Quality	Chapter 8 – Quality Management*
4.8 Safety	Not addressed in depth in PMBOK
4.9 Industrial Relations	Chapter 9 – Human Resources Management

Source: (Reproduced with permission of the editorial director: *Project Management Today*, July 1999, and based on an article by Carl Pritchard and J. Leroy Ward.)

Note: *These elements are covered in far greater depth in PMI's *Guide to the PMBOK*.

Leadership

A massive acceleration in technical and economic progress within many information technology organizations has brought about a significant awareness of the need for effective leadership. From observation of leaders in action, coupled with study of the work of contemporary behavioural scientists, it has become apparent that, if leaders are to be trained effectively rather than solely developed through experience, then an important question must be addressed. This question is not what must the leader *be* but rather what must the leader *do*? A key aspect of the information system project manager's job is to direct, instruct, encourage and motivate members of his team (including external personnel). To do this, the person must be totally committed to successful completion of the project. It is important that the individual project manager goes to great lengths to foster a team approach among those actively engaged in the project. The manager must motivate each member of the team to pursue the same aims, and must adopt a similar attitude himself. John Adair (1990) in *Understanding Motivation* identified six functions associated with leadership:

1. Planning: seeking available information; defining group tasks or goals; making a workable plan.
2. Initiating briefing the group, allocating tasks; setting group standards.
3. Controlling: maintaining group standards; ensuring progress towards objectives; prodding actions and decisions.
4. Supporting: expressing acceptance of individual contributions; encouraging and disciplining; creating team spirit; relieving tension with humour; reconciling disagreements.
5. Informing: clarifying task and plan; keeping the group informed; receiving information from the group; summarizing ideas and suggestions.
6. Evaluating: checking feasibility of ideas; testing consequence; evaluating group performance, helping the group to evaluate itself.

This model leadership approach, developed by Professor Adair, has been adopted by many successful organizations including IBM, GE, Microsoft and Logica. Adair's principles are encapsulated in a very simple form by Figure 2.1. Adair's crucial contribution was not so much in identifying the three components of leadership (objective, team, and the individual) as in insisting that they are interdependent. According to Adair's

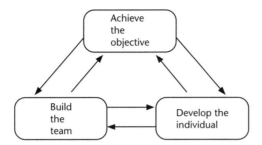

Figure 2.1 Leadership interrelationship functions

model, it is impossible to satisfy objective needs without adequate attention to team and individual needs. Similarly, team and individual needs are closely interlinked: the leader cannot adequately deal with one without also attending to the other.

One of the trademarks of outstanding leaders is that they are attentive to the needs of people. In 1992 Don Philips produced a provocative view of President Lincoln proposing that Lincoln was a leader from whom current leaders could learn a lot. Philips noted that though many have written about Lincoln's life and presidency, almost nothing exists about Lincoln the leader. Philips regards Lincoln as '. . . the greatest leader the US, and perhaps this world, has yet known.'

Lincoln was a leader who understood the concept of management by walking around, even though it was far more difficult for him than most modern day leaders (ASCE, 1994). His personal secretaries, Hay and Nicolay, noted that Lincoln would see as many people as often as he possibly could and reported that Lincoln spent 75 per cent of his time with people. He was one of the most accessible chief executives the US has ever known. Throughout the Civil War Lincoln would visit his generals and men in the field whenever possible. If he was unable to visit in person, he either spent time at the telegraph office, or sent special emissaries to the front. Philips also notes that Lincoln called on Congress regularly and was the first president in many years to attend a regular working session of the Senate. Lincoln knew that frequent human contact was essential in creating a sense of commitment, collaboration and community. He understood that human contact was needed to exchange vital information, and that information is crucial when making timely and effective decisions.

It can be argued that leaders have highly developed antennae for who is right and who is wrong for the job in hand. One of the most outstanding leaders in the software services industry is Ross Perot. A former IBM manager, Perot created a software company called EDS (Electronic Data Systems) some 25 years ago. Under his leadership it developed into the world's largest software company, ultimately merging with General Motors so that EDS acquired 16 per cent of the shares of another of the world's largest companies. People often ask how Perot was able to do this and what can be learned from his success. Those who profess to know him say that his brilliance lay in being able to pick a winning team. If a project is staffed with the best people for each role, less energy is spent in worrying about their performance, controlling their results and checking up on them. One hundred per cent of the manager's energies can be devoted to tackling new challenges and doing the right thing(s).

By examining leadership in the context of doing the right thing, Cleland (1998) identified a number of issues with which the information systems project manager must be concerned.

The first issue is the identification, development and communication of a vision for the project stakeholders who the leader wishes to lead. Project stakeholders include the members of the project team and other principals in the political, economic, social and technological (PEST), and competitive environments in which the project exists. A vision is a mental image produced by the imagination.

The second issue requires the project leader to identify the resources that will be needed to realize the vision. Having done this, the project manager designs a series of initiatives aimed at acquiring those resources and ensuring that they support the project and the organization.

The third issue is that of conceptualization and designation of the project's organizational design to align the people and resources to facilitate the accomplishment of the vision.

The fourth and final issue is that of gaining the commitment of the stakeholders to support the project manager's initiatives in the attainment of the vision. Gaining a commitment to the project vision requires the project manager to find the means and processes that will foster an environment in which team members will be motivated to work towards the vision. This commitment is not a destination, but an ongoing journey in terms of keeping people loyal to the vision, constantly striving for its attainment even during periods of adversity. The communication skills of the leader, and those of the followers, are important in gaining and retaining this commitment.

The need for emotional support

A project manager's life can be chaotic; the pace is normally fast (certainly in development projects with short life cycles) stress can be high, and rewards may at times seem illusory. The bigger the project, the greater the stakeholder participation, the chaos and the more intense the stress. In this environment of frantic uncertainty, the project manager needs someone to talk to, some outlet, someone who is trusted. Project managers are people too, and they need to belong. They especially need to know that others care for them as people and not just because they have power. A project manager's role requires a commercial attitude – they must be relatively sceptical and cautious in most interactions – and this means that they tend to develop a personal aloofness, or at least an apparent shallowness. Since they cannot generate much personal passion in their dealings with most others, they particularly need a small collection of people they can trust, people who will listen to their new ideas. A major reason for the development of a *core group* is the project manager's intense need for friendship and emotional support. Project managers who do not have this support more often than not suffer from severe stress.

Core groups

George Graen,[1] an eminent professor at the University of Cincinnati, spent several years studying the formation of core groups around people in managerial jobs. The following principles came from his research:

1. *The initial managing stage.* During this time, the manager instructs and assesses subordinates in the usual way: tasks are assigned and outcomes observed. Over time, the manager notes that some staff perform well, others are undependable. Among those who perform well, some seem to adopt the manager's own approach naturally, that is, they make about the same decisions, take the same actions and value the same outcomes. In general, they come to think and act like the project manager. Consequently, the manager becomes steadily more comfortable delegating responsibility to these people. This means that they move into the core group, especially if they are psychologically compatible with the manager, that is, if friendship comes easily. In this stage, the manager usually initiates most of the interactions that take place. For most subordinates, a relationship with the manager never advances beyond this stage since the interactions tend to be businesslike, dictated by the formal role each person is assigned. However, for those individuals with whom the manager feels comfortable, who share *similar motivations* with him, and especially those who have some particular talent or characteristic needed by the manager, the relationship ripens into the second stage.

2. *The mentoring stage.* One easily recognizable feature of this stage is a tendency for subordinates to take more initiative by acting as manager in terms of initiating projects, suggesting solutions and taking on responsibility. The follower begins to share in some of the action and excitement of the managerial role, being privy to inside information, exercising more flexibility in work assignments and feeling the frustrations involved in allocating power and resources. The relationship between manager and subordinate can now be better understood by considering the manager as a *mentor* and the follower as *apprentice* manager. If the relationship continues to grow and expand, if the apprentice manager continues to help the mentor solve larger and larger problems, if the organizational resources allow it, and if the two people see it as in their best interests, a third stage appears – the normalisation stage.

3. *The normalization stage.* Here the special relationship becomes normal, and perhaps even formalized in the organization's structure and in its policy manual. Apprentice managers tend to become special assistants, or receive some other formal title, being recognized as individuals with power in their own right, even as their special relationship with the manager continues. In this way, the programmer becomes an analyst and the bright young analyst becomes a project leader. Their special relationships with the manager become engraved on the organizational scroll. Hopefully, of course, the personal friendships continue to grow and flourish also.

Motivation

Paradoxically, information systems project managers are responsible for the well-being of their team. Team members will undoubtedly be drawn from various disciplines, for example systems analysts, programmers, software quality engineers, support engineers, and so on. Bringing together a group of professionals and forging them into a high performance team not only takes leadership but requires continuous motivation on the manager's part. The motivational aspects of management are often stressed by academics of business in many postgraduate business classes. It can be argued that all problems in management are people problems. From manufacturing software to poor client relations, people are the only ones who can fix problems. When we emphasize what a manager needs to do to motivate professional employees, we sometimes miss the problem. Many project managers do not deal well with the self-esteem and self-actualization needs of their team. Many project managers are by nature systematic and goal-oriented. This can be considered a good thing when the goals of others are recognized and encouraged. Too often, however, the need for others to achieve goals is overlooked.

The most popular model of motivation states that motivation begins with needs. If needs are unsatisfied, we establish a goal, either consciously or unconsciously, and take action to achieve that goal. There are, of course, exceptions to this view – some people simply do not take any action towards goals at all. Often, in fact, bad work experiences tend to diminish the ability even to perceive a goal, let alone formulate plans to reach it, however simplistic they may be. Some individuals (or team members) of this kind pay a high price for their inability to participate in goal objectives, even suffering complete alienation within the team. This in itself shows the profoundly deep-rooted relevance of goals: those who do not share the team consensus of their importance can risk isolation from the organization itself.

Figure 2.2 shows the relationship between individual needs, goals and action. Notice how the relationships shown depict a clear cycle. Notice also how each element (e.g. goals) depends at least partly on another. As an example, this model shows that actions are not taken arbitrarily, but are intended to achieve one or more specific

Figure 2.2 A motivational model derived from Herzberg (1968)

goals. There is substantial consistency in human performance. Like others, project managers want to succeed in whatever they attempt. For project managers, success tends to become habitual, just as winning races becomes habitual for star athletes. One of the most important and well-established psychological findings related to performance is that we tend to perform at roughly the same level as those people who are close to us. Groups of people working together (whether analysts, programmers, testers, etc.) set up informal norms of performance. These norms tend to be reinforced, usually in subtle ways, by the members of the group. Developers, for example, usually reach an unstated understanding of how much work they consider to be fair. The group subtly disciplines any developer who becomes overeager and attempts to exceed this norm. Code Jockeys, as they are sometimes known, are brought into line so that do not embarrass the rest of the group by showing them up.

Returning to the issue of motivation, Maslow (1987) argued that people have *basic needs* that must be met in order for them to feel fulfilled. He arranged these needs into a series of levels according to their importance. The first level, for example, was termed *biological needs* and referred to requirements such as food, water and shelter. Higher level needs included transcendence (helping others to find fulfilment) and self-actualization (achieving a person's full potential).

Traditionally, organizations have sought to meet only the lower level needs of their employees. Often, organizations have concentrated on issues such as safety in the workplace at the expense of other needs, such as helping people to develop their capabilities. The importance of esteem and self-fulfilment should not be underestimated; every organization can recount cases where highly talented members of staff have moved elsewhere to find more challenging and rewarding work, or because they felt undervalued.

Increasing motivation

In creating high performance project teams, it is not enough for the information systems project manager to act as the person who sets goals and enforces certain standards of behaviour. Herzberg (1968) referred to the factors causing dissatisfaction as *hygiene factors*, using the analogy that hygiene does not improve health, but does prevent sickness. Herzberg was able to identify a set of factors, which act as true motivators, making lasting fulfilment and commitment possible. These are:

- a sense of achievement from completing work;
- recognition from others within the organization;
- responsibility assumed;
- varied work, interesting tasks; and
- promotion prospects.

What are the implications of Herzberg for the individual project managers? Whilst the absence of these motivators will not necessarily cause team members to resign, an increase in their strength will lead directly to increased individual fulfilment. In turn, this will lead to sustained levels of high performance. Although it may seem simplistic, we can take this material as evidence to support the old cliché that a happy workforce is a productive workforce.

It is important to remember that we must see team members as unique individuals. What is acceptable to one person may not be to another. This simple truth is what makes motivation an interesting problem. We cannot evolve a panacea to motivational problems – each problem needs an analysis of the individual. Indicators of the different needs include:

1. *Basic needs*
   - team member wants reassurance about job security;
   - team member needs to have duties clearly defined;
   - team member expresses concern about money to pay for living needs;
   - team member avoids taking risk;
   - team member expresses concern about working conditions;
   - team member follows instructions and does not go beyond them; and,
   - team member may have domestic health problems.
2. *Acceptance needs*
   - team member likes helping others;
   - team member does not like upsetting people/confrontation;
   - team member enjoys team work;
   - team member seeks to be accepted through group involvement; and,
   - team member stresses the needs for good relations.
3. *Achievement needs*
   - team member shows enthusiasm for the job;
   - team member shows competitive spirit;
   - team member takes pride in his/her work;
   - team member wants recognition for work done;
   - team member likes to know how well he/she is doing;
   - team member shows initiative when working; and,
   - team member works well without close supervision.
4. *Power needs*
   - team member wins arguments;
   - team member seeks involvement in groups to influence people;
   - team member seeks leadership roles in informal groups;
   - team member values status which demonstrates importance;
   - team member knows what makes the organization tick; and,
   - team member is sensitive to internal politics.

As information systems project managers, we should be watching these indicators in our staff. They will form the basis for training, work assignment allocation, delegation, etc. They also provide an insight into what makes individuals tick.

Managerial styles

There is an English proverb which says: 'there are no bad students, only bad teachers'. It can be argued that this sentiment can also be extended to project managers: 'there are no bad team members, only poor project managers'.

The phrase managerial style has a number of related meanings. One meaning refers to a collective approach to participation, employee appraisal and control. Another meaning refers to the behaviour that the information systems project manager adopts when dealing with clients, sponsors, team members or subordinates. In this context, the particular style chosen will depend on personal inclinations, training, experience and environmental factors. It will influence the project manager's relations with their subordinates, group productivity, and patterns of interaction among employees. In the macro-organizational sense, management style helps determine formal structure (see Chapter 1), line relationships, whether the organization uses project teams, the frequency and character of project board meetings, and so on.

It could be argued that there is no such thing as the perfect managerial style. However, such a view would not sit well with the whole of the human behavioural school of knowledge, since it is based on the belief that it is possible to improve the way that managers work. Human behaviourists believe that a manager's style is based on the pattern of behaviour they exhibit in carrying out a leadership role over a period of time. An assumption is made that team members will work harder and more profitably for managers who employ certain styles rather than others. Rensis Likert (1961) in his book *New Patterns of Management*, outlined a model of managerial styles (or systems) that places managers within one of four basic categories. This model is shown in Table 2.3.

Tannenbaum and Schmidt (1958 and 1973) propose a similar model where the behaviour of a manager can be placed upon a continuum that ranges from authoritarian behaviour to democratic behaviour at the other. Figure 2.3 illustrates this model. The similarities between this model and Lickert's can be seen by

Table 2.3   Summary of Likert's managerial styles

SYSTEM 1 Exploitive authoritarian	SYSTEM 2 Benevolent authoritarian	SYSTEM 3 Consultative	SYSTEM 4 Participative groups
Under the exploitive and authoritarian regime, threats and punishments are employed and communication and team are poor	The benevolent authoritative regime is paternalistic and allows some opportunities for consultation and delegation	The consultative regime moves forwards to greater democracy and teamwork. Rewards are used instead of threats	The participative group regime is the ultimate democratic style, leading to commitment to organizational goals

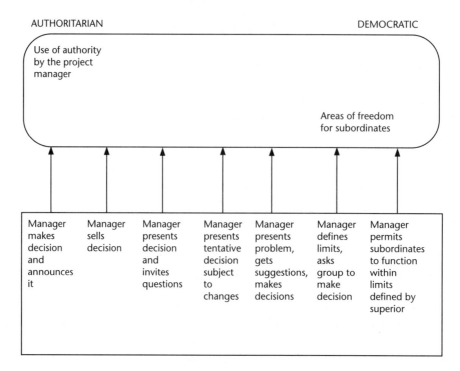

AUTHORITARIAN   DEMOCRATIC

Use of authority
by the project
manager

Areas of freedom
for subordinates

| Manager makes decision and announces it | Manager sells decision | Manager presents decision and invites questions | Manager presents tentative decision subject to changes | Manager presents problem, gets suggestions, makes decisions | Manager defines limits, asks group to make decision | Manager permits subordinates to function within limits defined by superior |

Figure 2.3 A continuum of management styles (adapted from Tannenbaum and Schmidt, 1958)

comparing the diagram with Table 2.3. Taken together, both models suggest that managers have a basic choice between an authoritarian or democratic approach to their roles.

Authoritarian style

Information systems project managers who are task-driven tend to be characterized as being strong, competent and dominant. Their style tends to be autocratic and their relationship with subordinates is mainly directional, that is, involves the issuing of orders. Information systems project managers who adopt this style of management usually find that their team begins to undermine them as morale drops. Project managers should be aware of the effects upon their team is using this style of management. Conventional theory indicates that the following may result:

- personal needs and interests of employees will have low priority – morale tends to suffer;
- hostility may be high, resulting in insubordination;
- employee creativity and initiative may be stifled; and
- if the project manager leaves, the project tends to suffer or fall apart.

Such an approach is often effective, but is not necessarily the most efficient way of managing a project. Although the project work may be completed in the way that the manager has specified, it does little to encourage creativity and innovation amongst team members.

Democratic style

In contrast, a democratic (person-oriented) project management style is characterized by the sharing of responsibility. A reliance is placed on the willingness of team members to take whatever actions are required of them without the threat of punishment. Democratic project managers use positive incentives to encourage team members to improve their work rate or reward them for notable performance. The person-oriented project manager also places an emphasis on decision making, problem solving, planning and control. Traditional theory indicates that with such a project manager the following will result:

- personal needs and employee interests will be given high priority;
- output and goal achievement will be higher in the longer term, than with the task-oriented approach;
- employee creativity and initiative will be increased;
- morale and employee satisfaction will be high; and
- commitment will be high.

Many theorists favour the democratic style of management. However, it is worth noting that projects sometimes cross cultural boundaries where such an approach may not apply. Although the democratic style is preferred in Western industrialized nations, it may not be suitable in other parts of the world. Given the cultural background of many autocratic project managers, adopting this type of management style represents a huge challenge if they are to operate effectively in the new environment. One information systems project manager participating in a seminar on cross-boarder project management in Europe, suggested that to be successful, '...you must believe in participating management and an intelligent team, committed to its objectives. Five or six years ago, you told people what to do and they followed your orders. Today, you have to convince employees that you are doing the right thing.'

Power and influence

A business must maintain appropriate relationships with other political, economic and social systems in its environment. Information systems project managers must also maintain manageable relationships within their project environment. This includes stakeholder groups such as external customers, internal clients, business users, internal employees, shareholders, government, suppliers, the local community and a number of other agencies. Figure 2.4 illustrates the project stakeholder community. All of these

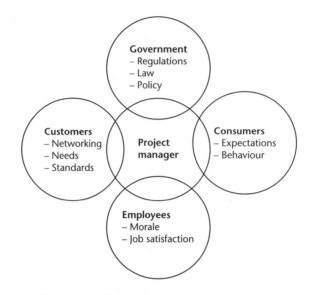

Figure 2.4 The project stakeholder community

parties may have a *stake* in the successful implementation of a project, so it is important to identify which stakeholders will have an impact on the work of the project team. For example, at the implementation phase of a project, the potential for misuse and malfunction of a proposed system must be analysed in terms of its impact on all of an organization's present and potential stakeholders (Mitroff and Mason, 1988). This kind of analysis not only clarifies that nature of potential problems, but may also lead to a practical solution.

In Chapter 1, we discussed how the political and social environment could influence project failure. It was noted that such failure is *not* addressed explicitly by traditional project management methods. As discussed, the transfer of lessons from the past into future practice can offer a crucial advantage. Unfortunately, this process is seldom implemented to its full extent and is often constrained by stakeholder participation or power politics.

Rosabeth Moss-Kanter (1985), writing in *The Change Masters*, describes power as 'the ability to get things done'. Although such a definition is straightforward, it has significant appeal in relation to the role of project managers. It is particularly helpful since much of the skill of a project manager revolves around the ability to manage the political power dimensions within and around the stakeholder community, so much so that failure to understand and control the political process has been the downfall of many good project managers. Politics is concerned with the way in which managers gain and use power and involves them in a range of activities, such as bargaining for resources, striking deals, forming coalitions with others, and so on. Clearly it is important for a project manager to have political skills in order to gain and keep power. Based on his own personal experience and analysis, Nico Machiavelli (Gauss, 1980) advised political leaders on how to acquire power, resist dissent and control subordinates. Machiavelli's cynical view of his fellow man is best summed up by his comment: 'Men are in general ungrateful, fickle, false, cowardly, covetous, but as long as you succeed, they are yours entirely'. For this reason, Machiavelli warns that, when power is at stake, questions of morality are irrelevant – lying, deceit and manipulation are all legitimate tactics.

From Machiavelli's perspective, winning the game by whatever means (power or otherwise) is all that matters. Power, however, is relative in the sense that the source of the project manager's power lies not in himself, but in his followers. The project manager can only exercise the power which his followers allow.

Social and behavioural researchers have identified several frameworks of power. The four major types of power which individuals develop or acquire are personal, legitimate, expert and political power. Each of these forms of power is considered in the next section.

Personal power

Personal power (or referent power) is possessed by certain individuals and is sometimes termed charismatic power. Some project managers have immense charisma and are able to build powerful personal relationships with senior managers and others. Other stakeholder groups look to these types of people to make decisions for them – they can be very forceful and determined. Project managers who use this type of power tend to sense the needs of their followers and provide a focus which meets those needs.

Legitimate power

This is based on people having positions within a structured framework. In a particular culture, power will be delegated to different managers. Since the manager's power is seen as being legitimately held, it will be accepted by others. The rights of the manager's role include the right to information which may come from above or below that organization level, the right of access to organizational decision-making bodies (for example, project boards and steering committees), and the right to organize work activities.

Expert power

Most information technology professionals are labelled knowledge workers. Expert power is based on the specialist knowledge possessed by certain individuals. It frequently arises when there is complex knowledge that can be gained only through professional training and education. In essence, expert power stems from, say, project managers having knowledge and skill in an area (for example, Object Development) that other managers do not. Other managers will be willing to accept the project manager's influence in the field of the project manager's expertise. Expert power in areas that are crucial to the attainment of success may give the power holder an important role with its associated position source. So, if the project manager's expertise is questioned by one of the stakeholders, it may be possible for him to resort to the methods associated with legitimate power. The level of expert power exercised will be related to the degree to which the individual can be substituted. If the person is difficult to replace, he or she is likely to be in a very strong position.

Political power

Political power stems from being supported by a stakeholder group. To gain political power the project manager will need to be able to work with people and social systems so that he can gain support and allegiance from them. Gaining true political power involves having an understanding of those factors most likely to encourage others to support you, as well as understanding how systems can be used in your favour. Political leadership also involves having access to sanctions and rewards. A number of tactics can be employed to obtain and retain political power. For example, project managers can develop formal and informal contacts with a stakeholder group, which will enhance their personal power base.

Decision making

Information systems projects by their nature tend be complex in nature and demand a high level of intellect and intervention by the project manager. Making decisions is by and large what project managers do. How well (or effectively) they make such decisions will be based on the criteria of *behavioural history, situational beliefs, personnel values, social and occupational norms, personality*, and *environmental constraints*. Project managers make decisions every day. Most of the decisions made will be routine and low risk. However, every decision, no matter how small, requires an assessment of objectives, alternatives and potential risks. This area is discussed in more detail in Chapter 4. In making decisions the project manager must settle the following important questions:

- What decision needs to be made?
- When does it have to be made?
- Who will decide?
- Who will need to be consulted?
- Who will ratify or veto the decision?
- Who will need to be informed of the decision?

Types of decision

As shown in Figure 2.5, decisions can normally be separated into two types. The first type is the forward-programmed (or forward-looking) decision which tends to be strategic in nature). As an example: do we hire additional staff in January 2003? The second type is made as we respond to a developing problem or crisis, which can either be technical (a software problem, for example) or involve people, for example moving the team to a different geographical location. These kinds of decisions tend to be tactical in nature.

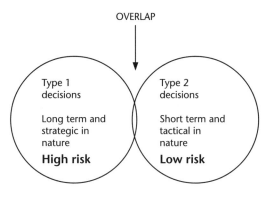

Figure 2.5 Decision profiles

A model of decision making

Simon (see Harrison, 1983), a prominent computer scientist, suggests that finding the solution to any problem can be divided into four stages:

1. Perception of decision need or opportunity (called the intelligence phase).
2. Formulation of alternative courses of action.
3. Evaluation of alternatives for their respective contributions.
4. Choice of one or more alternatives for implementation.

Simon's model of decision making is shown in Figure 2.6.

It is obvious from the above that decision making will depend on how well the facts and issues facing the business, client or project are understood. This is why information can be regarded as the life blood of any project manager. Project managers

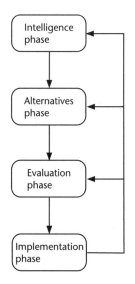

Figure 2.6 The decision making process

working in information technology have access to various business and information systems. Information systems can help in the intelligence phase by providing information about internal and external conditions that might require decision making by managers. In many organizations the use of project management information tools is an integral part of the decision-making process. As an example, such tools can undertake *what if? analysis* or produce pre-specified reports for managers on an exception basis. Information systems should help project managers to select a proper course of action and then provide feedback on the success of the implemented decision. Of course, this assumes that enough information was gathered during the intelligence phase, and a sufficient number of alternatives were developed and evaluated during the design phase. If not, the project manager may choose to return to these phases for more data or alternatives.

An alternative model of decision making

In his book, *High Output Management*, Andrew Grove (1984, p. 84) – a former President of the Intel Corporation – gives some interesting insights into decision making and suggests an alternative model for decision making based on a three stage process.

The first stage involves *free discussion*, in which all points of view are welcomed and all aspects of an issue are openly discussed. The greater the disagreement and controversy, the more important becomes the word *free*. Although this may sound obvious, it is not often the case that team members feel able to speak frankly and without fear of punishment. Usually when a meeting gets heated, participants hang back, trying to sense the direction of things, saying nothing until they see what view is likely to prevail. They then throw their support behind that view to avoid being associated with a losing position.

The next stage is reaching *a clear decision*. Again, the greater the disagreement about the issue, the more important becomes the word *clear*. In fact, particular pains should be taken to frame the terms of the decision with utter clarity. Again, there is a tendency to do just the opposite: when we know that a decision is controversial, we tend to obscure matters to avoid an argument. However, the argument cannot be avoided by our being mealy-mouthed; it is merely postponed. People who do not like a particular decision will become more angry and frustrated if they do not get a prompt and straight response.

Finally, everyone involved must give the decision reached by the group *full support*. This does not necessarily mean that every member of the group must be in full agreement. Providing that participants commit to back the decision that has been made, the outcome can be considered satisfactory.

One of the strengths of this model is that it seems easy to follow. However, Grove found that following the model came easily to only two classes of professional employees: senior managers who have been in the company for a long time, who feel at home with the way things are done, and who identify with the values of the organization; and the new graduates that Intel employed, because they used the model as students doing college work. For middle managers, the decision-making model is easier to accept intellectually than it is to use in practice. One of the reasons for this is that middle managers often have trouble expressing their views forcefully enough. They often find it difficult to make unpleasant or difficult decisions. They also find it difficult to accept that they are expected to support a decision with which they do not agree. However, the wrong decision must never be adopted simply because some people disagree or do not have the competence needed to do what is required. The decision adopted should always be amongst the genuine alternatives considered, that is, it should represent a course of action that is adequate to solve the problem. Sometimes, this may mean that we demand more of people than they are capable of giving. In these cases, people must learn to do more, or should be replaced by people with the required skills.

Rationality

Observers of organizational dynamics have indicated that decisions often occur in an atmosphere of limited political rationality. In this environment, conflicts of interest are rarely resolved fully, uncertainty is difficult to avoid, fire-fighting is common and decision makers learn as they go along. Where major decisions are needed, a balance is often made between rational, calculated thought and organizational procedures, regulations and politics. O'Brien (1990, p. 323) has noted that, given the resource constraints of the real world, most decision makers will choose to *satisfy* rather than *optimize* when faced with a decision situation. People will rarely act as rational beings who insist that all relevant information be gathered, that all rational alternatives are considered, and that only the optimum alternative be chosen. Instead, they will act with what Simon calls *bounded rationality*, that is, they will be satisfied to make a decision based on incomplete information and a limited number of alternatives, if it meets some of their subjective preferences and produces an acceptable level of results. Alexander George (1980, pp. 23–24), a political scientist, offers advice to decision makers who apply structured methods of thinking to ill-structured problems that rely on multiple points of view. His advice highlights when and where potential problems may occur:

1. When the decision maker and his or her advisors agree too readily on the nature of the problem facing them and on a response to it.
2. When advisors and policy advocates take different positions and debate them before the executive, but their disagreements do not cover the full range of relevant hypotheses and alternative options.
3. When there is no advocate for an unpopular policy option.
4. When advisors to the executive thrash out their disagreements over policy without the executive's knowledge and confront him or her with a unanimous recommendation.

5. When advisors agree privately among themselves that the executive ought to face up to a difficult decision, but no one is willing to alert him or her to the need to do so.

6. When the executive, faced with an important decision, is dependent on a single channel of information.

7. When the key assumptions and premises of a plan that the executive is asked to adopt have been evaluated only to advocates of that option.

8. When the executive asks advisors for their opinions on a preferred course of action but does not request a qualified group to examine more carefully the negative judgement offered by one or more advisors.

9. When the executive is impressed by the consensus among his or her advisors on behalf of a particular option but fails to ascertain how firm the consensus is, how it was achieved, and whether it is justified.

Problem solving

Good problem solving, like good decision making, depends heavily on experience and judgement. In both areas of project responsibility, however, it is only within the framework of a systematic procedure that experience and judgement produce successful results and a reputation for managerial excellence. In delivering information systems, project managers will face many situations which will require problem resolution. Some of these problems have already been identified and discussed in Chapter 1. Based on our observations over the years, we have come to the conclusion that many project managers work on the principle that 'if it's not broken, don't fix it'. This attitude of 'let's keep on doing what we're doing and if something goes wrong (breaks) then let's fix it and continue' is endemic within the information technology industry, and is obviously a key factor in project failure. Problem solving and critical thinking are both key project management skills. Research suggests that project managers will use one or a combination of three methods when forced to tackle problems. These methods are:

- Method 1: *Experience* – applying yesterday's solutions to today's problems, which may not be identified.
- Method 2: *Intuition* – allowing your subconscious mind to suggest a solution and applying it without looking for alternatives.
- Method 3: *Logical method* – using a systematic method to define the problem, create alternative solutions and choose the most advantageous. Figure 2.7 describes a model of problem solving based on this approach.

Stages in problem solving

When project managers set out to solve problems they often use the third method described above. It is worth looking at reasons for this in a little more detail. This

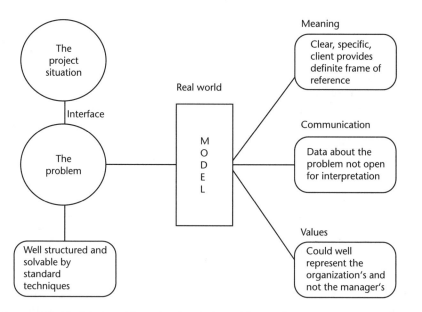

Figure 2.7 Model of problem situation (adapted from Eden, Jones and Sims, 1979)

method is perceived by managers to offer a higher success rate. The logical problem solving method takes several forms but basically falls into three parts:

1. Identifying the real problem (cause).
2. Choosing the best solution.
3. Implementing a solution.

1. *Identifying the real problem (cause).* A problem first reaches our attention as a situation, which can affect our ability to achieve an objective, for example a poorly functioning system might cause the loss of a client. The first step in solving a problem is to carry out a detailed examination of the situation as it is at present. This can be done using methods such as interviews, questionnaires, personal observation, examination of documents and modelling. During this stage it helps if information is classified for precision, validity, relevance and assumptions (based on fact, plausible and probable). Having completed gathering data, it can then be examined in detail. This should then allow the situation to be defined more clearly and it is a good idea to set down the details of the problem in written form. The search can then begin for the cause of the problem. Often, it will be found that the problem being investigated stems from one or more other problems that may not have been identified. In these cases, it will be necessary to work backwards, questioning why each problem or situation arose until it is not possible to go any further. At this point, the true underlying problem will have been uncovered.

2. *Choosing the best solution.* Having uncovered the real problem it is often tempting to pick the first solution that comes to mind. Although the chosen solution may well work, it may not have been the best solution available. Given this situation, we must

find ways to be certain that the solution chosen is the best one. One way of doing this is by comparing alternative solutions. Of course, this assumes that they are evaluated using the same criteria. For example, alternatives can be screened and ranked based on individual criteria or overall scores. This is usually done on the basis of formal or informal decision rules.

Table 2.4 gives an example of a ranking table, where a group of solutions are evaluated against a set of criteria. Each solution is assigned several scores, and the solution with the highest total score will be the one that is chosen. In the table, alternatives with an overall score of below 35 will be rejected (solutions A and C).

Developing solutions requires creative thinking and an ability to break away from tradition. Within reason, the more minds that can be applied to the problem, the more solutions will be suggested. In some cases, the problem being examined may not be clearly defined and may well cover more than a single issue. The important points for the project manager to note are:

1. Problem situations can contain a large number of interrelated problems. They may be based on personnel definitions of what is important, which may differ from the organization's view. They are more likely to be complex and ill-structured.
2. The manager may not always be able to communicate the nature of the problem effectively, for example, due to lack of verbal skills or a technical misunderstanding on both sides.
3. When presenting data about the problem, the manager will structure it in relation to his or her understanding of the situation and not the project manager's.
4. An individual's value-system is a frame of reference for selectively perceiving information from the environment and it helps to direct the construction of the problem.

3. *Implementing a solution.* Once a solution has been selected, it must be implemented. This, of course, can be harder than it sounds. There will almost certainly be a need to modify plans even as they are being put into action. In many instances, a project management effort will be required to implement the solution. If the solution affects an existing information technology project, the following items may need replanning: types of hardware and software, hiring of personnel, training of personnel, procedures and physical facilities.

Table 2.4 Example of evaluating alternative solutions

Criterion	Weighting	Solutions			Totals		
		A	B	C	A	B	C
Quality	3	5	3	3	15	9	9
Cost	4	2	5	3	8	20	12
Time	3	3	2	4	9	6	12
Totals	10	10	10	10	32	35	33

Communication

Two thousand five hundred years ago, Confucius wrote that, 'if language is not correct, then what is said is not what is meant; if what is said is not what is meant, then what ought to be done remains undone'. The same is perfectly true today in any project.

You will have realized from the previous section that all project managers act as protagonists in a complex social arena. Organizational peer managers very often have different points of view to those of project managers. There will also often be a difference in culture and objectives between peer managers. However, project managers will be interdependent on their peer managers and will often have to interact with them to achieve results. Given this, communication becomes a key factor in the success of managers working under such conditions. Vocabulary plays a key role in forming interpersonal relationships, for example managers must be careful to choose words that are sensitive to people's feelings. In terms of two people communicating with each other, perhaps in a manager-to-subordinate relationship, each person in the transaction has something to gain from a situation where communication is effective. For the project manager it may help to increase the team's understanding of the project objectives. For each team member, effective communication provides an opportunity to create a picture for him or herself of the contributions that are needed to deliver the project successfully.

In the body of knowledge needed for effective project management (listed earlier in this chapter, in Table 2.2), we identified communication as a key project management competency. All project managers need to have perfected good communication skills. Some project managers view communication as a *soft* management issue and as such a soft requirement. Those project managers who have come from a technical background see communication skills as intangible and inferior to technical competencies. The personal and business incentives are less obvious, and project managers are not effectively measured or rewarded on their communication performance. The three most common symptoms of poor communication are confusion/misunderstanding, duplication of effort or demand, and delay. Further consequences may be felt as demotivation, inefficiency and lost opportunity. Project managers (and others) can respond to the requirements for improved communication in projects in three ways (Howard, 1996):

1. *Basic communication behaviour*. Individuals make adjustments to their communications so that there is a greater alignment between project members. However, these alignments are carried out in such a way that they do not diminish the total autonomy of the individual who is still supreme and in control of communication interfaces.
2. *Symbiotic behaviour*. Communication occurs in such a way that individuals sacrifice part of their respective individual autonomies in order that the project entity of which they are part has a greater autonomy in its relationship with other projects and stakeholders in its environment.

3. *Fusion behaviour*. Individuals totally surrender their autonomy in communications so that the project becomes the superordinate system. Thus, the project has the maximum authority in its relationship with the larger development and organization development. Fusion has rarely, if ever, been reached.

Communication is not just a matter of making effective presentations, holding regular meetings, or handing down information. It is about creating trust and developing a climate in which open communication can take place. This atmosphere must be one of active listening, where suggestions are encouraged and constructive criticism can be offered openly. Above all, we should expect people to behave in a way that is consistent with spoken and written communication. According to a recent survey by Cawkwell (1998), many managers can find behaviour changes of this kind difficult, and they may well be apprehensive. Such concerns need to be recognized and addressed in a sympathetic and positive way.

We must also take account of the special requirements placed upon managers by communications technology. Technologies such as video conferencing tend to be regarded as being synonomous with face-to-face meetings and presentations. However, there are subtle differences that must be dealt with. As an example, video conferencing tends to disguise body language and other subtle cues that would normally be used to gauge the reactions of other people. In a similar way, e-mail should be seen as being somewhat different to internal memos or business correspondence since it tends to be treated less formally than other types of correspondence.

Choosing a communications approach

In Chapter 1, we saw that the culture of the organization is perhaps the biggest influence on what forms of communication are likely to work best. As we have seen, some organizations are predominantly command and control oriented whilst others are more collaborative in style. For the project manager, choosing a communication style will obviously be influenced by the organization style. There are many ways in which a *project communication strategy* can be developed. Table 2.5 proposes an overall strategy for handling communications within a project.

Table 2.5   Project communication strategy

Degree of advanced disclosure	Considerations:
	1. Advanced disclosure can cause uncertainty/ anxiety, but not disclosing can be equally unsettling – rumours and leaks are likely
	2. Advanced disclosure can be used as a way of getting feedback on ideas
	3. If you do communicate in advance make sure it is made clear what is *fixed* and what is *open* for disclosure

Table 2.5   Continued

Consultation or communication	Considerations: 1. The need to keep key people alongside you (even those who may be hostile to you) 2. You might actually be short of information 3. Consulted people are usually more involved and committed
The process	Considerations: 1. Prepare detailed communication plan 2. Prepare feedback mechanism
The message	Considerations: 1. Have a clear common message 2. Maintain the message rigorously to avoid doubts and reactions that can result from minor variations
The content	Considerations: 1. Put forward clear reasons for the objectives that you set 2. Declare a positive aim around which staff can unify and be energized 3. Identify the principles and approaches, which will be used within the project and the reasons for adopting them
The timing	Considerations: 1. Communicate as far ahead as possible and give time for staff and other managers to absorb the significance of the message and come to terms with the changes that are being proposed 2. Have a detailed timing schedule which will minimize the risk of staff and other managers being antagonized by being left out or receiving the message through the wrong channel
The people	Considerations: 1. Ensure that the message is given in the right way, at the right level, in the right language 2. Recognize that the person giving the message has some prior knowledge of the subject. Remember managers generally need time to absorb the message and discuss it with peers

Summary

▨ The work of a project manager can be described in terms of the processes that are completed during the life of the project. These processes are: visioning, developing goals and objectives; planning the project and optimizing effectiveness; monitoring, analysing, estimating and forecasting future states up to the conclusion of the project; and leading, directing, commanding or controlling the course of the project.

▨ The role of a project manager can also be described in terms of the basic job functions that are performed. These functions were listed in Table 2.1.

▨ Project managers are expected to develop a wide range of skills, knowledge and abilities. In the United Kingdom, the Association for Project Management sets out the body of knowledge required by managers (see Table 2.2).

▨ A key function of the project manager is to lead team members in their endeavours. This can only be achieved if the manager pays attention to the needs of both the team and its individual members. Project managers must be able to gain the commitment of stakeholders (clients, managers, team members, etc.) to the vision of the project.

▨ Project managers often establish core groups in order to obtain support for themselves, but the formation of a core group also brings other benefits, such as helping team members to develop their skills further.

▨ Most models of motivation are based around the concept that people have both basic and higher needs that must be fulfilled. Only when an individual's higher needs are fulfilled will that person give their full commitment and enthusiasm to a project.

▨ Project managers can adopt an authoritarian or democratic approach to their role. In general, a democratic management style is more effective than an authoritarian approach.

▨ Many working relationships are characterized by power. Individuals can obtain several different forms of power. These include personal, legitimate, expert and political power. Project managers must learn to handle these different kinds of power.

▨ Common models of decision making include four basic phases: perception of decision need or opportunity, formulation of alternative courses of action, evaluation of alternatives and choice of one or more alternatives for implementation.

▨ Grove's model of decision making is based on three stages: free discussion, reaching a clear decision and giving the decision full support. Although this model can be effective, it is not without its difficulties. As an example, middle managers sometimes find it difficult to accept decisions made using this approach.

■ There are several different approaches to problem solving. The logical method suggests that problem solving involves three stages: identifying the real problem, choosing the best solution and implementing a solution.

■ Effective communication is essential to the work of a project manager. Project managers can improve communications in three ways: basic communication behaviour, symbiotic behaviour and fusion behaviour. Managers should develop a project communications strategy in order to increase motivation and support the work of their teams.

Project checklists

Checklist 2.1 Project management

■ Have you agreed upon a methodology for delivering the project?

■ Have you a signed-off project plan?

■ Have you defined the organizational interface (communication plan, etc.)

■ Have you agreed a resource profile and schedule for the project?

■ Have you agreed a method of formal reporting?

■ Have you agreed a formal approach to configuration management?

■ Have you identified the project's critical success factors?

■ Have you prepared and agreed formal terms of reference for your staff?

■ Have you agreed what level of business assurance and project support is needed?

■ Keep the project simple:
  – define clear tasks;
  – perform validations at appropriate steps;
  – use appropriate evaluation criteria;
  – set reasonable criteria for validation;
  – set concise reachable deadlines;
  – keep an overview about the project as a whole;
  – keep in touch with the people associated with the project;
  – represent your requests by words and by your behaviour.

Checklist 2.2 Business review checklist

The following checklist provides a guide to some of the main considerations for business review.

1 Project significance

■ In the context of existing and other planned developments, does the scope of this project look reasonable? Should it be extended/limited?

■ Does the project take reasonable share of the current resources available? Resources include staff, financial budgets, machine time, etc.

■ What is the opportunity cost of the proposed development?

■ Are there political or other factors that override or diminish the cost/benefit view of the justification?

■ Does the project or proposed system conform to company and/or management style?

2 Existing system

■ Are the statements regarding the existing system correct?

■ Do the figures for volumes and running costs agree with known data?

■ Is there a single major problem concerned with the existing system, which if dealt with individually would do away with the need for a new system?

■ Are the users aware of existing systems problems, or is the impetus for change purely external?

3 System requirements

■ Is the proposed system volume dependent? If so, have expected volumes been clearly stated? Are peak volumes catered for?

■ Have the users been fully involved in assessing system requirements?

■ Have the users signified their acceptance of the suggested requirements (by participation in lower level Q-A procedures)?

■ If any special tools or techniques were used to assess requirements or measure rates and volumes, for example by simulations, were they satisfactorily constructed and carried out?

■ In suggesting system requirements, are there excessive or abnormal demands on:
  – computer operations staff;
  – data preparation or control staff;
  – user department;
  – development staff.

4 Proposed system

■ Are the base assumptions correct? Are they in line with technical standards?

■ Does the proposed system meet all the stated requirements? Are the reasons for not meeting any requirements fully justified?

■ Does the proposed system include any facilities not identified as part of the system requirements? Are any additional requirements fully justified?

■ Are features of the proposed system reasonably attainable? Are there any unreasonable assumptions made about:
  – staff capacities and abilities;
  – extraordinary working hours or conditions.

■ Is there a pioneering element in the proposed development? Has the risk been adequately assessed and justified?

■ Does the proposed system hang together? Is it workable? Are there any omissions, illogicalities or logistic errors?

5 Alternative approaches

■ Have all possible alternatives for the development been examined, costed and shown to be less attractive than the selected option?

■ Will the currently proposed system be invalidated by an alternative that may soon be available or more attractive?

6 Technical feasibility

■ Are management satisfied that the technicians involved have an in-depth understanding of the technical aspects of the project?

■ If technical pioneering is involved has the cost and time of the learning curve been adequately assessed?

■ Are correct assumptions made about:
  – data storage capacities;
  – run timings;
  – program languages;
  – development techniques.

■ For new hardware and software acquisitions are the claims of the supplier fully substantiated? Have they been validated by reference to other existing users?

■ Are suggested equipment and techniques either obsolescent or too sophisticated?

■ Have all aspects of fall-back and recovery been fully considered and satisfactory solutions presented?

■ Have all aspects of privacy and access been fully addressed?

7 User considerations

■ What new disciplines will the proposed system impose on the user department? Is there current experience of such departments' performance, and, if so, are the new disciplines likely to cause problems?

▓ Will the new system give rise to problems of morale?

▓ Is there adequate provision for user participation and liaison throughout the project life?

▓ Are the users enthusiastic about the system?

▓ Are user departments fully aware of the organization implications?

▓ Have they committed themselves to unrealistic time-scales and/or task performance?

▓ Is the implementation plan fail-safe?

▓ Have all possibilities for implementation failure been fully evaluated?

Bibliography

Adair J., 1990, *Understanding Motivation*, Talbart and Adaire Press, London.

ASCE, *Management Forum*, February 1994.

Cawkwell J., 1998, 'What Does Communication Mean to You?', Unpublished Research Paper, Leeds Metropolitan University UK, 1998.

Cleland D., 1998, *Project Management*, 3rd edn, McGraw-Hill Publishing Company, USA.

Dawson S., 1988, *Analysing Organisations*, Macmillan Education Ltd, London.

Eden C., Jones S. and Sims D., 1979, *Thinking in Organisations*, Macmillan Press, USA.

Gauss C., 1980, *Machiavelli The Prince*, New American Library, New York.

George A., 1980, *Presidential Decision Making in Foreign Policy: The Effective Use of Information and Advice*, Westview, USA.

Grove A., 1984, *High Output Management*, Souvenir Press, UK.

Harrison P., 1983, *Operational Research*, Mitchell Beazley, USA.

Herzberg F., 1968, *Work and the Nature of Man*, Staples Press.

Howard A., 1996, 'Improving System Development Methodologies: Tackling the Human Communications Issues', BCS, ISM Group Proceedings, September 1996.

Likert R., 1961, *New Patterns of Management*, McGraw-Hill Books.

Maslow A., 1987, *Motivation and Personality*, 3rd edn, Harper & Row, New York.

Mitroff I. and Mason R., 1988, 'Deep Ethical and Epistemological Issues in the Design of Information Systems', in *Expert Systems Review*, June 1988.

Moss-Kanter R. (1985) *The Change Masters: Innovation and entrepreneurship in the American corporation*, Simon and Schuster, New York.

O'Brien J., 1990, *Management Information Systems*, Irwin, USA (p. 323).

Tannenbaum, K. and Schmidt, W., (1958 and 1973), 'How To Choose A Leadership Pattern', in *Harvard Business Review*, March–April 1958, pp. 95–102, and May–June 1973, p. 167.

Further reading

Adams S., 1996, *The Dilbert Principle*, Bath Press, UK.

Galliers R., 1993, 'Research Issues in Information Systems' in *Journal of Information Technology*, No. 8, pp. 92–98.

Maslow H., 1971, 'Self Actualising and Beyond' in Maslow H., *The Farther Reaches of Human Nature*, pp. 41–53, Viking Press, New York.

McManus J., 1997, *The Role of the Project Manager, Management Briefings*, FT Pitman Publishing, London.

Morgan G., 1986, *Images of Organisation*, Sage Publications Inc., New York.

Useful websites

http://home.earthlink.net/~adebru/guerrilla/pmmain.htm
This website contains documents intended to be of help for anyone who gets the questionable honour of assuming a role as a project manager, team leader or any other leader in a fast-paced technical environment.

http://www.ee.ed.ac.uk/~gerard/Management/
This website contains the useful series of articles on basic management skills which appeared in IEE *Engineering Management Journal* bimonthly from October 1991 until April 1993.

http://www.projectnet.com
ProjectNet
The ProjectNet project management resource site by *Project Manager Today* magazine. Contains useful sources of information on managing projects.

Self-assessment exercises

1. According to Adair, what six functions are associated with leadership?

2. List Herzberg's hygiene factors.

3. According to Likert, which kind of managerial style accomplishes tasks through the use of threats and punishments?

4. In brief, explain the concept of expert power.

5. Simon's model of decision making involves four discrete stages. What are these stages?

6. According to Grove, why will some managers find it difficult to accept the decisions made by a group?

7. Why do most decision makers choose to satisfy rather than optimize?

8. If a project manager adopts an authoritarian management style, what kinds of problems are likely to occur?

Case study

This case study was originally published in Project Manager Today, April 1999, and was entitled 'Climbing the maturity ladder', part 11, by John McManus
We will call the Case Study Company the ACM Corporation, the company is currently valued at $5 billion – with operating interests in banking, insurance and asset management. In 1997 it spent some $200 million on information-technology-related products and services – including direct labour. A significant proportion of this cash went to external services providers. As part of the organization's future strategic direction, to enhance its market share in financial services, a decision was made to increase its inhouse IT software and back office capability. Although the company had a number of mature software processes, the IT board decided to reengineer a number of key processes. As part of this exercise the opportunity was taken to audit its people processes using the Capability Maturity Model (CMM).

First task

An initial audit was conducted in order to establish a base line. Working closely with external consultants a customized methodology and questionnaire was created, and a map developed to relate people capabilities with the company's key competency statements. Using the IT department for the trial, the staff groups were segmented by function, for example project management. Managers were identified from those departments that were the biggest users of its services (that is project-based work) to get feedback on the IT department personnel. The trial revealed a number of weaknesses in the organization's people and project processes. For example, a large percentage of personnel felt that staff development was not focused on the individual's needs. It was also perceived by some project managers that, although professionally developed, the appraisal system was too critical.

Empowerment

A key aspect of introducing change is staff empowerment. To show management support, and ensure buy-in from the organization, a group of key project staff were teamed up and empowered to determine how the people processes within the project department should be restructured. The team reviewed numerous aspects for restructuring including skill levels, current and future project workloads, environment, training, staff requests for assignments and even personality tests and team-building sessions.

By mapping the trial results to the baseline capabilities, a profile of each functional project group within the department was created. This gave the company the ability to review each group member's performance against both their department and group profile, and enabled individual improvement objectives to be set.

Putting the plan together

Following the initial trial and project mapping exercise, several plans were developed, beginning with an action plan for organization-wide improvement. The company needed a plan which identified people-improvement efforts in software development, software testing, product development, project management and general consultancy.

The process started with off-site workshops to develop a strategic programme for implementation. These sessions went well and included representatives from each of the supporting departments, a couple of senior project managers, and external facilitator and key management representatives from the board. The week ended with an agreed plan for implementation.

The plan defined:

- Roles and responsibilities (several groups were engaged to implement the plan, each group had a team leader, recorder and a scheduler who was responsible for coordinating the efforts of the groups).
- Objectives; the team had documented objectives and goals, for example increase people productivity within the system test phase of project *xyz*.
- Deliverables were reviewed and broken down using PRINCE statements.
- Schedule; each group developed and updated their schedule. Only the individual team leaders could evaluate their requirements and decide how long it would take them to finish their tasks.
- Rules; every team wrote their own rules. This included how often they would meet, when, where, how long, (meetings were often timeboxed, that is 2–3 hours).

Activities

With so many activities happening all at once, it became a challenge to keep everyone on the right track. Group leaders held biweekly meetings, but it was found that only so much could be comprehended at any one briefing. One method to help individuals adjust was through the use of checklists. External consultants had already developed several checklists they used for their audits and the group leaders decided some of their own. Checklists were created for many areas. Examples included items to consider in the preparation of checkpoint meetings and planning sessions. These checklists proved to be beneficial in assisting people through the early project stages.

Measuring success

The challenge for the company in initiating these strategic changes which incorporated both process and people activities, was to create an improvement strategy that allowed improvements guided by one level to help create an environment that supports improvements in other levels. At the same time, the organization had to balance the amount of change being undertaken whilst still managing its regular business activities. An organization needs to balance these tensions very carefully if it is to head off conflict.

Benefits

So what have these efforts provided the AME Corporation? The following are some of the project benefits:

- Project staff have focused clear objectives, which are specified, measurable, affordable and do-able.
- Discrete phases or steps are clearly defined and documented, e.g., requirements phase, high-level design phase, etc.
- Work products are specified for each phase, e.g., requirements document, high-level design diagrams, etc.
- Analysis procedures are established to ensure correctness of work products, e.g., proofs of key system properties.
- Reviews of major work products are scheduled, e.g., design inspections.

Questions

1. Define five competencies a project manager should possess and explain why they are important.
2. Explain what key factors would influence a project manager's style of management.
3. Explain why it is important to have a sound communication policy.
4. With respect to the case study in this chapter what implications do the benefits of well-defined people and project processes have for management and end users?

Note

1. G. Graen, University of Cincinnati, USA, 1982.

CHAPTER 3

Defining the information systems project life cycle

Introduction

Managers can not be expected to oversee a complex development project without a thorough understanding of the approaches and techniques available to them. This chapter provides an overview of the approaches and techniques used in software development projects. One of the aims of the chapter is to examine issues such as the selection of appropriate methods from the point of view of a project manager. A second aim is to demonstrate the range of tools and techniques available to managers. In addition, the chapter considers the selection of development tools according to the development approach adopted and the specific requirements of a project.

The first sections of the chapter look at traditional models of software development. The material discusses the nature of these models and examines the advantages and disadvantages of each. This approach allows readers to trace the development of these techniques over time and helps to highlight the differences between them.

A great deal of attention is paid to prototyping methods, such as Rapid Application Development. This reflects the importance and popularity of these methods in modern organizations. The discussion also considers the pitfalls of these methods from the point of view of project managers. This material leads on to a discussion of object-oriented development and highlights some of the many business advantages that can be gained by working in this way.

The final section of the chapter introduces the concept of a tool set model. Such a model can be used to formulate an overall strategy with regard to the selection of development tools.

Whilst some readers may already be familiar with some of the tools and techniques described, others will find that it provides a body of useful background material. In addition, all of the material is presented from the point of view of the project manager. The adoption of this viewpoint helps to distinguish this text from traditional publications since it enables a number of issues to be discussed from a managerial, rather than technical, point of view.

Learning objectives

Some of the topics covered include:

- An overview of approaches to software development, including the waterfall method, the 'b' model and the spiral model.
- An overview of prototyping methods with discussion of Rapid Applications Development, Joint Applications Development and Dynamic Systems Development Method.
- An overview of system methodologies with discussion of Structured Systems Analysis Design Method, Soft Systems Methodology and Booch Object Oriented Analysis Method.
- The use of a tool set model in developing a strategy for the selection and use of development tools.

At the end of this chapter, students will be able to:

- Explain different approaches to development, referring to established models such as the waterfall method.
- Identify and explain the major strengths and weaknesses of each method/approach.
- Identify methods and approaches suited to a variety of different problem situations, referring to methods such as Soft Systems Methodology.
- Select an appropriate approach to development, taking into account factors such as achieving early functionality and the nature of the problem to be solved.
- Apply the concept of a tool set model in order to select a variety of appropriate development tools. Justify the selections made.

The software project life cycle

It was stated in Chapter 1 that the project life cycle should be considered as a collection of phases each marked by the completion of one or more deliverables. There are principally four generic phases in the management of software development projects, these are:

1. *Birth* – the idea for the project is born within the client organization and its feasibility is determined. The method to achieve the original idea is planned.
2. *Adolescence* – the plans are converted into physical reality (the system) and the tested system is handed over to the client for use.
3. *Maturity* – the client makes use of the system.
4. *Demise* – the system is dismantled and disposed of at the end of its useful life.

Traditionalists advocate that each of the phases described above can be broken down into a series of smaller stages. As an example, the *birth* of a project could be decomposed into conception, feasibility (or analysis) and planning. Figure 3.1 shows how the software development process can be broken down into a series of smaller stages. The diagram also shows the stakeholders involved at each stage and the characteristics of the communication that takes place.

Many organizations require their project managers to produce formal plans to support the delivery process. Such plans will contain details of the proposed organization and resources. It will also contain estimates of costs, plans for controlling the

Phase one	Phase two	Phase three	Phase four
Birth	Adolescence	Maturity	Demise
1. Conception	4. Design	7. Operational use	9. Withdrawal
2. Feasibility	5. Implementation	8. Support	10. Disposal
3. Planning	6. Handover		
Main stakeholder groups within each phase			
Client	Client	Client	Client
Users	Users	Users	Third parties
Project team	Third parties	Third parties	
	Project team		
Communication action styles			
Strategic	Instrumental	Instrumental	Instrumental
Instrumental	Communicative	Communicative	Communicative
Communicative			

Figure 3.1 Generic phases within a software development project including main stakeholders and communication action styles

project budget and will define a method of assessing the progress of the project by the use of milestones and baselines. In addition, it will give details of the techniques which are to be used to ensure the quality of the final product. Such details will include methods for controlling change and how issued versions of software will be recorded (configuration management). These topics are discussed in more detail in Chapter 4.

The notion that a project has a life cycle made up of a number of different stages leads us on to consider some of the principal models used in software development.

Models and approaches to software development

In the late 1960s, the rapid increase in the size, cost and complexity of computer software projects, particularly on military projects in the USA, prompted a re-examination of the ad hoc approaches to the design and build approaches that had been used in the past. The cost of software was increasing so fast that the hardware platforms on which the software was running were actually becoming less expensive in comparison to the cost of developing the software itself. As software projects became more complex, it became necessary for organizations to employ a large number of highly qualified staff. Increased labour costs caused expenditure on software development projects to rise sharply.

One response to spiralling software development costs involved attempts to encourage professional practice in the development of software. The concept of a software life cycle model was first introduced within large military projects. The idea of a software life cycle model is a simple one: it is a model of the stages or steps, in which a software development project is initiated, developed and completed.

Although various models were developed, all were created with the goal of defining methods to facilitate a rigid, sequential progression throughout the software development process. This rigid, sequential process was designed to allow for the organization and management of the development process in a similar way to other well-understood production processes. This progression mirrors the production process that made the industrial revolution a success. The main objective of the early software life cycle models was to provide a structured division of the processes involved in the creation of a large software system. Such schemes were used as management tools that could be used to manage and track the development of software systems. The models used served as a basis for planning, staffing, coordinating, budgeting, and directing software development activities.

Checklist 3.1 can be used to ensure that software requirements have been specified correctly. By highlighting many of the issues that must be considered when specifying requirements, the checklist illustrates the need for a structured, comprehensive approach to software development. Note that the points contained in the checklist are general in nature, meaning that they apply to all software projects, regardless of the particular methodology used.

The waterfall method

The waterfall method was first introduced to software developers thirty years ago by Royce (McDermid and Rook, 1991), and is still widely used today. As shown in Figure 3.2, the model is based on the premise of sequential stages (or processes) represented by boxes, with each stage being completed before work starts on the next stage. For example, it will not be possible for a programmer to begin writing a program until the design specification for that program is complete. This method has both inputs and outputs – outputs tumble out of one stage and are used as inputs to the next. This method of software development is usually associated with projects that have a high degree of contract development. The waterfall model is a simple representation of what activity happens during a system development project, but it provides a good framework for introducing information systems development, since all the activities that are identified in the model occur in a typical project.

There are many variations of the waterfall model. All of these different variations, however, exhibit the same basic classical life cycle phases or stages. These common stages are discussed below.

Feasibility

The goal of feasibility studies is to evaluate alternative systems and to propose the most feasible and desirable system(s) for development. A feasibility document is produced. The feasibility of a proposed system can be evaluated in terms of four major categories:

- *Organizational feasibility*: how well a proposed information system supports the objectives of the organization's strategic plan for information systems.

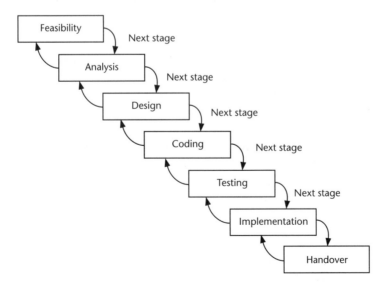

Figure 3.2 Traditional waterfall model of system development

- *Economic feasibility*: whether expected cost savings, increased revenue, increased profits, reductions in required investment, and other benefits exceed the cost of developing and operating a proposed system.
- *Technical feasibility*: whether reliable hardware and software capable of meeting the needs of a proposed system can be acquired or developed by the business in the required time.
- *Operating feasibility*: the willingness and ability of the management, employees, customers, suppliers, and so on to operate, use, and support a proposed system.

Analysis

The requirements for the system are investigated and formulated. A number of strategies are utilized in order to gather information about the client and the system to be built. Requirements are formulated, and expressed through a requirements document. A well-written requirements document is: correct, unambiguous, complete, verifiable, consistent, understandable, frozen (at the right level of detail), modifiable, traceable and annotated.

A correctly written requirements document should specify all system inputs, all system outputs, the relationships between the inputs and outputs, and all attributes of the system (for example: efficiency, reliability, ease of use, capacity). There are four primary purposes of a requirements document:

1. To serve as a means of communication among users, customers, analysts, designers, testers, and management.
2. To define the behaviour that the designers must build to.
3. To define the behaviour that the testers must test to.
4. To serve as a means of controlling the evaluation of the software system.

Design

The requirements document is interpreted, and a new design is generated. During preliminary design, the architecture for the software components and their interfaces is defined. Each element is then further refined into subcomponents, until a collection of relatively small units of software is left. During detailed design, algorithms are selected and documented for each component defined in the design (Gomaa, 1989). The design documentation produced at this stage is a clear and precise description of the system that will be created. Supporting documentation may be generated to describe the structure of the resulting design and outline the functionality of the new system in the form of a user manual.

Code and test

Coding is the physical creation of software programmes by developers. Testing normally occurs after some or all of the development as taken place. Test planning should proceed in the following sequence:

1. Write test plan.
2. Specify test data.
3. Review test plan.
4. Accept test plan.
5. Produce test data.
6. Review test data.
7. Test program or process.
8. Review results and if appropriate accept.

Testing has to be performed against some form of specification. Some system requirements are sufficiently detailed so that they can be simply marked up and used as the test specification. This test specification process is itself a form of testing, often finding many bugs and omissions. It forces the developer to draw back from the intricacies of how their code works, helps to refocus on the requirements and often flushes out scenarios or functionality that has been omitted (Challis, 1996). In essence, testing can fall into one of the following categories:

- *Module testing* – involves detailed testing of the functionality of a well-defined, but necessarily small, unit of code. Module testing is a detailed form of testing. By recording faults, problems can be analyzed and the development process improved.
- *Integration testing* – requires that code units are brought together, that the data flows and other interfaces between them are validated for correctness. Integration testing is often seen as unproductive and chaotic, but it represents the first time the units of a system are brought together to form a whole system.
- *Systems testing* – confirms the system delivers the functionality originally required. Once the system stays up for a useable period, the actual functionality it provides can be tested. Since this is the system test phase, it is important to return once more to the original system requirements, which on many projects form a contractually agreed document.

An important principle to understand is that the purpose of testing is to find bugs. A bug can be defined loosely as non-conformance to specification. Debugging is the process of fixing and correcting such bugs. It is useful to separate these two processes since they require different approaches. A test is considered successful if a bug is discovered since this demonstrates that the test was designed and applied correctly.

Figure 3.3 shows a modified version of the waterfall model that incorporates discrete testing stages.

Implementation

Implementation means putting the accepted system to work in its final environment, connecting it to any other operational systems and working with real data. Unlike operational running, the product is still under controlled conditions and not handed over to its final operators. A proper implementation plan, showing the steps involved and the entry/exit criteria for each, should be agreed between the parties involved. During implementation consideration should be given to:

- Correct functionality.
- The handling of errors and abnormal operating conditions.

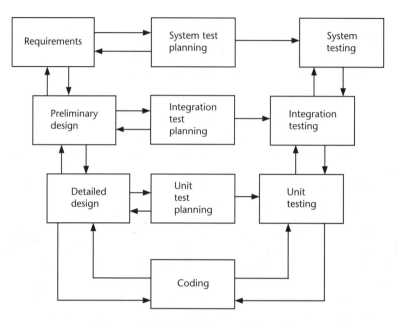

Figure 3.3 Elaborated waterfall model

- Performance (especially under peak or freak loads).
- Interfaces with other systems.
- Capacity to handle loads and volumes.
- Forced shut-down and backup/restore functions.
- Availability, reliability and maintainability.

As with acceptance, efforts by the customer to extend the scope or coverage of implementation must be resisted by the project manager and a definite cut-off point must be agreed. Other items, which might be reviewed during implementation, include the adequacy of the documentation, installation and build procedures.

Handover

This is the final stage and is where the client formally accepts the system and the project comes to an end (at least in principle), although in practice the software team will be expected to support the system for a short period of time in order to deal with minor faults, etc. Project managers should be wary of accepting handover arrangements that specify a period of fault-free running as a prerequisite, since problems could appear at any time and this could result in virtually open-ended acceptance. Warranty periods and continuing support contracts typically start at customer takeover or formal acceptance. Once the product or system is operational, a number of other aspects must be considered including: warranty, support, maintenance, enhancements and changes.

Advantages and disadvantages of the waterfall method

The benefits of using this type of model have been documented over the years by a number of practitioners. Readers are referred to the *Further reading* section of this chapter for additional sources of information. In essence, the strength of this approach lies in the fact that the complexities and problems of running a software project are broken down into separate stages which makes planning and control simpler. Completion of a stage can only be accomplished when the documentation produced at the end of stage is produced, accepted and signed-off.

Although this approach is favoured by many organizations, several writers have identified a number of cases where the adoption of this model led to major problems in the proposed solution. Gilb (1988), for example, cites instances where critical attributes of the system are obscured, rather than highlighted, by the requirements analysis. This is largely due to developers and users being separated by space, time and organization. As an example, he discusses the case of a corporate information system, which failed because the critical attribute of required processing power could not be met. Gilb highlights a major criticism of the waterfall method as follows:

> The fundamental assumption underpinning this approach is that the aim of the waterfall model in establishing comprehensive user requirements at the start of the project is simply not feasible – if only we had the intellectual capacity and the necessary knowledge to do these things accurately. In reality, we have to admit that we cannot tackle such tasks adequately for any but the trivially small projects.

Another major weakness of the waterfall method is that the system maintenance phase is not really covered. It is important to remember that maintenance accounts for 50 per cent of the cost of the software life cycle. Table 3.1 shows the approximate cost of each phase over the software life cycle.

In environments where the requirements are well understood and the business processes are mature, the waterfall method may be appropriate. In situations where the business requirements are not well understood and where the business processes are ad hoc, a different approach will be needed.

Table 3.1 Approximate costs of phases within software life cycle

Phase	Project size (small vs large)	
Architecture	S 5%	L 10%
Design	S 7%	L 10%
Coding	S 15%	L 5%
Testing	S 20%	L 15%
Implementation	S 3%	L 10%
Maintenance	S 50%	L 50%

Author's note: these percentages are averaged over a number of UK and USA projects and are based on statistics for 1996. For any specific project, these percentages might be quite different.

The 'b' Model

The 'b' model devised by Birrell and Ould (1988) was developed to overcome the shortcomings in the waterfall approach. As shown in Figure 3.4, the 'b' model incorporates both operational and maintenance elements. The diagram shows these elements as a series of cycles, each of which follows the same general sequence as the original development cycle outlined in Figure 3.2.

In the model, the maintenance phase of a project starts when the users have accepted (signed-off) the system. This phase involves evaluating, and modifying (analysis and design) the system to make any desirable or necessary improvements.

Some deficiencies

Whilst the 'b' model was undoubtedly an improvement on the waterfall model, it suffered from a number of practical deficiencies. One such deficiency is to be found in the analysis requirements phase since the size and complexity of modern software systems makes it difficult to get precise and complete requirements from the customer. For both the 'b' model and the waterfall model, a basic premise is that requirements can be clearly and completely specified. Although both models make allowances for changes in requirements later on, it is assumed that users know exactly what they want from the proposed system at the very start of the project.

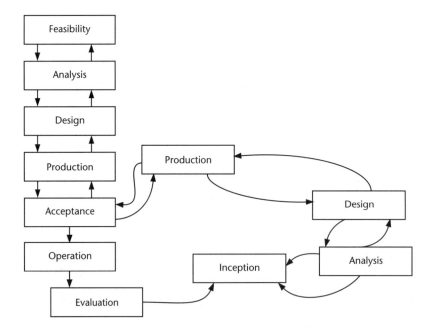

Figure 3.4 The 'b' model (adapted from Birrell and Ould, 1988)

Spiral model

The spiral model was introduced by Barry Boehn (1988) as a way of reducing risk. Each spiral in the model addresses a particular risk, with the most serious risks being addressed in the earliest cycles. The spiral model can be thought of as a meta-model since it can incorporate any other model within it. Models used with the spiral method are chosen according to the specific requirements of a stage and level of risk. Key features of the spiral model are an emphasis on the more problematic areas of the software development process and the use of an iterative, non-linear approach to projects.

Figure 3.5 shows the four stages of the spiral model. The four stages in the model are repeated until the objectives of a given phase of the development process have been met. The four stages comprise:

- Planning the next stage and selecting the development model to be used in that cycle (iteration).
- Determining objectives, alternatives and constraints.
- Evaluating alternatives, identifying and resolving risks.
- Developing and verifying a product.

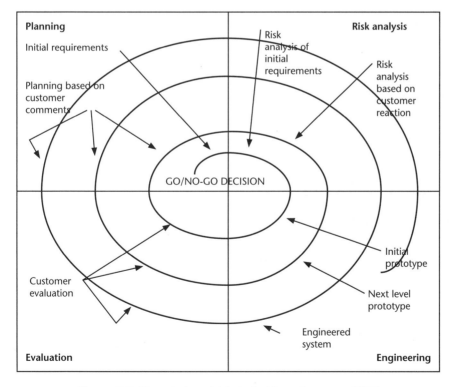

Figure 3.5 The spiral model (adapted from Pressman, 1997)

Although not widely used in the UK, the US advocates of the waterfall model argue that the model includes the best features of both the classic waterfall model and the prototyping approach. In addition the model introduces the important concepts of objective setting, risk management and planning into the overall development process. Clearly, these elements are very important from a project management perspective since they apply to factors that may affect the delivery of the system within the defined constraints.

Prototyping methods

A major criticism of earlier software development models involves the fact that coding does take place until late in the life of the project. In addition, there is no provision to allow requirements to be represented or clarified by prototyping. The spiral model described in the last section introduced software prototyping as a way of reducing risk. Other models, such as 'Evolutionary and Incremental Build', are based on an evolutionary prototyping rationale where the prototype is grown and refined into the final product. Figure 3.6 shows a simple prototype model of this kind.

The nature of prototyping means that requirements and specifications can be modified or improved as work progresses. Changes and additions can be made each time a new prototype is produced. In essence, prototyping focuses on what structured programming is lacking by addressing the need to improve productivity in analysis and requirements phases.

Schneider (1996) proposes a prototyping architecture where the prototype developer is the 'explainer' and the explanation receiver is the 'listener'. The strategy is to gradually turn this relationship into a two-way communication between equal partners. This is supported by Alavi (Van Vliet, 2000), who reports that users were more positive about the systems development using the prototyping approach.

Prototyping is appropriate for:

1. Data-oriented applications.
2. Applications with emphasis on the user interface.
3. Applications which are highly interactive.

Other reasons why prototyping is beneficial include:

- The prototype provides a vehicle for systems engineers to better understand the environment and the requirements problem being addressed.

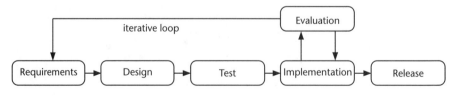

Figure 3.6 Prototype model

- A prototype is a demonstration of what is actually feasible with existing technology, and where the technical weak spots still exist.
- A prototype is an efficient mechanism for transfer of design intent from system engineer to the developer.
- A prototype lets the developer meet earlier schedules for the production version.
- A prototype allows for early customer interaction.
- A prototype demonstrates to the customers what is functionally feasible and stretches their imagination, leading to more creative inputs and a more forward-looking system.
- The prototype provides an analysis test bed and a vehicle to validate and evolve system requirements.

According to Dolan (1995), the prototype's primary purpose is to assist in the development of either a finished product meeting all of a customer's needs, or a preliminary product meeting a subset of those needs. The prototype software, in and of itself, is not usually designed with attributes such as efficiency, functionality, and maintainability as major quality factors.

A major difficulty with an approach based around prototyping occurs when the customer sees the prototype as an operational version of the software. Often, the customer is unaware that the prototype is held together 'with chewing gum and baling wire' and does not recognize that in the rush to get the software working, overall software quality or long-term maintainability issues were not considered. Customers may sometimes pressure developers into making the prototype into a working product. In such cases, the orderly development process originally planned by the developers can begin to break down. As an example, if the prototype is delivered as a working product, the project will move into the maintenance phase far earlier than expected. This can lead to a number of problems, ranging from increased costs to the total failure of the project.

It has been argued that management of prototyping is made problematic by its dependence on iterative activities (Baskerville, 1993). The basic management functions of planning and control are limited because plans are supposed to change with each cycle, and control is hampered by lack of meaningful progress measurement coupled with dependence on user cooperation. As an example, the project manager has only limited control over users and their interaction with developers. When the users dominate this interaction, they may inflate the scope of the project in an attempt to 'do it all' while they have the resources of the prototyping project available. When the developers dominate, they may deflate the scope of the project in order to reduce the programming work. These issues will be considered in more detail in Chapter 4.

Some of the weaknesses associated with prototyping have caused some researchers and practitioners to advise the use of this method only for small to medium-size systems, where the scope of the problem, number of users and the list of goals and expectations are reasonably manageable.

In closing this section, Table 3.2 highlights some common risks and problems associated with prototyping.

Table 3.2   Some risks associated with prototyping

1. Mistaken concepts of prototyping concerning definitions, objectives and correct application of the method.
2. Disagreement with users and customers regarding methodology, standards, tools and so on.
3. Out-of-control users who want to iterate and evolve a prototype into a system that does everything for everyone all the time.
4. Budget slashes and effort shortcuts – temptations brought about by use of the word 'prototype'.
5. Premature delivery of a prototype instead of a final (thoroughly documented and turned) product.
6. Over-evolved prototypes – substituting elegance and efficiency for flexibility.
7. When to stop – once the user sees that things can be altered, there is always the temptation to tweak one more thing and the person who calls a halt at any stage is seen as a fiend.

At this point, it is worth summarizing the relative strengths and weaknesses of the models discussed so far. Table 3.3 provides a summary that can be used to select an appropriate development approach for a project.

Table 3.3   Approaches to development: comparison of strengths and weaknesses

	Waterfall	Incremental	Spiral
Strengths			
Allows for workforce specialization	YES	YES	YES
Orderliness appeals to management	YES	YES	YES
Can be reported about	YES	YES	YES
Facilitates allocation of resources	YES	YES	YES
Early functionality		YES	YES
Does not require a complete set of requirements at the onset		YES	YES
Resources can be held constant		YES	
Control costs and risk through prototyping			YES
Weaknesses			
Requires a complete set of requirements at the onset	YES		
Enforcement of non-implementation attitude hampers analyst/designer communications	YES		
Beginning with less-defined general objectives may be uncomfortable for management		YES	YES
Requires clean interfaces between modules		YES	
Incompatibility with a formal review and audit procedure		YES	YES
Tendency for difficult problems to be pushed to the future so that the initial promise of the first increment is not met by subsequent products		YES	YES

Rapid Application Development (RAD)

Increasingly the traditional waterfall method of design has become inappropriate when constructing commercial business systems. It is being replaced by RAD methods where the objective is first to produce a visualization, then a prototype of the system so that users can quickly give feedback, after which the core functionality can be delivered quickly for maximum business benefit.

The RAD process defines a linear definition of steps. RAD begins by defining the desired product during an initial planning phase. During planning, a definition of the project scope is completed along with some preliminary data/process analysis, risk assessment and estimating. Next, a fixed period for building a fragment, increment or part of the application is determined. This fixed time limit is known as a timebox. Within the timebox, a spiral process occurs involving prototyping, modelling, architectural design, construction and testing. Each cycle within the timebox is repeated a number of times. Each iteration improves the solution, bringing it closer to completion. Figure 3.7 provides a model of Rapid Applications Development.

Kerr and Hunter (1994) describe RAD as:

> ... an approach to build computer systems which combines (CASE) tools and techniques, user-driven prototyping, and stringent project delivery time limits into a potent, tested, reliable formula for top notch quality and productivity.

The principles of RAD are based on the premise that fast, effective and efficient information systems can only be developed by the careful alignment of specific

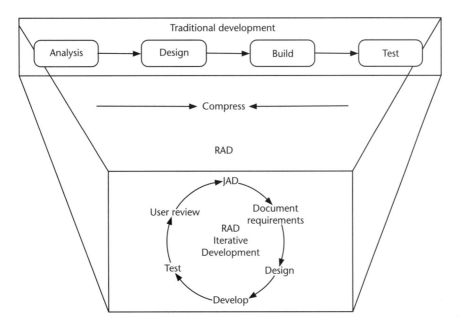

Figure 3.7 RAD model

development methods and techniques with suitable application tools. There are four main principles inherent within the RAD approach. These are:

1. Improving the speed of systems development by using tools and techniques appropriate to the business organization and its competitive environment.
2. Using an iterative prototyping approach to systems development.
3. Emphasizing concentrated end-user participation and involvement in the whole development process via structured workshops and end-user meetings.
4. Using a number of known modelling tools and techniques that are collected together in the form of a resource toolbox.

RAD is sometimes associated with the Faster, Better, Cheaper trilogy. However, Martin (1991) points out that faster, better, cheaper does not necessarily mean 'quick and dirty'. The need for fast and efficient design and implementation means that time-intensive activities must be automated or, at the very least, supported by appropriate technology. The gap between design and implementation is one area where effort is time intensive. Computer Aided Software Engineering (CASE) tools are generally used in order to provide a seamless connection between the two and speed up the development of code from design specification. CASE tools are examined in more detail in Chapter 4.

User involvement

Managing user involvement within a RAD project in terms of time, deliverables and commitment becomes increasingly important, and has been known to make established project managers feel uncomfortable. The traditional task-driven approach does not work, clear objectives for the team must be set and teams must be empowered to achieve these objectives in their own way. These objectives have to be measurable however, for example, if the objective is a prototype it will only have been met if accepted by the users. Systems belong to the users, not developers. Management must therefore commit users who have the authority, desire, responsibility and knowledge to make decisions on behalf of the rest of the community. It is also important to keep the users' feet firmly on the ground; their expectations must be kept in line with current technological capabilities and budgets. Setting expectations correctly with senior management is one of the project manager's most important tasks.

Timeboxing

Timeboxing is an essential project management aspect of RAD. It forces the development team to anticipate reducing the scale of product delivery, increases focus on end-user priorities, and assumes continual change will occur. A timebox is a mechanism to control resources and delivery scope. Multiple timeboxes can be used sequentially, in parallel or staggered. Timeboxing forces the project team to have a market and product orientation. Planning product components by timebox, rather than thinking in terms of tasks, activities and deadlines, is an effective means of delivering real value.

Strengths and weaknesses

Although considered an excellent method, RAD is not suitable for all types of project. As an example, RAD may not be suitable if the system is likely to have a long life expectancy. Table 3.4 provides a simple checklist that highlights some of the issues that must be taken into account when considering the use of RAD.

Table 3.4 A checklist for determining the suitability of a RAD approach to a typical development project

Suitability factor	Suitable (Y/N)	Comments
1. Does the sponsor/senior management understand and accept the RAD philosophy?		Buy-in to the approach is essential
2. Will the team members be empowered to make decisions on behalf of their communities?		An essential feature for RAD
3. Is there senior user commitment to provide end user involvement?		Identify whether there is a clearly defined and empowered user group and the commitment for them to be fully involved in the development process
4. Can the organization accommodate the frequent delivery of increments?		Configuration and release management procedures are required
5. Will it be possible for the developers to have access to the users throughout the project?		Do they need to colocate or will a lower level of involvement be sufficient?
6. Will the development team remain the same throughout the project?		The stability of the team including the user representatives is important
7. Will the development team have the appropriate skills?		These include technical skills, knowledge of the business area and interpersonal skills
8. Will the individual development teams consist of six people or less?		Teams should contain no more than six people including users
9. Is there a supportive commercial relationship?		Between the IT development staff and the users
10. Will the project use technology suitable for prototyping?		The development platform needs to allow for iterative and, where necessary, reversible development
11. Is there a highly demonstrable user interface?		Screens, reports, file prints, etc.

Table 3.4   Continued

12. Is there clear ownership?	Is there a champion who will progress political issues and ensure resources are provided? Is there a clearly defined user group?
13. Will the development be computationally non-complex?	The more complex the development the greater the risks involved
14. Can the solution be developed in increments if required?	80:20 solution, i.e. releases deliver some benefits early. If large, possesses the capability of being split into smaller components
15. Has the development a fixed time scale?	Is the solution needed quickly? Is it business critical?
16. Can the requirements be prioritized?	Can the MoSCoW rules be applied? Cannot only have 'must haves'
17. Are the requirements not too detailed and fixed?	Will users be able to define requirements interactively?

In common with other approaches to development, RAD offers a number of strengths and weaknesses. The major advantages and disadvantages of RAD are given in Table 3.5.

Table 3.5   RAD advantages and disadvantages

Advantages
1. Encourages interaction between users and developers
2. Increased rate of development
3. Encourages feedback and learning
4. Iteration reduces risk and uncertainty

Disadvantages
1. Inadequate preparation
2. Harder to gauge success – no classic milestones
3. Less efficient code
4. Fear of return to the early days of uncontrolled practices
5. More code defects
6. Standardize look and feel
7. Successful efforts difficult to repeat
8. Unwanted features through use of CASE tools
9. Reduced features
10. Prototyping may not scale-up
11. Interests of user and developers may diverge from one iteration to the next

Joint Applications Development

A critical success factor in a any RAD project is how requirements are defined and generated. Joint Application Development (JAD) is a technique that allows developers, managers and customer groups to work together to build a RAD product.

The purpose of a JAD session is to define the user and application interfaces for a specific component of the RAD project. There will be one or more JAD sessions per project. The JAD group will normally include a session leader/facilitator, two or more end-user representatives, a representative from the client, one or more developers, and a scribe. Each person must attend every JAD meeting. The JAD session should accomplish each of the following goals:

- refining requirements;
- developing a work-flow description;
- identifying the system data groups and functions;
- designing the screens and reports;
- identifying external interfaces for other systems.

Figure 3.8 provides a simplified view of the JAD process.

If multiple JAD sessions are implemented for a project, these goals may be broken up into separate sessions. JAD sessions confront one of the riskiest portions of the RAD process – creating the user interface.

In order to manage the JAD process, a person experienced in group facilitation, systems analysis and collecting requirements is needed. The JAD facilitator must produce the following deliverables:

1. Identify all stakeholders and clarify executive goal.
2. Scope out the general requirements (project mission and product features) from each of the users' perspectives (business abstract).
3. Reconcile each user's view of the product with the executive goal into one summary (project abstract).
4. Define the interaction of the product with users, other products or systems, and the organization (context diagram).

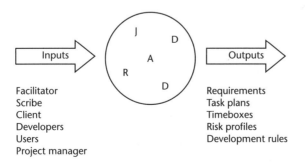

Figure 3.8 The JAD process

5. Concur on business justification, timebox, and costbox for project (preliminary business plan).
6. Define the ways in which the users will interact or use the new product (use cases). Collect samples of desired inputs and outputs from users. Stick to business processes first, then drill down for data needed and known ('knows and does' list).
7. Prioritize the use cases by collective user preference and risk (Delphi technique).
8. Validate and review the use case scenarios.
9. Organize the use cases, constraint, assumptions, and other requirements into a rigorous Software Requirements Specification (SRS).
10. Design (with technical help) the screen and report layouts. Prototypes are handy for this.

JAD has been shown to be highly efficient when used with RAD best practice. A major advantage of the JAD approach is that it allows for the simultaneous gathering and consolidating of large amounts of information. Moreover, discrepancies are resolved immediately with the aid of the facilitator. JAD can also provide useful information for process improvement efforts. Other benefits include:

1. Saves time, eliminates process delays and misunderstandings, thereby improves system quality.
2. Reduces function creep, most of which results from poor initial requirements.
3. Cultural risk is mitigated by using transition managers and appropriate users.
4. Avoids bloated functionality, gold plating, and helps designers delay their typical 'solution fixation' until they understand the requirements better.
5. Lays the foundation for a framework of mutual education, separate brainstorming, binding negotiation, and progress tracking.
6. Avoids requirements becoming too specific or too vague, both of which cause problems during implementation and acceptance.

Dynamic Systems Development Method (DSDM)

The DSDM Consortium includes major organizations in both the public and private sectors, large IT corporations, smaller tool vendors and consultancy companies. The DSDM Consortium developed the Dynamic Systems Development Method in 1994 in an attempt to provide a public domain, non-proprietary methodology for Rapid Application Development (see Figure 3.9).

In the UK, DSDM is well regarded since it is in keeping with traditional development approaches, such as SSADM. Where DSDM differs from traditional methods is in the assumption that business requirements are not fixed and are almost certain to change over time. DSDM recognizes that 'change is the only constant' and that the development process should be creative and exploratory, albeit within constraints.

Although DSDM does not prescribe tools and techniques, it addresses the issues of the full software development life cycle in a clear and comprehensive way. A key strength of DSDM lies in the fact that it is built solely on the experience and knowledge

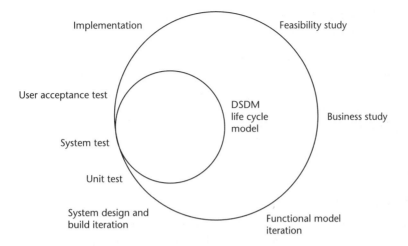

Figure 3.9 DSDM life cycle model

of best practice which reside in members. Lessons of experience embodied in DSDM mean that it has many of the characteristics of RAD. These characteristics include the following:

- prototyping is incremental,
- there is a focus on delivering business functionality,
- project teams of developers and business people must be in control of the development process.

DSDM principles

There are nine major principles that underlie the DSDM methodology. These principles are:[1]

1. Active user involvement is imperative.
2. DSDM teams must be empowered to make decisions.
3. The focus is on frequent delivery of products.
4. Fitness for business purpose is the essential criterion for acceptance of deliverables.
5. Iterative and incremental development is necessary to converge on an accurate business solution.
6. All changes during development are reversible.
7. Requirements are base-lined at a high level.
8. Testing is integrated throughout the life cycle.
9. A collaborative and cooperative approach between all stake holders is essential.

Of DSDM's nine principles, some will have already been taken on by most organizations. Others, such as the recognition that volatile business requirements and very tight timescales should not be problems for a methodology, contain the essence of DSDM and are considered key strengths.

DSDM sets up a framework that asks important questions about the project to be undertaken. The usual considerations are:

1. Definition of the problem to be addressed – is it understood?
2. Technical feasibility of the project – do we have the right skills?
3. Impact on the business – is the project worth undertaking?
4. Is there sufficient cash to see the project through?
5. Is DSDM the right methodology for the project?

Within DSDM, the feasibility study has two products. The first is an outline of the desired outcome. The second is a fast prototype of the system.

Prototyping within DSDM

Once its suitability for a project has been agreed, DSDM begins with a high-level functionality specification. Two cycles then follow: (a) detailed functionality development and non-functional requirements definition, and (b) design and build. The first cycle is primarily concerned with eliciting requirements and the second involves ensuring that production-quality software is produced. Both cycles are iterative and prototype-driven. It is also important to note that there is no demarcation between cycles. As an example, work on some components may have just started, whilst others have already been completed.

There are two ways in which DSDM suggests that the prototyping of an application may be sliced: horizontally or vertically. Either an entire system is built at a high level to confirm its fit to the project scope, or small parts of an application are built incrementally until fully understood. In reality, a mixture of low-level and high-level work will inevitably take place simultaneously. DSDM identifies four types of prototype, each with a particular focus:

1. Business functionality.
2. Usability of user interface.
3. Performance and capacity.
4. Capability/technique (for experimentation with design and tools).

Only unsuccessful capability/technique prototypes will be discarded. Each prototyping cycle has four phases:

1. Identify prototypes.
2. Agree schedule.
3. Create prototype.
4. Review prototype.

The key to defining a prototype is differentiating between what is essential to it and what is not. This will obviously be business-driven, and will determine what must be achieved on schedule.[2] 'Timeboxing' is the process of setting tight deadlines (typically no more than two weeks), not for completing a task, but for meeting a business object-ive. The timebox is the lowest level of planning in DSDM, and therefore the level at which progress will be monitored. If there is slippage, the scope of the prototype should be reduced, rather than the deadline extended. The main benefit of this approach is that it results in frequent delivery to the users. Prototype review has two main objectives: to ensure that development is fundamentally on the right track, and that users at all levels are satisfied.

Team roles

DSDM teams are based upon roles. Individuals may perform more than one role and one role may be split between two people. A typical DSDM project will consist of a Visionary, Project Manager, Ambassador User, Advisor Users, Technical Coordinator, Senior Developer, Developer, JAD Facilitator and Scribe. The structure of a DSDM team is shown in Figure 3.10.

Given some understanding of DSDM practices and philosophy, each of these roles shown should be self-explanatory, but their scope should be noted:

- The Visionary is responsible for ensuring that a project's high-level business needs are not forgotten.
- The Advisor can be brought in for key prototyping or testing sessions to broaden end-user involvement in, and acceptance of, what is being developed.
- Specialists may be brought into a DSDM team on an ad hoc basis. Such Specialists might include a Workshop Facilitator, a Systems Integrator and/or an Operations Coordinator.
- An expert Facilitator and Scribe allow DSDM to benefit from Joint Application Development (JAD) techniques for requirements elicitation, analysis and prioritization.

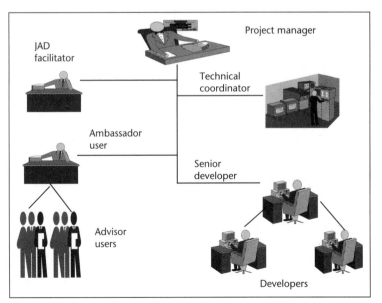

Figure 3.10 DSDM team for RAD

Advantages and disadvantages

We can summarize the main advantages of DSDM as follows:

- It focuses on building software that is fit for purpose.
- It allows users a voice during development.
- Development is timeboxed for efficiency.
- Testing is done early in the cycle.
- Tracking progress is made easier due to the shorter life cycles.

The major disadvantages of DSDM can be summarized as follows:

- Conflict between users and developers can sometimes be an issue.
- Software configuration management must be tightly maintained.
- RAD tools are not always up to the job.
- It is sometimes difficult to get management buy-in.
- Quality is sometimes an issue.

System methodologies

In broad terms system methodologies are a collection of procedures, techniques, tools and documentation aids. However, some writers, such as Avision and Fitzgerald (1996), suggest that a methodology is more than merely a collection of these things. Unless an approach is based on some philosophical view, it remains nothing more than a method, like a recipe. According to Professor Peter Checkland (1990) '... a methodology will lack the precision of a technique but will be a firmer guide to action than a philosophy'. We can therefore suggest that a methodology should be described as a series of philosophical views accompanied by one or more methods.

In the last 20 years, a number of methodologies have been developed for use in commercial environments, such as large organizations and software houses. Such methodologies can be classified into three broad groups:

1. Structured methodologies (for example, SSADM).
2. Soft systems methodologies.
3. Object oriented methodologies (for example, Booch method).

Structured Systems Analysis Design Method (SSADM)

Perhaps the most widely known and used structured method, Structured Systems Analysis and Design Method (SSADM) was launched in 1981 and has been used by the UK Government in computing since that time. It was originally developed by LBMS (Learmonth and Burchett Management Systems) for the UK's Central Computer and Telecommunications Agency (CCTA). Since its first appearance, the method has undergone numerous changes and is now used widely throughout industry as well as by the government and public sector organizations.

The current release of SSADM is version 4.3, which was launched in 1996 and is targeted at the development of applications with graphical user interfaces. 'SSADM' and 'Structured Systems Analysis and Design' are registered trademarks of the Government Centre for Information Systems (CCTA). The CCTA specify that the methodology should be self-checking, should use tried and tested techniques, and should be tailored and reachable. The purpose of SSADM is to:

- Improve systems project planning and control.
- Increase the effectiveness of experienced and inexperienced staff.
- Produce better quality information systems.
- Enhance communication between developers and users.
- Enhance its usability through computer-based tools.

SSADM is an analysis and design method that ensures information systems specification is correctly defined and monitored. It provides a complete framework for capturing and analysing requirements and specifying a system design. There are five modules and seven stages within SSADM. These modules and stages are shown in Table 3.6.

Within each stage of the model there is a sequence of numbered steps which in turn are divided into numbered tasks. At the bottom level, SSADM consists of approximately 230 tasks, not all of which may be executed in any one implementation of the method. Figure 3.11 provides an example of the various components that comprise SSADM. SSADM attempts to catalogue a system from three perspectives. Namely:

1. How the data items in the system move through it.
2. How the various data items are related to each other.
3. How any one of the data items changes over time.

Within SSADM there are three separate techniques for dealing with each of the above aspects:

1. *Data flow diagrams* (DFD). DFDs attempt to describe pictorially how information flows around an organization. Checklist 3.2 can be used to check the accuracy and consistency of data flow diagrams.

Table 3.6 Modules and stages within SSADM

Module	Stage
Feasibility study module	0. Feasibility
Requirements analysis module	1. Investigate current environment
	2. Business systems options
Requirements specification module	3. Definition of requirements
Logical system specification module	4. Technical systems options
	5. Logical design
Physical design module	6. Physical design

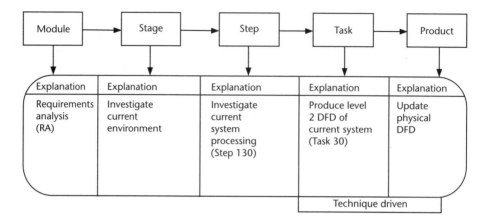

Figure 3.11 Components of SSADM

2. *Logical data structuring* (LDS) including entity relationship modelling and conceptual modelling. These techniques are designed to show how the different data items relate to each other.
3. *Entity life histories* (ELH). Using structure diagrams, this method shows how a data item comes into being, how it is modified throughout its life and how it comes to be deleted when it's finished with.

Project managers must ensure that two key products are created: a required system logical data model and function definitions. The logical data model is probably the key component of the entire SSADM development process. It drives the design of the eventual database and all processing is specified with reference to it. A data model produced to poor quality standards will undermine the specification, design and construction of the entire system. Function definitions identify the system processing which must be implemented and how this processing should be packaged to provide effective support for users.

SSADM does not result in products, which user representatives can readily understand and review. Merely sending SSADM models to users and asking for their comments will prove very ineffective. At all times, the emphasis should be on presentations by the project team to ensure that the user representatives are aware of the issues which must be validated and agreed by them.

The structural model for SSADM contains no specific activities relating to implementation of the system. This can result in all implementation issues being ignored until very late in the development process, with the result that system implementation is largely unplanned, poorly coordinated and badly managed. Project managers should ensure that implementation issues are addressed as early as possible. Unfortunately, the default structural model leaves all mention of implementation activities until Stage 6 (Physical design).

Soft Systems Methodology

Soft Systems Methodology (SSM) is a systematic process based around the construction of a model that takes perceptions of the real world into account. By including the real world in the model, it is possible to learn more about the system to be constructed and gain a clearer understanding of complex problems.

There are seven stages involved in SSM:

1. Finding out about the problem situation. This is basic research into the problem area. Who are the key players? How does the process work?
2. Expressing the problem situation through rich pictures. As with any type of diagram, more knowledge can be communicated visually than verbally or in written form.
3. Selecting how to view the situation and producing root definitions. From what different perspectives can we look at this problem situation?
4. Building conceptual models of what the system must do for each root definition. If root definitions can be described as 'what?', then these models can be described as 'how?'.
5. Comparison of the conceptual models with the real world. Compare the results from stages 2 and 4 and see where differences and similarities lie.
6. Identify feasible and desirable changes. Are there ways of improving the situation?
7. Recommendations for taking action to improve the problem situation. How would you implement the changes from stage 6?

Figure 3.12 shows the stages involved in SSM. Notice that a dotted line is used to separate the 'real world' from the problem being examined. Although the diagram shows each stage in logical order, it is possible for analysts to start at any point in the model.

SSM stages

Since SSM can be difficult to understand for some groups, it is worth taking a little time to explore each of the stages shown in the diagram.

Stage 1: The problem situation (unstructured)
The intention of this stage is to collect as much information as possible from a wide range of people who are relevant to the system. Analysts gather a large and varied body of information since every person has a different view of the problem. In this way, the analyst will gain a deeper understanding on the problem and the possibilities opened up.

Stage 2: The problem situation (expressed)
Having gathered some information, the analyst will create a rich picture to describe the situation. A rich picture is used as a means of communication between analysts and users. The diagram provides a summary of all that is known about the problem situation. A typical picture will show the organizational structure, organizational goals,

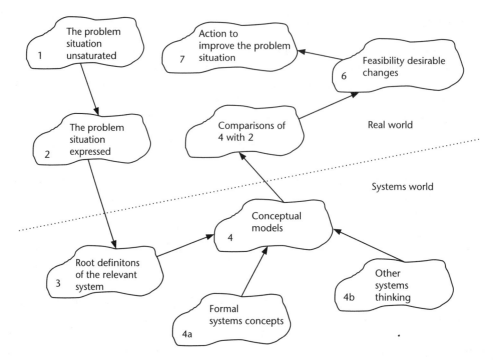

Figure 3.12 Soft systems road map

control of resources, issues, problems, and sources of conflict. One might start to draw the rich picture by looking for elements of structure in the problem area, such as the departmental boundaries, product types, and the geographical layout. The next stage is to look for the elements of process, i.e. what is going on, such as the information flow, the flow of goods. The relationship between structure and process shows the climate of the situation.

It is important to remember that the rich picture will show both 'hard' and 'soft' information. Hard facts might include the number of departments in the organization, whilst soft facts might include subjective views, such as issues that staff feel concerned about.

Stage 3: Root definition of relevant systems (CATWOE)

Root definition is the process of formalizing a hypothesis to aid in the development of a conceptual model that will eventually be used to create a new system (or amend the existing one). Each root definition will contain a particular viewpoint and assumptions, and each will affirm different parts of the rich picture. A root definition will contain a number of different elements:

- *Customers* are the beneficiaries or victims that are affected by the activities of the system. These individuals can be inside or outside of the system. Examples might include customers, suppliers, academic staff, students, and so on.

- *Actors* are agents of change. They carry out the activities of the system.
- *Transformation* is a process or task and describes the actual work performed by the system.
- *Weltanschauung* is the set of assumptions needed to make the root definitions meaningful.
- *Owner* is the person with overall responsibility for the system. This person reserves the right to halt the whole activity.
- *Environment* is the environment in which the activity of the system takes place.

Stage 4: Building the conceptual model

The rich picture and root definitions provide a complete view of the organization. In order to complete the analysis of human activity systems, a conceptual model needs to be constructed. The model will show what the systems need to do, how various activities are interrelated, and how they ought to be logically arranged and connected. The conceptual model shows what ought to happen in attaining the objectives specified in the root definition. It is constructed in terms of what must go into the system. It may involve several layers that show the model at different levels of detail. Conceptual models are likely to contain the following components:

- Purpose.
- Measure of performance.
- Decision-making process.
- Component systems, which interact.
- An environment, separated by a boundary.
- Resources.
- Continuity, and stability.

The model has three aims:

1. It is a set of instructions to the builders.
2. It is a significant element in the architect's design activities.
3. It is a medium of communication between architects and clients to allow the right design to be chosen.

Stage 5: Comparing the conceptual model with reality

This stage is the most important one since it compares the conceptual model with the real situation. The real world is often too complex and thus the model aims to provide a framework to make sense of the real situation. Some of the techniques used to perform the comparison include structured data collection, tabulation and model-to-model techniques.

STRUCTURED DATA COLLECTION AND TABULATION. This is the most basic technique used to perform the comparison. It can be carried out with any type of relevant system and any mode of use. It is particularly useful at the explanatory stage in order to assess the relevance of the model in the context of the problem being investigated. The steps in an explanatory comparison are:

- list all activities in the model;
- define the outputs from each activity;
- investigate the situation and gain evidence that something exists which matches the output; and
- interpret and evaluate the results produced by the matching process.

MODEL-TO-MODEL. In some situations it may be important to look at one conceptual model versus another. This is useful if there are two or more different versions of what might be happening in the situation, or if the models are fairly similar. Assessing similarities and differences leads to a better understanding of the situation.

Stage 6: Assessing feasible and desirable changes
This stage relates to the analysis of proposed changes from Stage 5, which are considered both possible and desirable. In this stage, ideas for such changes are written into a plan.

Stage 7: Action to improve the problem situation
This stage recommends the action to aid the problem situation. Note, however, that the methodology does not specify the methods needed to implement solutions. It only provides a better understanding of problem situations, rather than a rigid scheme for solving a particular problem.

SSM is a useful methodology for dealing with unstructured or semi-structured problems. It is of particular value when there is a need to focus on people, or where a problem has aspects that need to be viewed subjectively. Although the approach provides practitioners with a great deal of freedom, some structure is imposed on the process through the creation of root definitions and abstract models. Of course, the greatest strength of this approach lies in the concept of human activity systems. SSM remains the only widely used methodology that concentrates on people. This approach allows developers to tap into a rich body of knowledge (that is, experience, perceptions and attitudes) that other techniques tend to ignore.

However, SSM also contains several weaknesses. A reliance on subjective information can cause analysts to become side-tracked, losing sight of the real issues that need to be examined. In addition, analysts must be intuitive and must have great skill in eliciting information from people. The freedom offered by SSM means that it is possible for the process to lose coherence, falling into an unstructured shambles that fails to solve the problem being examined.

The Booch object oriented analysis method

The object oriented analysis (OOA) approach to system design extends and improves on the previous methods of system development. Object oriented (OO) techniques effectively capture and display system requirements in a way that more closely reflects the real world. OO models reflect a more natural partitioning of the problem, are more flexible and resilient to change, and can be developed more rapidly at a lower cost. Booch (1994) describes OOA as follows:

> ...the method that leads us to an object-oriented decomposition; object-oriented design defines a notation and process for constructing complex software system, and offers a rich set of logical and physical models with which we may reason about different aspects of the system under consideration.

In the early 1990s, Booch was instrumental in developing an iterative model of software development which helped to popularize software, reuse and make it economically feasible to use. His book, *Object-Oriented Analysis and Design with Applications*, describes the theory, notation, process, and pragmatics of object oriented technology. The Booch method is a widely used OO method, that helps design systems using the object paradigm. The Booch method covers the analysis and design phases of an OO system. The phases of Booch's approach are shown in Table 3.7.

Systems developed using the Booch method use a single paradigm that facilitates architecture and code reuse. This is particularly important, as software projects increase in size and complexity, and as shorter development cycles become a business necessity. The method defines different models to describe your system.

Booch's method starts by defining class and object diagrams. These diagrams are then refined in a series of steps:

1. The logical model (problem domain) is represented in the class and object structure.
2. In the class diagram, the architecture is constructed (the static model).
3. The object diagram shows how the classes interact with each other. This diagram captures some moments in the life of the system and helps to describe the dynamic behaviour of the system.

Table 3.7 OOA and design overview

Architectural planning	Tactical design	Release planning
1. Cluster similar objects in separate architectural partitions 2. Layer objects by level of abstraction 3. Identify relevant scenarios 4. Create a design prototype 5. Validate the design prototype by applying it to usage scenarios	1. Define domain-independent policies 2. Define domain-specific policies 3. Develop a scenario that describes the semantics of each policy 4. Create a prototype of each policy 5. Instrument and refine the prototype 6. Review each policy	1. Organize scenarios developed during OOA by priority 2. Allocate corresponding architectural releases to the scenarios 3. Design and construct each release incrementally 4. Adjust goals and schedule of incremental release as required

4. The module and process architecture describes the physical allocation of the classes to modules and processes.
5. State transition diagrams show the dynamic behaviour of classes. The state transition diagram is used to show the state space of a given class, the events (messages) that cause a transition from one state to another, and the actions that result from a state change.

The process of object oriented development

Like RAD and DSDM methods, Booch supports the iterative and incremental development of a system. Relationships are developed in an iterative way. First, a general association and the roles of the classes are defined. Later, when it is known how the classes interact with each other, the relationship is refined to a users relationship.

Booch OOA strengths and weaknesses

The Booch methodology is sequential in the sense that the analysis phase is completed and then the design phase is completed. The methodology is cyclical in the sense that each phase is composed of smaller cyclical steps. There is neither explicit priority setting nor a non-monotonic control mechanism. The Booch methodology concentrates on the analysis and design phase and does not consider the implementation or the testing phase in much detail.

Table 3.8 summarizes some of the strengths and weaknesses of this approach.

Table 3.8   Strengths and weaknesses within the Booch OOA method

Advantages	Disadvantages
1. Improve user – developer communication 2. Model static and dynamic behaviour 3. Use class categories to define a logical system architecture 4. Uses modules and sub-systems to map logical architecture to physical architecture	1. The method is sometimes criticized for its big set of different symbols to document almost every design decision 2. Lack of a tool set that supports the full life cycle 3. The method is complex to use

Unified Modelling Language (UML)

The Unified Modelling Language was developed in 1993 by the Rational Software Corporation. In only a relatively short period of time, UML has become extremely popular and is used throughout the world. Although it is only just starting to gain significant popularity in the UK, UML is well-established in the US. Much of the popularity of UML can be attributed to the support it has received from Microsoft – UML tools are supplied as key components of all Microsoft development packages. However, this does not detract from UML's strength as a well-rounded development technique.

UML focuses on object oriented software development and emphasizes the use of high-level programming tools. Applications designed with UML are divided into three basic parts called tiers. The three parts are known as the Business Services, Data Services and User Interface tiers. The use of tiers helps to divide the application into sections that make it easier to perform activities such as design, coding, implementation and maintenance. As an example, all access to data is performed within the Data Services Tier, according to rules and specifications set out in the Business Services Tier. If the method of database access is changed, only the Data Services Tier of the application needs to be modified – the Business Services Tier will remain unchanged.

UML makes use of three types of diagrams in order to provide a comprehensive view of the proposed system. These diagrams can be termed static, dynamic and container diagrams. Static and dynamic diagrams show the proposed system in different states. Container diagrams package together elements of the system into a single, simplified diagram.

The diagrams used in UML are listed in Table 3.9. For most entries in the table, the purpose of each diagram should be evident from the name assigned to it.

A significant element of UML is the use of textual descriptions of activities that are called Use Cases. These statements can be used to describe the needs of users in various levels of detail. They are also used as the basis for the Use Case Diagram that bears similarities to the data flow diagrams and entity relationship models used in SSADM.

Some of the strengths of UML can be summarized as follows:

- The method is intended to complement the high-level programming languages used by most large organizations.
- All aspects of system design are dealt with, from user interface design to deployment.
- The method bears a number of similarities to other approaches, such as SSADM. This helps developers to learn UML quickly and easily.
- Developers with experience of object oriented design or programming tend to find the method easy to learn and simple to understand.

Major weaknesses of the method include:

- UML focuses primarily on system design and pays little attention to management issues, such as risk management.

Table 3.9 Types of UML diagram

Dynamic	Static	Container
Use case diagram	Object diagram	Package diagram
Class diagram	Component diagram	
Sequence diagram	Deployment diagram	
Collaboration diagram		
Statechart diagram		
Activity diagram		

- The method places a high level of reliance on cooperation from users.
- The method is not suitable for all development projects, for example very small projects.

Object systems development (paradigm variations)

It is widely accepted that systems of the future will be designed and developed using business objects that are event-driven, concurrently executing and running in a heterogeneous environment. The inherent complexity of the business objects development process requires a different kind of developer who can demonstrate an abstract approach to problem resolution. Object orientation (OO) development is built on two principles, namely: encapsulation and inheritance, although one could add abstraction as a third.

ENCAPSULATION. Encapsulation is not unique to OO; it has been variously called data abstraction or information clustering. In essence, encapsulation is a packaging strategy which combines related data, process and state information a single indivisible component. OO languages provide machinery for encapsulation. In many OO programming languages, encapsulation of objects (e.g. classes and their instances) is systematically and semantically supported by the language. In others, the concept of encapsulation is supported conceptually, but not physically. Whatever its shortcomings, encapsulation is a relatively low-cost way to improve system conceptualization and implementation.

INHERITANCE. By belonging to a common class, an object inherits its properties from and takes its behaviour from its parents. In effect, inheritance formalizes a relationship among real world and software objects (Figure 3.13). Some OO languages support multiple inheritance, that is, an object may acquire characteristics directly from only one other object. Some OO languages support multiple inheritance, that is, an object may acquire characteristics from two or more different objects. The types of characteristics which may be inherited, and the specific semantics of inheritance vary from language to language. Figure 3.13 provides an example of inheritance.

The object paradigm can be used in at least three different ways. They are divergent at the back or technology end of the life cycle, because they are effected by the programming language used and the environment.

1. Object oriented development is characterized by OO analysis, design and implementation in an OO language which provides facilities for encapsulation and inheritance.
2. Object based development is characterized by OO analysis, and possibly design tools and an implementation which does not support the full object abstraction.
3. Object structured development retains the object abstraction for analysis and uses some OO design principles, but shifts to an object-like design using structured

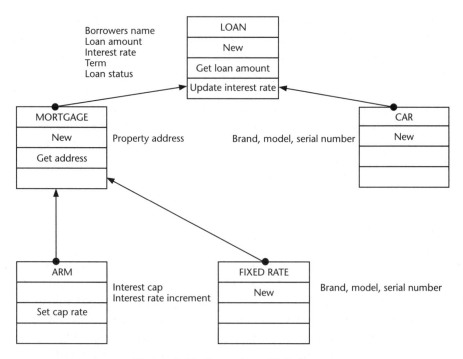

Figure 3.13 Illustrations of inheritance

design notation and principles. Implementation is in a standard language (Fortran, C or Cobol, for example). These languages provide no direct encapsulation or inheritance machinery.

The modelling technique (SSADM) which most developers will be familiar with is based on defining function in one model and the information on which they operate in another. The function model describes a hierarchy of functions where the lowest level represents elementary business functions. In contrast, in OO systems development, we tend to build an information system from the bottom up, starting at the server layer where the model parts are held (Prins, 1996).

The skill base needed to encapsulate business process into business objects and determine the appropriate levels of granularity is crucial to OO development projects. Developers and their project managers need to be able to determine:

- What do I need in an object?
- What do I need to tell the objects to do?
- How do I want other objects to interact with this object?

As described earlier, modelling business objects and business processes yields the functional requirements of an information system. However, there are many non-functional requirements that must also be dealt with. These non-functional requirements specify the infrastructure on which the information system must run.

Examples are server platforms, client platforms, network type, database mechanism, presentation form, national languages supported, security provisions, international standards, and so on. In systems analysis, the emphasis is on the functional analysis but in design and implementation most of the work is on the non-functional requirements. Building a business object can be likened to creating an iceberg. As it floats around in the company information system, all that is visible is the 10 per cent that implements the functional requirements. Most of it is hidden from sight; 90 per cent of the volume is needed to meet the non-functional requirements (Prins, 1997). It is worth remembering that for a given business information system, the non-functional requirements are constant across otherwise different business objects, such as product, customer, and account.

Component standards

One of the main issues that designers of OO systems need to address is that of establishing component standards. Standards are an essential part of the basis for reusable and interchangeable components. It is envisioned that application development in the future will require two types of developers: component builders who design and build the core reusable business objects and components; and solution builders who assemble applications from existing components. However, organizations will need to put greater emphasis on analysis and design if the benefits of simplifying maintenance and reuse are to be achieved. The promises made for OO systems include:

- Higher quality systems (robustness, reliability, extensibility, maintainability, and usability).
- Greater productivity through reusability.
- Higher quality development process.
- Ability to build bigger or more complex systems.

Development tools

As discussed, the need for quality software developers and a considered development approach is paramount. However, the selection and application of a suitable development tool set has a significant impact on the successful delivery of a system and its ongoing support. The focus here is the identification and selection of development tools to meet specific organizational or project requirements.[3] Associated with any development are organizational, project and application constraints. The successful application of a tool set needs to consider all of these constraints and, in the most extreme cases, these constraints may actually determine the tool set to be used. Whilst discussing the previously mentioned areas, suggestions are included to indicate how the risks associated with development and specific approaches can be managed. Ultimately, regardless of the approach taken, the business imperative is still cost effective, timely, and quality of delivery.

Tool set model

To understand the implications of using individual tools or undertaking specific types of projects, it is helpful to develop a generic tool set model. Such a model is given in Figure 3.14.

The model shown draws from the three-layer client–server architecture prevalent in many of today's tools and has been enhanced to reflect specific development requirements. Each of the components in the model provides services and maps onto discrete tool set functions or utilities. By mapping the facilities provided by a specific tool onto the model, it is possible to assess its suitability for development projects. Similarly, the needs of specific applications can be mapped against the model and used to identify a suitable tool set.

The core elements of the model are interface design, storage design and business modelling. These elements are augmented by the configuration management and deployment components. Ideally, all of the components communicate via a repository component.

Implicit in the model is the need for a coherent tool set architecture. This may vary from a framework that enables tool set components to communicate, through to a complete application architecture that provides large elements of generic system functionality, such as a security or online help sub-system.

Given that between 20 per cent and 30 per cent of any application is relatively standard, the provision of a comprehensive application framework can significantly reduce the overall development effort required. It also provides a standard framework within which developers can work, mitigating the informal system design undertaken in development projects.

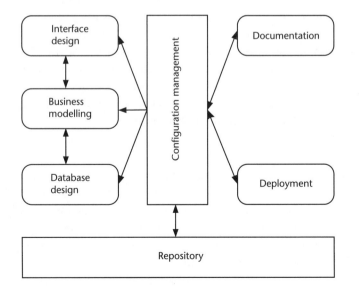

Figure 3.14 Tool set model

Components of the tool set model

Lawrence D. Bell once remarked, 'show me a man who cannot bother to do little things and I'll show you a man who cannot be trusted to do big things'. During the technical design phase details are important and cannot be taken for granted. No loose ends should exist when system programming begins. In their book, *Corporate Management in Crisis: Why the Mighty Fall*, Joel Ross and Michael Kampi stated their belief that: '... attention to details is not nitpicking but an essential and vital part of successful management'. This is an important message for the system builder. Paying attention to details is not an easy job since it takes discipline as well as tact. The project team must keep a keen focus on the details during the upcoming design process.

Although a solid 'vision' (see Chapter 4) describing what the system will do, and what the major components will look like may be in place, a vast gap will remain between this 'vision' and the actual technical realities of implementation. Bridging this gap is technical design. This phase focuses on making the system a reality. By the completion of this phase, no detailed questions should remain about how a screen will operate, where information will come from on a report, how a program will perform required calculations, or any other technical issue.

Interface design

The key to RAD and OO development projects is for users to touch and feel the functions associated with their requirements and subsequently provide feedback to refine these requirements. Consequently, the interface design component is a critical element of any development tool set. The need to develop and deliver complex screens rapidly is increasingly being satisfied by the component assembly of sophisticated graphical widget sets. Screens are realized as aggregations of graphical objects specialized to provide the required functionality. Given the increasing complexity of operating systems, it is vital that the tool set abstracts the complexities of the underlying windowing system. Ideally, screens can be developed independent of their target platform and windowing system. As the interface design component drives much of the development process, its seamless integration with the other tool set components is vital. Consequently, many tool sets provide facilities to define storage and business objects with which interface objects may communicate.

Storage design

The storage design component provides facilities to define the storage structures accessed by the other components by abstracting the complexities of underlying databases. It also manages access to a range of external databases, ideally, supporting access to several different databases at the same time. When undertaking a RAD or OO project, storage design takes an evolutionary approach that is driven by the need to support specific functionality. Consequently, the ability of a tool set to associate screen functionality with differing storage structures is vital. This also extends to database stored procedures. Database access is provided either using proprietary database interfaces, or standard database independent middle-ware supporting standards such as ODBC. Whilst ODBC facilitates database independence it occasionally restricts the facilities available from a specific database and may also impact performance. The database design facilities provided by the tool set may vary from complete integration including storage management through to the association of screen fields with database columns. In general, the more sophisticated a tool set, the better the database integration. When using object oriented tool sets, the facilities provided to map between object and relational technologies are key. The preferred approach is for a tool set to define the database schema, storage mapping objects and standard storage services based on high-level developer input.

Business modelling

The business processing performed in the majority of development applications is limited in complexity to business algorithms and calculations. This is because many tools lack a business modelling component and tightly couple the interface design and storage design components. A significant constraint on the complexity of any systems development using development tools is the need visually to demonstrate system functionality. Many tool sets provide minimal facilities to develop business processes visually and integrate them with database and screen functionality.

The complexity of business processing required by an application has a significant impact on the suitability of a specific tool set. Most development applications currently contain minimal computational complexity and large elements of online functionality which is suited to the delivery of tactical applications. To develop major systems using RAD or OO requires sophisticated repository-based tools with facilities to integrate screens, business processes and data storage. This is starting to happen with the development of enterprise client–server tools and modelling tools that provide bridges to a variety of development tools.

Configuration management

A secure repository to hold the information associated with the other tool set components is vital given the need for effective configuration management and change control. As the number of developers increases, the need to record and control software changes becomes increasingly important. Equally important is the ability to define software baselines as in conventional projects. However, there is an added requirement to be able to back-out complete changes. As the complexity of the tool set and application increase so does the overhead of being able to remove changes. An element of change control that is often glossed over is the need for impact analysis. As minimal time is spent in defining the architecture of a system, the potential for complex interactions and missed impact when implementing changes is significant. Consequently, facilities to provide rudimentary impact analysis can be of great benefit. A peripheral consideration is the need to hold system baselines and associate them with specific software baselines. Typically this includes the original requirements document, change requests and system documentation. Testing is undertaken throughout the development cycle, culminating in the acceptance test of a deployed application. In view of this, a test tool interface is required to support the association of software baselines and test baselines and enable regression testing.

Deployment

The deployment of applications may include the compilation of executable images, the use of interpreted files or the creation of a proprietary run time environment. The options available may have a significant impact on system performance, although executable files are normally the preferred option. Increasingly, there is a need to deploy applications across several platforms. Ideally, when using RAD for instance, systems are developed using their deployment platform. This minimizes the time required between developing and demonstrating functions and reduces the risk of functional or performance differences. In some cases, it may be necessary to develop on one platform and deploy on another platform. In these cases, the deployment process should be as transparent as possible and the application demonstrated on the target platform at the earliest opportunity.

Given the growing use of client–server technology and the need to install software on user workstations, software management and distribution are becoming increasingly important. The creation and rollout of software releases needs to be controlled by the configuration management of workstation configurations and software baselines. An aspect of conventional projects normally left to the end of a development project is the creation of system and supporting documentation. There is a need to be able to create overview documentation describing an application and its underlying database automatically, using the meta data held by the tool set and information associated with software components during their development.

Technology characteristics

The focus of a development project needs to be the delivery of a business system. This requires significant effort to translate user requirements into application functionality and to manage the scope of the work being performed. The overhead of using a new development tool set de-focuses development staff and introduces risk. The size and type of projects undertaken typically lend themselves to tactical or departmental applications. Ideally the systems developed are standalone, without significant linkage to other systems. This is necessary to reduce the system design and application design required during development.

Whilst it is possible for novice developers to deliver significant elements of functionality using entry level tool sets, the delivery of major systems using RAD or OO requires experienced professional developers. Neglecting to appreciate the implications of change control and scope management will result in failure. A variety of technology architectures may be used to undertake systems projects depending on specific project requirements. The key considerations are to manage risk, by selecting mainstream proven technologies, and to consider deployment and potential scalability requirements.

Pitfalls

As previously discussed, inadequate project evaluation and preparation appears to be a major reason for the failure of system development projects. Given the delivery imperative facing most organizations, methods such as RAD are often seen as a route to solving many problems and are applied in entirely the wrong situations. Familiarity with the development tool set is vital to ensure development staff remain focused on delivering the required business functionality within the constraints of the chosen technology. In addition, developers may be able to use existing software from similar projects with which they have been involved. Coordinating the changes being developed by a project team to avoid adverse impact between system components is vital. Poor communication, change control and an inadequate requirements baseline will all contribute to a failure to deliver the required system. Whilst most technology vendors insist that their products will work together, the use of a complex multi-platform architecture increases the risk of problems. In addition, the more complicated the technology architecture the greater the need to design the system correctly and the greater the overheads associated with debugging and testing.

Tool set selection

The development tool set market can be considered as comprising model based tools, 4GL based tools and OO based tools. Typically, model and 4GL based tools are better suited to RAD as they abstract the detail of their underlying technology.

The market contains many vendors providing products suited to RAD and OO system development. Despite the array of products available, the main criterion for selecting a tool set is that it can be productively used to quickly deliver stable systems. Many mainstream development tool sets can be used for both RAD and OO projects.

Industry trends

Modelling tools with links to application development environments are continuing to emerge. This will have a significant impact on development as it is currently constrained by the lack of visual tools to develop complex business processes. Object orientated technology will have an increasing influence on the evolution of development tools, as it is particularly suited to developing application driven software, such as GUI's, and modelling complex behaviour such as business processes.

The availability of object oriented database management systems means that development tools are likely to become repository based. However, these tools will still be reliant on RDBMS to store information and to generate functions based on a data model. Many first generation client–server development tools will struggle to deliver major scaleable applications. Arguably they will be constrained by an underlying two-tier architecture that fails to decouple business components from interface and storage components. This is giving rise to the emergence of more sophisticated second generation tools employing a three-tier distributed architecture.

Many project managers have suffered as a result of placing their success in the hands of the promised 'experienced' programmer or the 'intelligent' code generator. The temptation is to leave the details until later in order to gain time within the phase. However, the unexpected often happens, such as a key analyst leaving the project, and this can lead to major difficulties. In such cases, not only are extraordinary amounts of time necessary to stay on top of the construction effort, but the possibility of key requirements being overlooked increases dramatically. Whilst it is sometimes possible to overcome these kinds of problems, they can often lead to disaster.

Summary

■ Development projects are made up of four basic stages: birth, adolescence, maturity and demise. The notion that a project has a life cycle is the basis of many software development approaches.

■ The waterfall method tends to view software development as a series of discrete stages, where each stage is carried out in strict sequence. Although highly structured, this approach assumes that all user requirements are fixed and will be known at the start of the project.

■ The 'b' model was introduced as a way of overcoming some of the problems associated with the waterfall model. However, this model also suffers from some of the same disadvantages, such as assuming that user requirements will be known at the start of the project.

■ The spiral method is an iterative technique that allows stages to be repeated in order to refine ideas and products. The model allows the use of any development technique (e.g. RAD) since it defines an overall approach to development. The spiral method introduced the important concepts of objective setting, risk management and planning into the overall development process.

■ Many approaches do not allow requirements and specifications to be modified as work progresses. In addition, with some approaches, coding does not begin until late in the life of the project. Prototyping solves both of these problems by producing working models of a system very early in the life of the project. However, prototyping also suffers from a number of disadvantages, such as being dependent on high levels of cooperation from users.

■ Rapid Application Development (RAD) is a form of prototyping that uses the concept of a timebox to provide control over activities. A timebox is a fixed period of time for building a part of the application or achieving a given outcome. RAD is a popular technique but is not suitable for all types of project.

■ Joint Application Development (JAD) is a technique that allows developers, managers and customer groups to work together to build a RAD product.

■ The Dynamic Systems Development Method (DSDM) draws upon the experience of large organizations, tool vendors and consultancy companies. DSDM specifies an overall approach to RAD that does not proscribe specific tools or techniques. DSDM is well regarded in the UK and continues to grow in popularity.

■ System methodologies describe an overall approach to development and the tools/techniques used to develop a system.

■ Structured Systems Analysis and Design Method (SSADM) is one of the best-known and widely used system methodologies. SSADM is made up of a number of stages, each of which is made up of several steps. Tools used by SSADM include data flow diagrams, entity relationship models and entity life histories.

■ Soft Systems Methodology (SSM) focuses on building a model of a problem situation that takes into account individual knowledge, experience and perceptions. Tools used by SSM include rich pictures and root definitions.

■ Object Oriented Analysis (OOA) approaches to system design, such as the Booch method, try to capture and display system requirements in a way that more closely reflects the real world. This approach is based around concepts such as inheritance and encapsulation. In turn, this supports code reuse and the creation of robust software applications.

■ A tool set model can be used to understand the implications of using individual tools or undertaking specific types of projects. Such a model will take into account all of the tools used during different stages of a project, for example user interface design, database design, deployment and so on.

Project checklists

Checklist 3.1 Software requirements

Requirements content

■ Are all the inputs to the system specified including their source, accuracy, range of values, and frequency?

■ Are all the outputs from the system specified including their destination, accuracy, range of values, frequency, and format?

■ Are all the report formats specified?

■ Are all the external hardware and software interfaces specified?

■ Are all the communication interfaces specified including handshaking, error checking, and communication protocols?

■ Is the expected response time, from the user's point of view, specified for all necessary operations?

■ Are other timing considerations specified, such as processing time, data transfer, and system throughput?

■ Are all the tasks the user wants to perform specified?

■ Does each task specify the data used in the task and data resulting from the task?

■ Is the level of security specified?

■ Is the reliability specified including the consequences of software failure, vital information protected from failure, error detection, and recovery?

■ Are acceptable tradeoffs between competing attributes specified, for example, between robustness and correctness?

■ Is maximum memory specified?

■ Is the maximum storage specified?

■ Is the definition of success included? Of failure?

■ Is the maintainability of the system specified, including the ability to respond to changes in the operating environment, interfaces with other software, accuracy, performance, and additional predicted capabilities?

Requirements completeness

■ Where information isn't available before development begins, are the areas of incompleteness specified?

■ Are the requirements complete in the sense that if a product satisfies every requirement, it will be acceptable?

■ Are you uneasy about any part of the requirements? Are some parts impossible to implement and included just to please your customer or boss?

Requirements quality

■ Are the requirements written in user language? Do the users think so?

■ Do all the requirements avoid conflicts with other requirements?

■ Do the requirements avoid specifying the design?

■ Are the requirements at a fairly consistent level? Should any requirement be specified in more detail? Should any requirement be specified in less detail?

■ Are the requirements clear enough to be turned over to an independent group for implementation and still be understood?

■ Is each item relevant to the problem and its solution? Can each item be traced to its origin in the problem environment?

■ Is each requirement testable? Will it be possible for independent testing to determine whether each requirement has been satisfied?

■ Are all possible changes to the requirements specified including the likelihood of each change?

Checklist 3.2 Design/review of data flow diagrams

Introduction

A checklist of review points for Data Flow Diagrams follows. In addition to these points, it should always be remembered when reviewing DFDs that they are primarily a means of communicating the system's main activities.

Basic review of data flow diagrams

■ Has a system boundary been included in the diagram?

■ Are all data sources and recipients external to the boundary?

■ Does each process name start with a strong verb, and include a noun that the verb acts upon?

■ Has the location part of the process symbol been specified in physical system diagrams, and left blank in logical system diagrams?

■ Does each process have input and output data flows?

■ Is there an input and output to every data store (if data stores are duplicated then this may occur at different places in the DFD set)?

■ Data stores should only be connected to processes (by data flows)?

■ Have the data store reference letters been correctly defined, i.e.
  D for permanent computer data;
  T for temporary computer data;
  M for non-computer (manual) data storage?

■ External data sources or recipients should be directly connected to processes in the system. (Where helpful to communicating an understanding of the system, sources or recipients may be connected to each other outside the system boundary.)

▨ Sources or recipients should not refer to people by name – use position or title.

▨ Can the diagram be simplified by amalgamating many recipients of one output into one generic 'output distribution list' (and them documenting the receivers elsewhere)?

▨ All data flows are named. Does each data flow start or end with a process? The only exception to this is between external sources and recipients.

▨ Flows that are within the system should be drawn within the system boundary. Is the diagram well laid out:
  – are the symbols equally spaced?
  – are data flows short, so that the symbols the flow connects are 'visually' close?
  – does the diagram have a uniform style (e.g. straight data flows or flows with a right-angle incorporated)?
  – data flows should not cross wherever possible?
  – are data stores and source/recipients duplicated to reduce number of crossing flows, and also the length of data flows?

▨ Are any of the diagrams or parts of a diagram too detailed for the diagram level?

▨ The DFD diagrams should not be a documentation of computer programs.

▨ A process should not represent a decision – the decision is part of a process.

▨ In a logical data flow diagram, have all physical references in the data flow and process names been removed, e.g., locations, physical medium or time frames?

Business review

Boundary of system
▨ Ensure that the boundary is correct. Are any functions of organizational departments erroneously included or excluded?

Processes
▨ Do all the outputs require all the inputs to a process, and vice versa?

▨ Does each process have a distinct output?

▨ Are the processes a true reflection of the activity in the business system? Are any necessary manual processes or analytical processes included?

▨ Are housekeeping activities or custodial activities to maintain reference data, included in the diagrams?

▨ Could the process be better 'levelled' to communicate the analyst's understanding?

▨ In a logical data flow diagram:
  – have all redundant processes been removed?
  – has all unnecessary process sequencing been erased?

– have all unnecessary processing cycles been removed?

– is the process partitioning based purely upon business functionality, with no reflection of any current organizational structure?

– does each process have one major output?

■ There should be minimal portrayal of reporting or inquiry processing on data flow diagrams as this frequently causes cluttered diagrams. Inquiries should be documented as Functions.

■ Include reports that are by-products of other processes as output data flows from that process.

Sources and recipients

■ Are the sources and recipients depicted the correct ones for the associated data flows?

■ Are the sources/recipients complete – should there be any more for a given data flow?

■ For a given source/recipient are there any further inputs, or outputs to be received?

■ In a logical DFD, is the source/recipient shown the actual generator or user of the data flow information, or merely the interface to the system?

Reviewing process descriptions

Basic review

■ Is the input clearly stated – both in reference and descriptive terms?

■ Is the main output of the process clearly stated?

■ Are the sources and receivers of the data clearly stated?

■ Has the reference data required been documented?

■ Have any additional outputs been referenced, such as audit reports?

Semantic checks

■ The process description should be used to add additional information that the DFD format is unsuitable for:

– has the frequency of the input been stated, both the average and peak volumes included when these occur?

– functional need for this process, i.e. its role within the system?

■ Is the information correct?

■ Is there any additional information to be added to clarify that the processing had taken place?

Bibliography

Avision D. and Fitzgerald G., 1996, *Informations Systems Development: Methodologies, Tools and Techniques*, 2nd edn, Blackwell, UK.

Baskerville R., 1993, 'Semantic Database Prototypes', in *Journal of Information Systems*, pp. 119–144.

Birrell N. and Ould M., 1988, *A Practical Handbook for Software Development*, Cambridge University Press, UK.

Boehm B., 1988, 'A Spiral Model of Software Development and Enhancement', in Computer, No. 21, pp. 61–72, May 1988.

Booch G., 1994, *Object-Oriented Analysis and Design with Applications*, 2nd edn, Benjamin Cummings, Redwood City.

Challis J., 1996, 'Improving the Testing Process: Part 1', in *Computing*, September 1996.

Checkland P. and Scholes J., 1990, *Soft Systems in Action*, John Wiley & Sons, Chichester.

Dolan K., 1995, *Prototypes*, Research Analysis & Maintenance, Inc., El Paso, TX.

DSDM Manual Version 3, DSDM Consortium, 1997.

Gomaa H., 1989, 'Structuring criteria for real-time systems design', in Proceedings of the 10th International Conference Software Engineering, Pittsburgh, USA.

Gilb T., 1988, *Principles of Software Engineering Management*, Addison-Wesley, USA.

Kerr J. and Hunter R., 1994, *Inside RAD*, McGraw-Hill Publishing, USA.

Martin J., 1991, *Rapid Applications Development*, Macmillan Press, New York.

McDermid J. and Rook P., 1991, 'Software Development Process Models', in McDermid J. (ed.), *Software Engineer's Reference Book*, Butterworth-Heinemann Ltd, Oxford.

Pressman, 1997, *Software Engineering: A Practitioner's Approach*, McGraw-Hill, New York.

Prins R. *et al.*, 1997, 'Family Traits In Business Objects And Their Applications', in *IBM Systems Journal*, Vol. 1, No. 1, p. 36.

Prins R., 1996, *Developing Business Objects: A Framework Driven Approach*, McGraw-Hill International Ltd, UK.

Schneider K., 1996, 'Prototypes as Assets, not Toys – Why and How to Extract Knowledge from Prototypes', in Proceedings of ISCE, 18, pp. 522–531, IEEE.

Van Vliet H., 2000, *Software Engineering: Principles and Practice*, 2nd edn, John Wiley & Sons, Chichester.

Further reading

Booch G., 1997, *Object Solutions: Managing the Object-oriented Project*, Addison-Wesley, USA.

Davis A., 1990, *Software Requirements: Analysis and specification*, Prentice-Hall, USA.

Flynn D., 1992, *Information Systems Requirements: Determination & Analysis*, McGraw-Hill, USA.

Pressman R. and Ince D., 2000, *Software Engineering: A Practitioner's Approach*, 5th edn, McGraw-Hill, UK.

Robertson S. and Robertson J., 1990, 'Mastering the Requirements Process', in Davis A., 1990, *Software Requirements: Analysis and Specification*, Prentice-Hall, USA.

Stapleton J. and Constable P., 1997, *DSDM The Method in Practice*, DSDM Consortium.

Useful websites

http://www.dsdm.org/
This website is managed by the DSDM consortium and contains information relating to the Dynamic Systems Design Methodology.

http://www.iconixsw.com/Spec_Sheets/OverviewOOMethods.html
This website contains information relating to the Booch methodology. The site also provides details on e-learning materials.

http://www.duneram.com/books/winbooks.html
This website contains details of books and other related material to do with the Unified Modeling Language (UML).

http://members.tripod.com/SSM_Delphi/ssm4.html
Home page for Softs Systems Methodology in the world wide web. A very useful source of information on soft systems.

Self-assessment exercises

1. The text states that a successful software test is one that discovers a bug. Why?

2. A project can be said to have four distinct phases. What are these phases?

3. In the waterfall method, a new stage can only begin once the previous stage has been completed. True or false?

4. What is economic feasibility?

5. In simple terms, what is the difference between module testing and system testing?

6. What is the approximate cost of maintenance over the entire life cycle of a project?
   (a) 20 per cent
   (b) 30 per cent
   (c) 40 per cent
   (d) 50 per cent
   (e) 60 per cent

7. The 'b' model does not assume that users know exactly what they want from the proposed system at the very start of the project. True or false?

8. The spiral model provides little support for risk management and planning. True or false?

9. In simple terms, what is evolutionary prototyping?

10. List at least three disadvantages related to prototyping.

11. What is a timebox?

12. What are the four main principles apparent within RAD?

13. The purpose of a JAD session is to define the user and application interfaces for a specific component of a RAD project. True or false?

14. DSDM suggests that the prototyping of an application may be sliced in two ways. What are these two ways?

15. What is shown by an entity life history?

16. With reference to SSM, what is CATWOE?

17. What is encapsulation?

18. What are the three core elements of a tool set model?

Case study

(This Case Study which is reproduced with permission, was originally published in *Management Services*, April–May 1998, and was entitled 'The Future of Software Development in Large Organisations' by Richard Girling and John McManus.)

The application of RAD in a waterfall systems cultural environment

Introduction

In the traditional, linear or 'waterfall' approach to development, users are consulted only during the initial analysis phase. Design, development, testing, and deployment are executed in series, and end users don't see the developers' work until the application is deployed. But, what if the design phase uncovers requirements that are technically unfeasible, or extremely expensive to implement? What if errors in the design are encountered during the build phase? The elapsed time between the initial analysis and testing is usually a period of several months. What if business requirements or priorities change or the users realize they overlooked critical needs during the analysis phase? These are many of the reasons why software development projects either fail or don't meet the user's expectations when delivered.

Rapid Applications Development

Increasingly the traditional 'waterfall' method of design has become inappropriate when constructing commercial business systems. It is being replaced by 'Rapid Applications Development' (RAD) methods where the objective is first to produce a visualization, then a prototype of the system so that users can quickly give feedback, after which the core functionality can be delivered quickly for maximum business benefit.

The fundamental aspect of this method is the splitting of the development work into smaller pieces, (or iterative development cycles) each of which is the responsibility of a small group of users, analysts and developers. User involvement is essential in RAD, as well as the use of modelling and the automatic generation of solutions. This has a number of distinct advantages over the traditional sequential development model. Iteration allows for effectiveness and self-correction. Studies have shown that human beings almost never perform a complex task correctly the first time. However, people are extremely good at making an adequate beginning and then making many small refinements and improvements. We should encourage and exploit this rather than fight it.

Integrated RAD teams

RAD projects are typically staffed with small integrated teams comprising developers, end users, and IT technical resources. Small teams combined with short, iterative development cycles optimize speed, unity of vision and purpose, effective informal communication and simple project management. An important, fundamental principle of iterative development is that each iteration delivers a functional version of the final system. It is a properly developed, fully working portion of the final system and is not the same as a prototype.

RAD teams would not necessarily have to be from the same department within an organization. Each team member could be from any area where information systems expertise is found. This cross-section of personnel would be able to capitalize on diverse system knowledge. However, before considering initializing a RAD team, it may be prudent to examine the nature of the project to determine if RAD development could be used (not all projects are suitable for RAD). One practical method is to survey the organization's short-term business requirements. RAD could be looked at as an option to deliver any such requirement. I will now discuss how the RAD methodology was used to deliver a Client–Server application within a major European Transport Company.

The case study

The organization concerned had for 20 years delivered software systems using the traditional system development life cycle methodology with mixed results and benefits. The major weaknesses were perceived to be:

(a) too rigid, slow, sequential and inflexible to deal with change;
(b) too lengthy, often costly, and laborious;
(c) underplays end-user involvement in the development process;

(d) fails to deliver business requirement and system user needs;

(e) and, inappropriate for small- or medium-scale systems development.

These failings led to the belief that a new systems development paradigm was needed. The result was the adoption of the alternative systems development method RAD, arising with general and common aims of:

1. Reducing development time and cost of systems development.
2. Improving the delivery of business, systems and user requirements.
3. Delivering the imperative of rapid systems development time frames.
4. Dealing with the dynamic nature of business activity in the organization.

Caution

Although RAD is an approach that is inherently designed to provide fast information systems development with better quality results than the traditional waterfall approach to development. It is perhaps worth pointing out that the choice of a RAD method, and the approach used, is an important and critical business decision; the process of systems development can be time consuming and costly to any organization. The predominant objective of any business systems development project should be to build information systems that meet the requirements of a particular strategic business unit, and its end users, in order to deliver the optimal benefits of information systems.

The RAD project

The software systems project selected for this approach was defined as:

1. Building a fault recording and incident system, which will incorporate real time updates as changes occur.
2. A Graphical User Interface (GUI), which will access data from a RDMS for text input.
3. A flexible reporting system which will provide historical statistics.
4. Available to run on a Client 486.
5. System should not impact performance of existing systems. The system must be capable of showing data entered within 15 seconds.

A key characteristic of any RAD project is gaining user acceptance to what you are trying to accomplish. The management team had identified a number of key personnel whose cooperation would be vital to the success of the project. Knowing this the RAD management team arranged an informal away day. The objective was to outline the methodology, risks and benefits of the RAD approach. On the whole, the day was a success, however a number of issues were put on the table, namely:

- How do we liberate personnel from their day-to-day functional roles?
- How do we organize and pay for training in the RAD method?
- How do we manage the user selection process?
- If it goes wrong how do we deal with the blame culture?
- How do we manage the hidden costs which are not factored in?

It became apparent that this project would only succeed with the full and united cooperation of the organization senior management team. Several weeks of hard selling (under a difficult political corporate climate) and bargaining finally resulted in the team getting the investment funds to undertake the project.

Creating the environment

The project acquired a dedicated suite of rooms in which to undertake the Joint Applications Development (JAD) sessions and ensuing development work. One of the rooms was designated a JAD area, however due to the nature and number of the JAD exercises taking place a traffic light system was initiated to avoid unnecessary interruptions. A relaxation room was also provided for users, developers and the project manager to recover from burn-out JAD sessions (and to get to know the users better).

To promote the RAD concept promotional literature was fixed to the walls of the main room. We encouraged people to drop in and look round our displays – it also allowed users to get up to speed and read the latest news without disturbing the team too much. The project team installed a dedicated Local Area Network (LAN). The network supported 15 PCs utilizing two top-of-the-range file servers. The choice of which RAD tool to use was a complex issue. Assuming you are an IT practitioner – if you were asked to name a popular RAD tool, you'd probably cite either Borland, Delphi, CA Visual Objectives, Microsoft Visual Basic or PowerBuilder. In selecting the tool, consideration was given to existing skills within the team, ease of use, type of support offered and cost. Consideration was also given to reusability and quality of object code. Eventually PowerBuilder was selected, mainly for its adherence to objected orientation techniques, skill set availability and whole life-cycle cost of use.

The project team

The business review stage had already been concluded some time before the RAD team was put together. The RAD management team consisted of an experienced IT project manager, a professional business analyst and technical design authority who provided RAD counsel and quality assurance expertise throughout the project life cycle. Due to lack of internal development expertise in the RAD tools, a decision was taken to employ a number of experienced developers from the external market. An initial test of the market however, proved futile. After several discussions agreement was reached to approach a short-listed group of software houses in order to procure the experienced developers needed. During these approaches it became evident that the so-called inhouse RAD experience provided by some of the suppliers either did not exist or was to be obtained from our first choice the external market. After several weeks the management team eventually found the developers it needed.

The selection process

Whilst no single selection process is guaranteed to deliver the people you are looking for, the management team decided to minimize its risk by undertaking a three-tier selection process. Tier one: Belbin self-assessment questionnaire. Most systems projects of this nature require people to work together in small groups for intensive periods of time. To do this effectively it is useful to understand something about how individuals may behave. Each of the 20 short-listed candidates was asked to complete a Belbin questionnaire to ascertain which of the Belbin categories they conformed to – for example, Implementer, Resource Investigator, Team Worker, Completer Finisher, Coordinator, Shaper, Plant or Monitor Evaluator. Generally the ideal team will consist of:

1. A good spread of the eight roles.
2. Little duplication and few gaps.
3. Individuals shift to secondary roles if the group is unbalanced.
4. New members recruited or coopted to fill gaps.
5. Members are aware of the importance of complementing each other's role.

The completed questionnaires were then grouped into their identified types. But no action was taken with the results at this stage. Tier two: this tier consisted of an in-depth technical interview with each member of the management team. Each interview lasted between 30–45 minutes against an agreed technical script. Tier three: this final phase of the selection process involved reviewing each of the identified outputs from phases one and two. The critical attributes identified were:

- At least 18 months' experience with PowerBuilder.
- Good interpersonal skills – able to lead individual JAD sessions.
- Able to cooperate with other team members.
- Ability to work on own initiative without getting too stressed out.
- Able to socialize after working hours with the other team members.

From those people interviewed seven were finally selected to work with the team. Interestingly 70 per cent of the candidates interviewed had the correct technical skills, but over half failed on the soft interpersonal skill set. Belbin gives a clue here – at least 40 per cent of those interviewed were Monitor Evaluators with weakness traits described as: little inspiration and the ability to motivate others.

User participation

A crucial ingredient of RAD is core business knowledge. Within the project several user roles were identified. Two of these roles were deemed absolutely critical to the success of the project. The two key roles were the advisor user and champion advisor user. The terms of reference for each role were: to provide core business knowledge, to participate in JAD and prototyping sessions and to provide counsel to other users and developers. The selection criteria used to assess the suitability of personnel to fill these positions was:

- Ability to apply business knowledge.
- Ability to communicate (both written and verbal).
- Ability to work within a small multi-skilled team.
- Ability to solve practical problems and issues.

The personnel appointed remained with the project until completion and were instrumental in shaping the outcome of the development work. Each individual underwent training in RAD methodology (this was undertaken by a recognized and approved UK training organization). Where appropriate training was also provided for members of the management team, this training proved invaluable.

Joint Application Development sessions

JAD is the means by which the business requirements are augmented within RAD – this involves the bringing together of users and developers in a workshop environment. The objective is to define deliverables within a controlled framework. The elected framework was Timeboxing and the use of *MOSCOW* lists. This stands for:

Must have (available by the planned date shown).
Should have (should be available by 30/10/99).
Could have (could be available by 30/10/99).
Won't have (will be considered for a future phase after 30/10/99).

During the course of 16 weeks some 20 JAD workshops were held and knowledge of 50 users was applied in the final system design. A lesson learned in the early JAD workshops was the need for formal rules. Although not exclusive to this project the rules given in Table CS3.1 were applied.

Documented requirements from the early JADs were used to prioritize requirements into a MOSCOW list – several iterations of asking *Why* questions such as 'if this was not included would the system not function?' This shifted priorities, for example some of Must have's became Could have's. The base line data model was developed outside the user environment, however, this was added to through the JAD sessions with users. The RAD team would go through with the users what they had done in the previous sessions and review it (after they had thought about it). The new model would be approved to the users before commencing a new JAD session including a description of all the data elements and the relationships documented in business terminology.

Prototyping within RAD

From the MOSCOW list the RAD development team started off with a plan of the prototypes it needed to build. The users set the pace by what they wanted to see. Timeboxing was used to

Table CS3.1   JAD rules of engagement

1. Success requires commitment from all participants
2. All participants are equal
3. Preparation is important
4. Prompt start and finish times must be adhered to
5. Participants must be willing to participate
6. Technical jargon should be kept to a minimum
7. An agenda must be produced and agreed with all participants
8. All open-ended statements must be dealt with offline
9. Let facilitators facilitate
10. Keep a sense of proportion and have fun

control the output levels from the RAD sessions – a typical timebox was 10 elapsed days for a major deliverable (for example an input screen). The timebox regime was used utterly and without deviation to control the productivity of the development process. When we were running late, something would go out of the timebox. There were a few obvious possibilities, in the end the user advisors had to decide. Changes to the timebox were monitored and function point productivity was adjusted (although in some instances reluctantly). As part of the quality assurance process, each prototype was received by the end users in conjunction with the champion and advisor users. The prototypes were continually refined until an acceptable product was achieved. All prototypes were reviewed by the project manager and his quality assurance team.

During the prototyping sessions a number of benefits and disbenefits were observed. It is perhaps worth pointing these out Table CS3.2.

RAD software metrics

The technique of Function Point Analysis (FPA) was used in two major areas to monitor weekly development process, and to size MOSCOW list items. Weekly development progress was monitored by providing an estimate of the size of the final system and by measuring the work done in function points each week. A graph was produced, each week, showing actual effort against estimated effort. Care had to be taken to distinguish between new functionality and re-work. The size of individual MOSCOW list items were estimated in function points to allow similarly-sized requirements to be given a lower priority should higher priority items come to light. The implementation of a metrics program is not a trivial task. Summarizing the team's experience in using software metrics it is advisable to:

- Determine what you want to control – select metrics appropriate for the situation.
- Realize that measurement is a political issue – measurement will be resented, find the right allies.
- Plan the goals properly – undertake a small pilot.
- Appoint (if affordable) a metrics specialist.
- Document effort involved in carrying out the metrics program.

Testing within RAD

Experience suggests that as many as 55 per cent of all defects can be caused prior to the first line of source code being written. A major goal of RAD is to anticipate and remove defects in the software before integration and implementation takes place. The methodology used by

Table CS3.2 Prototyping strengths and weaknesses

Benefits	Dis-benefits
Most users felt involved	Some users didn't take to the process
Reduced risk of non-acceptance	Could not always accommodate users
Testing was introduced early in the cycle	Quality was sometimes questionable
Cut development by a third	Burn-out was an issue
Changes were augmented quickly	Function points were sometimes missed

the team to test the RAD products was developed prior to the JAD sessions and was tested in local conditions using a test environment.

For the testing phase, the objectives were to demonstrate to users that the system would meet the requirements and satisfy agreed acceptance criteria. To this end a thorough plan was drawn up for how the system would be tested. For each type of activity, a detailed test plan was created. All the outputs which needed testing were listed and a detailed test script was created. The tests were carried out by the group – the transaction types and characteristics of each test case were listed. The test plan was reviewed with the end users to ensure nothing was forgotten. The sequence of tests were planned to allow for phasing in, one sub-system at a time. Errors were classified as major, minor, cosmetic and systems testing was only deemed as being complete when all major and minor errors were corrected (Table CS3.3).

Lessons learned

In conclusion the organization, and to some degree the project team, took a risk in adopting the RAD method, however, the project manager and his team do believe they made the right choice in selecting the RAD approach. After testing was concluded the whole team (including the users) held a workshop to discuss what lessons had been learnt from the process. These are summarized in Table CS3.4.

Table CS3.3   Areas of system testing

1. Data conversion
2. All functional areas including:
   – data capture
   – security and access levels
   – reporting
   – interfaces
   – error handling
   – performance including volume testing
   – destructive testing

Table CS3.4   Points recorded in the lessons learnt session

1. Politics count – get managers and users on your side
2. Don't oversell the concept of RAD
3. Don't plan an ambitious system
4. Don't under estimate the work involved – do use software metrics
5. Don't undervalue testing – do all stages
6. Pay attention to detail – get the requirement right
7. Get the right resources on the project – RAD trained personnel are a must
8. Don't put off solving problems
9. Listen to what your users are telling you
10. Take expert advice – obtain advice from professionals

Table CS3.4   Continued

Some shortcomings
  1. The project was perhaps too big – it could have been split into smaller units
  2. The prototype timeboxes were perhaps too big
  3. More review sessions could have been held (perhaps twice daily)
  4. Users often wanted to re-visit the project scope – this led to stress within the team
  5. Function point productivity sometimes suffered
  6. Gaining consensus was sometimes a conflict between management and users

Questions

  1. Explain what would influence your choice to use RAD.
  2. Explain what is meant by timeboxing.
  3. What advantages does RAD have over the traditional waterfall method?
  4. Explain the basic concepts of DSDM.
  5. Why is it important to have user involvement in RAD projects?

Notes

  1. *Source*: DSDM Manual Version 3, DSDM Consortium, 1997.
  2. *Source*: Butler Group Report on DSDM, 1996.
  3. This material was initially presented at a British Computer Society, Project Management Specialist Interest Group, Autumn School in November 1996. The subject of the presentation was the application of RAD development tools. The material was presented by Nigel Murkitt, of Alani Ltd, Oxford, and is edited and produced with permission.

CHAPTER 4

Managing the information systems project life cycle

Introduction

Chapter 3 was concerned with the overall process of software development and considered common approaches to analysis and design. This chapter moves on to examine the management of projects, concentrating on issues such as planning and scheduling. The material presented here marks a transition from technical issues, such as conducting an analysis of the proposed system, to managerial issues, such as controlling resources and monitoring progress.

Several methodologies for project management are in common use and it would be difficult for any text to consider all of these in depth. In view of this, the material presented here focuses on PRINCE, an approach that is accepted as the *de facto* standard in the United Kingdom. Fortunately, this approach shares many of the features found in other methodologies. Furthermore, the features considered here provide good examples of best practice that can be applied to a wide variety of projects. It is argued that managing the discussion in this way serves two distinct purposes. Firstly, it provides relatively detailed coverage of a project management methodology that most, if not all, project managers will be required to use at one time or another. Secondly, it provides a clear discussion of the key features, strengths and weaknesses of project management methods in the context of the *tasks* managers are required to carry out.

A relatively detailed discussion of planning looks at methods such as work breakdown structure (WBS) and product-based planning (PBP). This material leads on to look at scheduling in depth. A particular emphasis is placed on handling problem areas, such as schedule conflicts and implementing sudden changes to schedules.

The final sections of the chapter examine issues related to control, handover and closure. A great deal of emphasis is placed on the need for accurate and timely management information. It is stressed that efficient reporting mechanisms are essential to the success of a project.

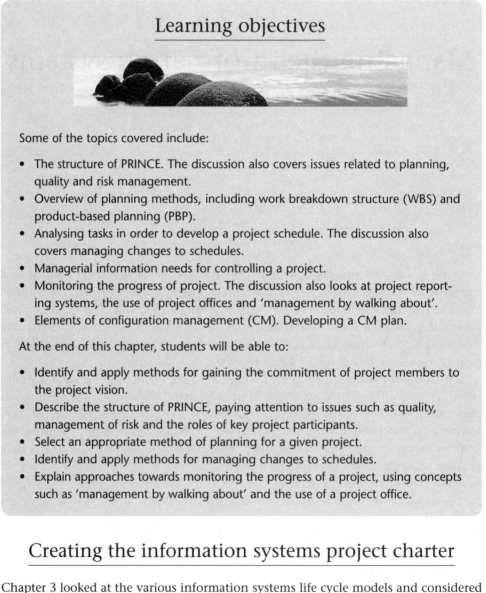

Learning objectives

Some of the topics covered include:

- The structure of PRINCE. The discussion also covers issues related to planning, quality and risk management.
- Overview of planning methods, including work breakdown structure (WBS) and product-based planning (PBP).
- Analysing tasks in order to develop a project schedule. The discussion also covers managing changes to schedules.
- Managerial information needs for controlling a project.
- Monitoring the progress of project. The discussion also looks at project reporting systems, the use of project offices and 'management by walking about'.
- Elements of configuration management (CM). Developing a CM plan.

At the end of this chapter, students will be able to:

- Identify and apply methods for gaining the commitment of project members to the project vision.
- Describe the structure of PRINCE, paying attention to issues such as quality, management of risk and the roles of key project participants.
- Select an appropriate method of planning for a given project.
- Identify and apply methods for managing changes to schedules.
- Explain approaches towards monitoring the progress of a project, using concepts such as 'management by walking about' and the use of a project office.

Creating the information systems project charter

Chapter 3 looked at the various information systems life cycle models and considered their relevant strengths and weaknesses. Academics and information systems practitioners often ask how they should go about starting to implement information technology systems. In this chapter, we provide a response to this question by looking at what is needed to deliver information systems projects. Although all projects are different and have distinctive characteristics, there are elements which are common to all but a few. Such elements include planning, organizing, directing and controlling. Each of these elements will be discussed here.

Within most project management methodologies the process of starting up a project expects the existence of a project mandate which defines in high level terms the reason for the project and what outcome is sought. Such a mandate is often associated with a project charter. A project charter may be described as: 'a document consisting of a mission statement, including background, purpose and benefits, a goal, objectives, scope, assumptions and constraints'. A project charter clearly documents a definition of the project in order to bring a project team into necessary agreement (Lewis, 1995). In essence, a project charter should aim to answer the following questions:

1. Why are we undertaking this project in the first place?
2. For whom do we do it – who are the stakeholders and customers, and what are their expectations for the project?
3. How do we go about meeting the customer expectations?

All activity on the project should be supported by a clearly described project mission. As a project progresses through its life cycle, it is often necessary to take a step back and realign individual project elements with one another and with the project mission. Successful projects strike a balance among customers and stakeholders. Table 4.1 demonstrates the encapsulation of vision, mission, customer and stakeholder statements for a university services department.

In developing charter statements it is important to amplify the voice of the customer. As an example, it should be made clear who will be paying for the project and who will actually be using the systems and processes designed. The charter should

Table 4.1	Elements of project charter
Vision	Exceed customer expectations by providing university services in a supportive, team-based environment, any time, anywhere, anyway.
Mission	Create and implement an improved and integrated, multi-access, team-based, customer-oriented service environment. Focusing on information services.
Customers/stakeholders	Students, parents, potential students, staff, faculty, school counsellors, alumni, tax payers, government agencies, Office of Higher Education, unions, university administrators and departments, suppliers and vendors.

clarify the business priorities of customers and their criteria for success. Project managers must actively and emphatically communicate this charter.

The information systems vision

Chapter 2 discussed the role of leadership in project management. A key component of leadership is vision. A vision, however, is of little use if it is not communicated to others. Only when the vision has been understood and adopted by the team does its usefulness begin to emerge. A project management visionary plays a vital role in making this happen. The willingness of the project manager to share his insights and understanding of the steps needed to arrive at a desired outcome tend to be dependent on two factors. These are the level of confidence the project manager has in his ideas, and his ability to tolerate close scrutiny and criticism of those ideas. Regardless of personal risks, a professional project manager must strive to be a systems visionary. With each passing phase of the project, the project manager must constantly develop and communicate his or her vision of both the system functionality and the project approach. Putting forward this vision assists in accomplishing two important results. First, it creates a base line foundation for continuing discussion. In many cases, the original system approach vision may not survive for long as better ideas are presented and improvement discussions occur. Second, the vision promotes constructive, critical thinking. It often helps if the vision statement is depicted graphically, for example in the form of a rich picture.

Gaining commitment to the vision

It could be argued that the presentation of a base line vision stimulates incremental modes of thought. If the visionary can relinquish ownership of the vision and encourage it to become the property of the group, the effectiveness of the process can be enhanced even more. The project manager serves to plant the starting point ideas, and the team members, customers and other stakeholders assist with, and take responsibility for, the ultimate direction and composition of the shared vision.

Gaining a commitment to the project vision requires the project manager to find the means and processes that will foster an environment in which team members will be motivated to work towards the vision. This commitment is not a destination, but an ongoing journey in terms of keeping people loyal to the vision, and constantly striving for its attainment, even during periods of adversity. The communication skills of the project manager, and the followers, are important in gaining and retaining this commitment.

Project stakeholders

Chapter 2 provided a brief discussion of the relationship between the project manager and the various stakeholder groups. Information system project managers are seldom part of an organization's senior management team. In order to ensure access to the resources he requires, the project manager will need the support of at least one project champion. The shrewd project manager understands the need to support his champion by building an external coalition of senior managers who will support the project in the highest councils of the organization. It is critical in any information systems development project to establish good lines of communication between stakeholder groups. In a software development project, these parties include users, management, suppliers, business assurance, systems designers, programmers, operations personnel and, of course, the project sponsor.

Managing these key stakeholder communities is vital to any project success. In gaining buy-in from stakeholders and meeting expectations, the following practical advice is offered:

- Put your own objectives in the wider context of the company. Customer requirements must be uppermost in your thinking and service delivery.
- Communicate clearly with your sponsor and suppliers about the required levels of performance, and deliver on promises in this respect.
- Lead by example, of your own effort and commitment, not demanding more of your subordinates than they are willing to give of themselves.
- Develop relationships with line managers and subordinates which create a climate of confidence as to the constructive nature of criticism received or given.
- Make work enjoyable and fulfilling, developing a working environment combining humour and respect, in which people know they will be listened to and treated fairly.
- Encourage stakeholders to contribute to decisions, but act decisively when necessary, accepting responsibility for their actions at all times.
- Represent your company in both formal and informal contexts, presenting the organization favourably and honestly; know about strengths and success and also how weaknesses are being tackled.

Remember for the project manager, success or failure (however measured) is often not the issue – it is the perception of success or failure in the eyes of the stakeholders which counts. This perception can be expected to govern the rewards which the project manager receives in the form of remuneration. Even though it is an indirect and imperfect measure, pay is still today considered to be the best available way of measuring performance across projects.

The information system project management life cycle

The management of large and complex information systems can be visualized as an engineering feedback control system with functions of monitoring, evaluating, and control elements. The effects of these elements are controlled by methods and tools utilized by the information systems project manager. From experience, the necessity of having a stable, well-tried, well-understood project management methodology in place is essential to inform project members (and stakeholders) and allow real cost and time scales to be predicted.

In selecting an appropriate project methodology for discussion, we are particularly keen to highlight the management principles behind the methodology. It is also important to remain mindful of the soft issues of management, the relationships between systems people and groups of people. It is our experience that to attempt to use any model mechanistically usually results in some level of failure. Project management methodologies should use frameworks that help individuals share a common language. The effective use of a methodology requires a common understanding of the philosophy and relational management approach. In information systems project management, the language we use is noticeably different from that traditionally used by other professionals, such as management consultants. Although the methodology selected looks anything but soft in appearance, our message is this: 'there is softness in the rigour of this methodology'.

In addition to the theory outlined in this chapter, the checklists provided at the end of the material are intended to provide *practical* guidance in carrying out many of the tasks associated with the design of a new system. The areas covered by the checklists include normalization, the design of user screens, entity life histories and system architecture.

As mentioned earlier, the purpose of this chapter is to discuss a methodology for project management in the field of information technology and information systems. The value of such a methodology will be enhanced if it can also be used in a more general sense. In attempting to describe such a methodology, and in attempting to provide some practical guidance for project managers, our starting point is PRINCE.

What is PRINCE 2?

PRINCE[1] (Project In Controlled Environment) was developed by the CCTA (Central Computer and Telecommunications Agency) in 1989 as a UK standard for IT project management. Since its introduction, PRINCE has become widely used in both the public and private sectors and is now the UK's *de facto* standard for project management. Although PRINCE was originally developed for the needs of IT projects, the method has also been adopted for many non-IT projects. The latest version of the method, PRINCE 2, is designed to incorporate the requirements of existing users and to enhance the method towards a generic, best-practice approach for the management of all types of projects. It is especially useful in the field of complex programmes composed of individual information technology projects.

In all information technology projects, the main objective is to establish control over resources, time, and quality. PRINCE 2 is a process-based approach for project management providing an easily tailored and scaleable method for the management of all types of projects. Each process is defined with its key inputs and outputs together with the specific objectives and activities to be carried out. The method describes how a project is divided in manageable stages, enabling efficient control of resources and regular progress monitoring throughout the project. The various roles and responsibilities for managing a project are adaptable to suit the size and complexity of the project, and the skills of the organization.

Project planning using PRINCE 2 is product-based, which means the project plans are focused on delivering results and are not simply about planning when the various activities on the project will be done. A PRINCE 2 project is driven by its Business Case, which describes the organization's justification, commitment and rationale for the project's deliverables or outcome. The business case is regularly reviewed in conjunction with the project's progress to ensure the business objectives, which may well change during the life of the project, are still being met.

Scope of PRINCE 2

PRINCE 2 is designed to provide a common language for all of the parties involved in the project. Bringing customers and suppliers together typically involves contracts and contract management. Although these aspects are outside of PRINCE 2, the method recognizes the need to provide projects with the necessary controls and breakpoints to work successfully within a contractual framework. The processes include starting up a project, directing a project, planning and managing stages. There are eight components:

1. Organization
2. Planning
3. Controls
4. Stages
5. Risk management
6. Quality in a project environment
7. Configuration management
8. Change control

The structure of a PRINCE project is shown in more detail by Table 4.2. Note that the term 'stage' within PRINCE 2 has specific meaning and is significant in the PRINCE 2 approach.

There are a set of fundamental elements which need to be present in the conduct of a project in order to describe it as running under PRINCE 2. These elements are:

1. A project board which takes responsibility for the success of the project.
2. Product-based planning with product descriptions for the end products (user deliverables).
3. Declaration, monitoring, control and exception reporting using project tolerances.
4. Independent assurance of quality, business, technical and user aspects of the project.
5. Frequent reference back to the business case to ensure that the planned business benefits are being realized.

Table 4.2 PRINCE structure

Organization
- Key customer and personnel make up a project board
- Project manager reports to the project board
- Project assurance provides independent assurance to the project board
- Can be adapted to fit corporate or inhouse style
- Places emphasis on involvement of committed user and customer personnel

Planning
- Structured into the project and stage plans
- Product-based
- Exceptional plans produced when the project is forecast to exceed its tolerance

Controls
- Formal project initiation
- Highlight reports written by the project manager
- End stage assessments
- Exception reports and optional mid-stage assessments
- Formal project closure
- Reporting by exception is a central theme

Stages
- Mandatory initiation followed by stages appropriate to the particular project
- Stage breaks coincide with key decision points, external dependencies, product deliveries

Risk management
- Risks classified as business or project risk
- Project board members own risks which originate externally
- Risk management takes place throughout the project

Quality in project environment
- Mandates independent project assurance
- Project/quality plan is part of project initiation document (PID)
- PID refined and stage plans produced for each stage
- All major products have a product description including quality criteria
- Structured product quality reviews
- Emphasis on configuration management and change control

Configuration management
- Configuration management of products is a natural extension from product-based planning
- Products classified as management, quality, or specialist
- Management of products recommended to fall within the remit of the customer's central support organization

Change control
- Specialist products are governed by request for change and off specification documents are handled as project issues

Organization

The PRINCE 2 organization is based on a customer/supplier environment where the customer wants the product or service and the supplier builds or provides it. Key roles of senior user and executive come from the customer (user) organization. These combine with the senior supplier (typically from the supplier organization but can be the inhouse IT function) to form the three key roles within the project board.

The board commissions the project, receives progress reports and is responsible for the continuation of a PRINCE 2 project through its stage boundaries. The project manager reports directly to the board.

The project assurance team (PAT) provides valuable assistance to the project manager as well as an independent view that gives the board greater confidence.

The PRINCE 2 organization can sometimes appear to be heavy but it should be remembered that processes and components can be tailored to suit the project. As an example, one person might undertake several PRINCE 2 roles. One of the main advantages of PRINCE 2 is the emphasis it places on the role of users within the project organization. The involvement, of committed user and customer personnel throughout a project is key to delivering a successful product.

Planning

Planning is one of the most important skills of a project manager. Two aspects of PRINCE 2 are of particular note with regard to planning:

PROJECT AND STAGE PLANS. PRINCE 2 encourages a structured level of planning. The overall project plan is presented at initiation, or start-up, and identifies the ultimate goals. Stage plans are drawn up with more detail to show each stage in turn. The stage plan becomes operational and is used for recording effort spent and new forecast estimates. New stage plans are drawn up for each stage in turn when authority to proceed is given.

PRODUCT-BASED PLANNING. PRINCE 2 encourages the project manager to consider the outcome of tasks within the plan – these are products. Product descriptions are drawn up at the start of each stage and clearly show the level of detail, composition and quality acceptance criteria. A product flow diagram is also drawn up to show the interdependencies between products. This leads to a better understanding of the activities to be considered in planning.

Product planning is worthy of further note. In the context of a classic waterfall development or RAD approach, products may be well defined within a supplier's quality system. However, consultancy-type projects, or those of a more unusual nature, will often benefit from having defined a product description at the outset. This is to establish clear terms of reference that can help manage expectations of the customer or user.

The exception plan is produced where forecasts show that the project will exceed its tolerances. It is the responsibility of the project manager to flag up a project in exception and communicate this to the project board. In this way, the board will be reasonably assured that the project is proceeding to plan unless the project draws attention to the exception reports.

Controls

PRINCE 2 is predicated on management by exception to determine the level of reporting and communication with the board. PRINCE 2 controls include:

1. Project initiation when the full plan, benefits and risks are discussed.
2. Highlight reports, which are written by the project manager.
3. End stage assessment, when the outcome of the current stage is reviewed before embarking on the next.
4. Exception reports, written in cases where forecasts indicate the project is exceeding its tolerances.
5. Mid-stage assessments which are called by the project board in exceptional situations to consider action and make decisions.
6. Project closure, where the debrief also considers lessons learned.

The principle of reporting by exception is a central theme of PRINCE 2. The project start-up and project initiation stage establishes clear objectives and tolerances for the project manager. Considering these controls, there is no further need for regular reporting to the board unless specific events dictate. Where forecasts show that the project cannot be delivered within tolerance the manager must write an exception report and produce a new plan (the exception plan) to show how it is brought back on track.

End of stage is a key reporting point for the project manager when the board decide whether the project is still meeting its business case and risks are reviewed before launching the next stage. This is a significant step and thus the importance of choosing stage delineation points can be seen. The review of risks at end of stage shows how risk management is bound into the normal control and reporting patterns for PRINCE 2 projects.

PRINCE 2 stages

In PRINCE 2, each project is divided into a number of decision points and this defines the stages. The initiation stage is mandatory but thereafter each stage is chosen to best suit the project, for example:

1. Key or significant points which naturally arise, for example investigation results may give rise to options which should be considered by the board;
2. With links to related projects, especially within a programme development; or
3. Based on product delivery forming a natural review point.

Stages must be selected carefully in order to ensure that the project can be monitored properly and that it remains under control. As an example, choosing PRINCE 2 stages as 'Analysis' and 'Design' means that, at end stage assessment, the board may be considering 'just started' and 'nearly complete' products. This should be avoided if possible and care should be taken to define those parts of products that are incomplete so that the board can take decisions based on accurate and meaningful information.

Quality

PRINCE 2 identifies a number of specific elements that relate to quality. There is a particular need to monitor all aspects of the project's performance and products independent of the project manager. This is the project assurance function. The specific assurance roles to be filled are at the discretion of the project board, but typical roles are that of quality assurance, technical assurance and business assurance.

The overall project/quality plan is produced as part of the project initiation document. Subsequent versions are produced at the end of each stage to reflect changes in circumstances as the project progresses. At the beginning of each stage, more detailed stage plans are produced identifying planning and quality details pertaining to that stage. As an aid to quality assurance and control, PRINCE 2 identifies a number of essential requirements:

1. The need for a control document for every major product in the project. This is known as the product description. It is produced as part of the planning process before the product is developed. The product description includes the quality criteria for the product, which define how the quality of the product is to be checked.
2. The need for reviews. PRINCE 2 includes a generic quality check, called a quality review. This is a structured technique designed to ensure a product's completeness and adherence to standards.
3. The importance of configuration management and change control. An approach to change control is defined, based on the identification of all potential changes as project issues.

Management of risk

Under PRINCE 2 risks are classified into two types that are called business risk and project risk. A business risk is one where the resultant product may not deliver its intended benefit. A project risk is one that threatens the ability of the project to deliver to time and budget. All plans, management expertise and control techniques are geared towards minimizing risk. The project manager, of course, exerts day-to-day control and thus is central to the management of risk.

The project board also plays a key role in managing risk. Risks that are identified as being particularly threatening are given 'owners' and board members play an important role owning risks that originate from outside the project. In PRINCE 2, a risk analysis is carried out to identify and quantify the nature of risks. Risks are recorded within a risk log. Risk management takes place throughout the project but the stage boundaries within PRINCE 2 offer natural checkpoints for risks to be given more attention. Risks that are identified at the start of a project are documented in the plans and these may roll over at each stage or may be eliminated. The management of risk will be explored in more depth in Chapter 6.

Configuration

Within PRINCE 2, a central theme is product-based planning. It is therefore a natural extension to ensure proper management of products through version control and change. The products are the assets of a project and these can be:

1. Paper or document (even if electronic), e.g. reports, studies and plans.
2. Intrinsically electronic (as in the case of software source and executable code).
3. Hardware.

   PRINCE 2 products are classified as management, quality or specialist. Management products are those created for the purpose of running the project; they are about the project itself, for example the plans and highlight reports. Quality products describe standards and quality criteria, for example product descriptions. Specialist products are those designed to deliver the benefit, to be used in some fashion by the customer's business, for example operating instructions and application code. PRINCE 2 advocates that management of the assets is likely to fall within the remit of the customer's central support organization and there are strong ties with the PAT and change management.

Change

During a stage, the project is deemed to be within tolerance and on target unless, a state of exception is reported. Thus versions of stage plans will not arise unless an exception is triggered. Note that the project manager may have a set of subordinate detailed plans in operation depending on the size of the project. These detailed plans must be subject to strict change control to ensure they support the stage plan. Specialist products are under configuration management and link with change control principally through two mechanisms:

1. A Request for Change describes a modification required of a product. This triggers a full, planning style, impact assessment of the change. The board can decide if the business case is still valid.
2. An off specification is a term denoting that a product is incorrect and does not meet the need.

Requests for change and off specifications are handled as project issues, which is a general term encompassing these and other issues, such as questions and suggestions that the project manager must attend to. Project issues are logged, discussed and actioned – this provides clear visibility to the originator of the issue. The product descriptions, business case, project plans and tolerances given to the project manager form a framework within which all changes can be assessed. Coupled with configuration management techniques, this defines the PRINCE 2 approach to change management.

Key project participants

The methodology defines specific responsibilities for project participants and promotes responsible communication among programmers, systems analysts, quality assurance personnel, users, project manager, and the project steering committee. Responsibilities and duties are established at the outset of the project and provide for performance and management accountability. Management control of the project is ensured by formally assigning responsibilities.

The main participants in a software development project are described in the following sections.

Project steering committee

To ensure top management control during the entire course of the Software Development Life Cycle (SDLC), a project steering committee should be formed regularly to oversee and review progress, and make decisions at each critical stage. The committee should decide whether to initiate, continue, revise, or terminate the project and should consider any strategic matters affecting the project, provide overall direction, and establish both accountability and primary management controls. The committee should meet regularly to review and analyse progress and performance, and to approve completed work and plans for the next phase before the project proceeds.

User

These individuals are responsible for identifying the business need for a new system or a major enhancement. The user should identify alternative solutions for the need and determine the feasibility and cost/benefit of the various alternatives. The user is also responsible for conducting a risk analysis to assess the potential vulnerabilities of the system or application being developed. The sponsor/user is ultimately responsible for the 'go/no go' decision for the systems and should provide approvals at the end of each phase of the life cycle. These individuals should have the skills necessary to identify functional requirements and prepare comprehensive acceptance test cases. The user must be empowered to represent the user community.

Project manager

The project manager is responsible for seeing that the system is properly designed to meet the user's requirements and that the project adheres to an appropriate schedule. The project manager has overall responsibility for ensuring that all documentation is prepared as the system progresses through the SDLC phases. The project manager is accountable to the user and the project steering committee.

Systems analyst

The systems analyst is responsible for analysing user requirements and determining the approach for systems design.

Programmer

The programmer is responsible for the coding and initial unit and systems testing.

Quality control specialist

The QA staff are responsible for assuring the user that the application system is developed in accordance with the system's stated objectives, contains required internal controls and security to produce accurate results on a consistent basis, and operates in conformance with requirements and data processing procedures.

Contracts manager

When contracting with vendors to provide part or all of the system development activity, this individual is responsible for awarding and managing contracts. The contracts manager is responsible for ensuring that the vendor or contractor comply with the terms of the contract.

Figure 4.1 shows the overall structure of PRINCE, including the roles of participants and the range of documents produced over the project's life cycle.

Benefits of PRINCE

Prince is a structured project management methodology. It includes both management and technical tasks and the specialized techniques needed to support them. Although

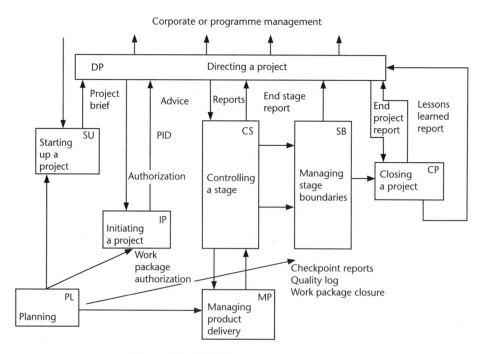

Figure 4.1 PRINCE structure (source: CCTA)

PRINCE is a total management framework, which covers most types of project encountered in information technology departments, it is important to emphasize that it is applied only at the level required to exercise effective control over any particular project.

The key features of PRINCE are:

- Its concentration on the products of the project.
- The subdivision of the project into stages.

These features help to ensure that the project delivers what the business user requires. The project board are involved in the initial planning process, and thereafter maintain control at a high level, passing detailed control responsibility to project management. The benefits of using PRINCE are that it:

- Identifies products and helps ensure that they are produced on time and to budget.
- Focuses attention on the quality of the products.
- Separates the management and technical aspects of the organization, planning and control.
- Facilitates control at all levels.
- Makes the project's progress more visible to management.
- Provides a communication medium for all project staff.
- Ensures that work in progress is in the correct sequence.
- Involves senior management in the project at the right time and place.
- Involves users in the project at the right time and place.
- Allows the project to be stopped and re-started, completely under management control, at any time in the project's life.

Project objectives and planning

Where a project charter lays out the mission in broad terms, the project plan defines in detail the basic means by which the stated goals will be achieved. A plan should be created as soon as the core team and project manager have been designated and given the go-ahead by senior management or the project board.

Planning objectives

In planning the delivery of an information systems development project, a number of what?, who?, when?, and how? questions must be answered in relation to the key or stated objectives. Such objectives will include planning for design and build, test, implementation and subsequent handover to the user.

Plans must be considered as the principal communication device of any information systems project, no matter how large or small. They need to be planned in detail and the right amount of time should be allocated for their preparation and subsequent agreement. If PRINCE is being used then a narrative summary is usually called for. This summary will detail the project's environment and intended implementation approach, will identify the stages and will refer to any product delivery or milestones. The project manager must also ensure that all stage dates are explicitly stated and are not more than six months apart. The project manager should also ensure that the project board and end stage meetings are agreed in advance.

In practice a project plan is usually drawn up at the requirements phase. The individual documents within the plan will usually develop gradually, for example stage plans will progress from a crude phasing of work to detailed task schedules, and estimates will evolve into detailed cost plans.

Purpose of the project plan

The project plan has a number of purposes.

1. To demonstrate that proper consideration has been given to the management and execution needs of the project, as well as the potential interfacing problems which could arise between the different stakeholders involved.
2. To those directly involved in the project, it defines the overall management strategy, responsibilities, authorities and specific procedures to be followed.
3. To those not directly engaged, it gives a basis for assessing the impact of the project on their own areas of responsibility.
4. For the customer (or end user), the plan establishes project objectives, scope and functional requirements, and demonstrates broadly how, when and at what cost these will be met.
5. It assists in fostering the creation and maintenance of a team approach by providing a common planning basis, and defining the contributions and relationships of all participants in the project.
6. It will draw attention to potential limiting factors outside the control of the project team, and assess the risk of their occurrence for the project concerned.
7. The project plan will indicate procedures and assign responsibility for the resolution of all problems threatening to impede progress on the project.
8. The plan also establishes benchmarks against which the total project performance can be monitored whilst the project is progressing. It will also include arrangements for auditing following the completion of the project.

Methods of planning

The basic tools and techniques used in planning information systems projects have remained the same for many years. Table 4.3 lists a variety of traditional tools and techniques. Although methods of planning and control, such as computer-based

Table 4.3   Traditional Project Management Tools and Techniques

Tool or technique	Usefulness[2]
Work breakdown structure	Refer to following discussion
Product-based planning	Refer to following discussion
Responsibility matrix	Integration of the project organization with the WBS – assignment of responsibilities
Bar charts or Gantt Charts	Simple representation of the project schedule. Does not show the precedence relationship
Project network techniques: PERT, CPM, PDM, GERT	Network techniques for work scheduling. Provide the analysis of the scheduling impacts that activities have on each other and the determination of critical activities and float time. Basis of cost estimation, resources allocation and management and risk analysis
Cost schedules	Identification of the capital requirements for resources. Estimates of realistic budgets that provide standards, against which project performance is measured
Project control: variance analysis, PERT/cost, earned value, etc.	Assessment of project performance with the generation of performance indices. Provided for the detection of project overruns and the need of corrective actions. The WDS, Gantt charts and other scheduling techniques are usually incorporated in the project control process

PERT or Gantt charts, are still used in almost all projects, there are several additional methods that are essential, especially for projects of higher technology, and where considerable changes are involved. Two such methods are the work breakdown structure (WBS) and product-based planning (PBP).

Work breakdown structure (WBS)

A WBS can be described as a deliverable-oriented grouping of project elements that organizes and defines the total scope of the project. Generally speaking, work not in the WBS is outside the scope of the project. As with the objective statement, the WBS is often used to develop or confirm a common understanding of project scope. Each descending level represents an increasingly detailed description of the project elements. An example of WBS planning is given in Figure 4.2.

In decomposing tasks (or activities) the project deliverables need to be split into manageable units of work to generate a hierarchical structure of tasks where any one task is a child of a parent of one or more child tasks lower in the structure. An existing WBS can be helpful in identifying tasks for new projects, where similar work

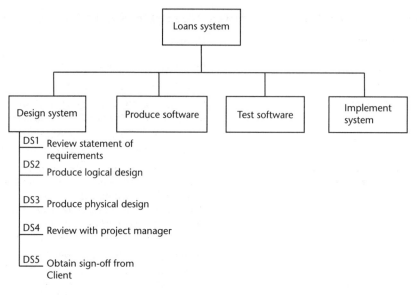

Figure 4.2 Example of simple WBS product based-planning (PBP)

has been done in the past. A checklist of activities for a typical software project is given in Table 4.4.

In many project planning offices, WBS is used as a means to estimate and track financial costs associated with the components or sub-systems of the project. From a client perspective, this document has a contractual significance since it helps the funding business case manager keep track of how money is being spent. For development purposes it is also used for a number of purposes including allocating development-to-cost targets, error analysis, resource allocations, and so on. In practice, some changes will be made in the WBS during the project's life cycle. It is extremely important however, to follow its condition continuously and carefully (Lackman, 1987).

The process

The WBS process can be broken down into a number of stages. These are described below:

1. *Develop/update WBS logic.* Logic development is the establishment of all predecessor/successor relationships between tasks in the WBS. The relationships should be developed/refined by the project team. The basic task relationships are as follows:
   (a) Finish–Start (FS): a task must end before another task can begin.
   (b) Start–Start (SS): two or more tasks that can start at the same time.
   (c) Finish–Finish (FF): two or more tasks that can end at the same time.

Table 4.4   WBS activity checklist

Requirements phase	Data flow diagrams
	Data requirements
	Functional requirements
	Network models
	Presentation requirements
	Interface requirements
	Prototyping
	Development of requirements
	Sizing of alternative solutions
	Expenditure estimates
	Resource Estimates
	Reviews
Detailed design/planning	Detailed design
	File layouts
	Detailed design and interfaces
	Logical design
	Physical design
	Security design
	System control tables and codes
	Data validation of logical procedures
	Audit tracking
	Software/hardware installation plan
	System test plan
	Training plan
	Documentation plan
	Implementation support plan
	Contingency plan
	Quality plan
Development and system configuration	Cleanup of data
	Coding
	Table building
	Procurement of vendor packages
	System testing
	Unit testing
	Capacity testing
	File conversion
	User acceptance testing
Implementation and deployment	Development of business procedures
	Production user documentation
	Installation of software, hardware, and data communications
	Implementation of new interfaces
	Conversion of data
	User training
	Introduction of support services

2. *Establish/update lead or delay time.* Most project planning tools allow lead and/or delay with any of the above relationships; for example, a particular task can end and the related task can begin several days later.
3. *Define/update constraints.* All tasks should be established with a constraint type of as-soon-as-possible, unless otherwise mandated. The reason for this is to allow for flexibility within the plan. If a plan is updated with actual start and finish dates which differ from the planned start and finish dates, the approved project planning tool will adjust the schedule accordingly; for example, if certain tasks finish earlier than the planned finish, the tasks which are dependent on that task would begin sooner. There will be occasions, however, when a project manager will use constraint types such as must-start-on or must-finish-on. An example of this would be a contract award. If this does not occur by a particular date it will delay the rest of the project.
4. *Give each task a duration.* Project team members should provide input to the project manager on the time they expect it will take to complete their assigned tasks. Combined with the logic established by accomplishing the steps above, this will establish a schedule. If there is to be subcontracting on the project, pay particular attention to the cycle times for preparing, reviewing and processing acquisition documents. Duration should be shown in 'days' rather than hours.
5. *Apply resources to the tasks.* The project management tool will indicate if a resource is over-utilized. If so, it will help in doing resource levelling and indicate how that will impact the schedule.
6. *Several iterations* of steps 3, 4 and 5 may need to be done to establish a valid critical path. These steps do not indicate chronology and may be done concurrently.

Product-based planning

Top-down hierarchical analysis and design considers a system as a whole and then identifies subsystems which, together, make up the whole system. Each sub-system is treated in exactly the same way as the original system and the process continues until a desired degree of resolution is achieved and the system can be uniquely and completely specified. In essence, product-based planning uses the same methodology.

The concept of product-based planning (PBP) attempts to identify the end deliverables of a project and breaks them down into a series of component products. In theory, each component of the project will have the same properties and each may also be subject to the same operations. Although every component has to be a product in its own right, the content of each component will need to be defined.

In defining what form a product should take, it is prudent to state that whatever form is given to one product must also be given to all products in order to conform to the convention. To comply with the accepted practices of configuration management, each product should have a set of states. Typically, the states required are similar to those described for the WBS. Each product will be started at some time and will eventually be completed. The actual start and finish dates are therefore self-explanatory. Many products, once finished, will require to be changed for one reason or another, even though every attempt is made to avoid it. The principles of configuration management, which are discussed below, require this fact to be recorded. In addition, it is desirable to establish the consequential effect of change and it seems prudent to plan a structure with the facility for doing this.

Benefits of WBS and PBP

The benefits of using WBS and PBP approaches can be summarized as follows:

- They provide the basis for control during the project life cycle.
- They enable quality to be built in at an early stage.
- They help to verify milestone targets.
- They help to identify risk and potential problem areas.
- They assist in resource provision.
- They help in communicating ideas to users and project team members.
- They help to set project objectives.

Planning failures

It is worth while pointing out that, even with the best planning tools, a good plan can occasionally fail. Often, the key failings of project plans lie in one of several areas:

- The plan did not allow sufficient time to deliver the results or the expected results were not even stated. The target completion date of the implementation plan passed and users and/or management became impatient with the result that the plan was abandoned.
- The plan tried to implement every function of the chosen project management system simultaneously. Without being able to stabilize one area of the project management process at a time, the system never produced consistent results and was deemed unstable. A similar problem occurs when the implementation plan calls for working with several new technologies during the implementation. An organization trying to implement a wide area network and client–server database in order to make project management software work is taking on a project that is an order of magnitude more complex. One technology or the other is bound to have teething problems and by the time it is corrected, the users will have deemed the system unstable and have moved on.
- The plan tries to bring the entire organization online simultaneously. This is analogous to wiring a thousand-person company for a local area network simultaneously as opposed to working one room at a time. Sometimes the schedule tried to implement with the loudest-complaining, least happy users

first. Only after struggling for months is it determined that these users are unhappy with more than just their current software, so the implementation stalls and is ultimately abandoned (Vandersluis, 1995).

Milestone planning

A paper by Turner and Cochrane (1993) identified four types of project which they classified using a 2 × 2 matrix. This matrix can be used to position differing types of IT project. See Figure 4.3

- **Type 1:** Well-defined goals and methods.
  On these types of projects the goals and methods to achieve the project are known and have been tested on many previous projects.
- **Type 2:** Well-defined goals but methods are poor.
  On these types of projects, one knows the goals but cannot say precisely how they will be achieved and by what methods. Rapid application development application projects typically fall into this category.
- **Type 3:** Methods are well defined but the goals are not.
  On these types of projects, it is known what types of activities will be undertaken, for example design and build a reporting database, but because the goals are not well defined, it is not known in precisely what sequence the activities will occur. This results in poor planning and resourcing of projects.
- **Type 4:** Goals and methods are both ill-defined.
  These type of projects are typically failures since they lack structure and are frequently subject to ongoing changes. Management has little or no control over what is taking place.

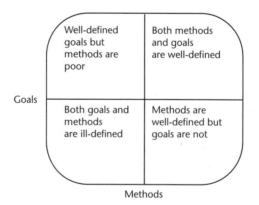

Figure 4.3 Goals and methods matrix

Organizing the project

Once the WBS is complete, it is usually good practice to define an organization structure that will support the delivery of the project. It is very important to create a project organization with clear lines of accountability and authority. There are a number of options available for a IT project organization. Figure 4.4 provides an example of an organizational structure for a complex system. Key features of this type of structure include:

- Clear decision making hierarchy.
- Project board is accountable for overall project.
- Project manager has in-depth technical knowledge.
- High degree of cooperation required between subordinate managers.
- Overall project plan managed by the project manager.

When planning the project organization, defining who will be part of the team is critical. Members of the project team need the right skills for the work they will be assigned. To make sure that this is the case, it is necessary to identify the skills required by the project and to evaluate the skills available within the project team. It is sometimes helpful to use a skills inventory matrix, such as that shown in Table 4.5. A matrix

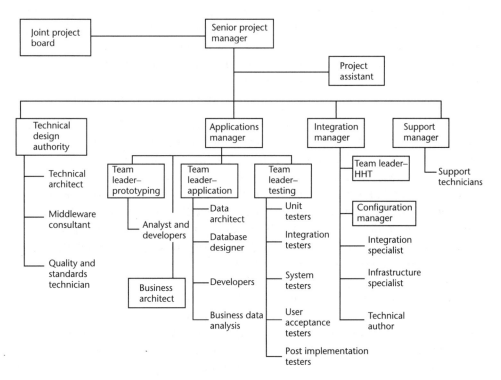

Figure 4.4 Example of an organizational structure

Table 4.5   Resource requirements matrix

Criteria	Explanation
Position	Database designer, business analyst, developer
Skills required	Database design skills, programming in C++
When required	The date you will need them from. For example June to November 2001
Days per week required	5, or 4, or 3, or 2, or 1
Allocated dates	From January to April 2001
Grade and Rate	SPM1 £600 per day

such as this is helpful for identifying areas where there is not sufficient expertise so resources can be requested early on.

Once the resource needs are understood by level or resource type, the time has arrived to determine the actual people who will fill the specified roles. This endeavour is usually easier said than done. Competing priorities, fixed responsibilities, and future availability all play an important role in initially determining who the potential candidates are for consideration. Once this has been accomplished, the next step is even more difficult. Each project team candidate's personal and technical strengths and weaknesses must be weighed against their anticipated project role. Also, various potential combinations of individual team members should be examined, and any apparent advantages or disadvantages of each of the groupings should be considered. Project size plays an important role here, and influences the way resources are allocated. Paul Melichar identified four basic system development (or project) strategies for resource allocation: monolithic, release or version, fast track, and hybrid.

- *Monolithic*. This involves developing the system as a whole with each phase as a standalone activity. Subsequent phases are not commenced until the preceding phases are complete. This strategy is for small, low-risk projects.
- *Release or version*. This involves breaking the system into semi-independent sub-systems and producing an entire operational sub-system or product as version one or release one, then a second sub-system added as version two or release two, and so on. According to Thomsett (1998), the user will be given semi-operational components of the system. As an example, version one could be all the input components that create live data files. Whilst version two, the output components, is being developed the users can access the live data via query languages. In version three, the full database facility could be added. This is termed sequential release. Alternatively, the project team is broken into sub-teams, each of which produces a sub-system in a parallel or concurrent manner. This is termed concurrent release. Each release uses the methodology as per the phased strategy.
- *Fast track*. This involves producing a production prototype of the system. This can be achieved by minimizing adherence to standards and/or by use of application

generators or high level languages. The first operational prototype is redeveloped through a series of rewrites. Clearly, this is a high risk strategy and requires extensive negotiations with management and project stakeholders.

- *Hybrid*. This is a version of concurrent release. The hybrid strategy really involves a series of release or subprojects, with each subproject or release using a differing development strategy. As an example, a high risk subproject may be developed using the fast track strategy, while a low risk subproject is developed concurrently using the phased strategy.

Generally speaking, with a team size of greater than six people, the project has to use one of the variations of the release or hybrid strategies. It is usually more efficient to add additional people to subdivided project/tasks.

Project scheduling

Project scheduling may be described as the determination of the best means of achieving a project's general and specific objectives. This involves identification and optimization of the project's overall requirements, resource availability and internal and external constraint and activity sequencing. To a degree, creating the schedule can require a combination of foresight and educated guesswork. In general, the smaller the project, and the more similar it is to other projects which have already been implemented, the easier it is to develop a realistic schedule. If the project is very large, it may be appropriate to use the rolling wave approach, which breaks the project down into small enough phases that can be realistically managed for the first phase. At the end of that phase, time can be taken to determine what needs to happen next. Whether a schedule is created for the entire project or the rolling wave approach is used, the schedule should be refined and expanded as the project proceeds. The tasks listed in the project schedule will be the tasks required to accomplish each deliverable listed in the plan. In other words, the deliverables in the plan should provide a road map for creating the task plan. As an example, for the deliverable test strategy the tasks might include:

1. Hold kick-off meeting
2. Define test strategy
3. Prepare test strategy document
4. Review with users
5. Obtain feedback and make amendments
6. Appoint test team
7. Create test scripts
8. Review test scripts
9. Make changes if necessary
10. Make ready test environment
11. Execute system tests
12. Review results and log results

13. Repeat tests if required
14. Sign-off tests

Task interdependencies

When creating the schedule, it is important to record which tasks are dependent on the start and completion of others. The more clearly relationships are defined between tasks, the more useful the project schedule becomes as a mechanism for project tracking and control. One way of viewing these relationships is by creating an activity network. An activity network depicts sequential relationships and dependencies among activities. This allows the activities that impose the greatest time restrictions on the change activity to be identified. In creating the activity network, each task should be examined in terms of how it relates to other tasks and milestones. Having determined task interdependencies, tasks can be linked together as required to create an activity network. Task relationships can be viewed using a PERT or Gantt chart. This allows the identification of incorrect/omitted links so that corrections can be made. In addition, any resource or schedule conflicts can be identified and resolved. A Project Management Tool (PMT) such as *Microsoft Project* is useful here since many plans and schedules go through several iterations.

Figure 4.5 shows how Microsoft Project can be used to schedule a wide range of project activities. Note that the package also allows a range of charts and diagrams

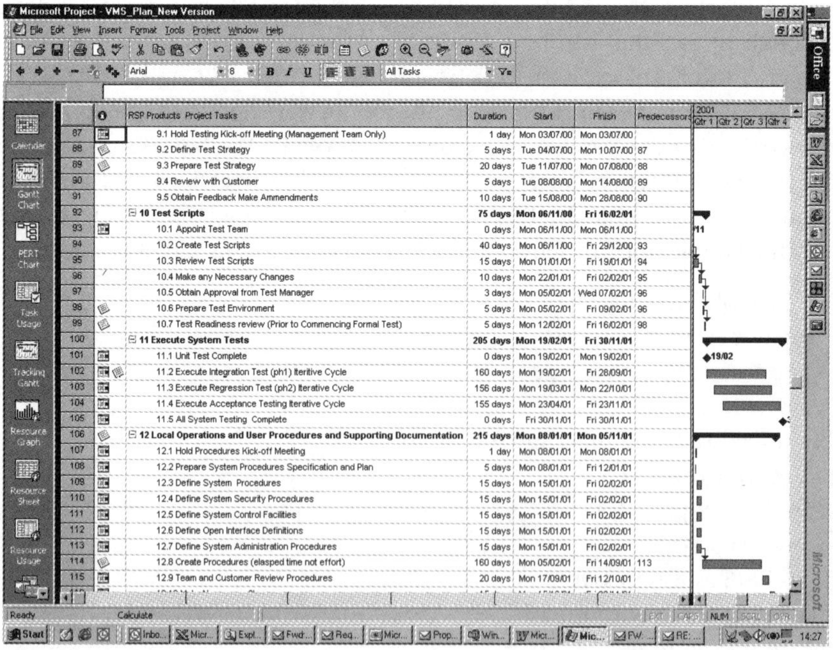

Figure 4.5 Example of a project management tool – Microsoft Project

to be produced from the data entered by the user. The diagram, for example, shows how a simple Gantt chart has been created to represent the overall structure of a project.

Identifying the critical path

Identifying and analysing the critical path helps the project manager to determine the earliest date on which the project can be completed, and allows all of the following questions about the project to be answered:

- What is the duration of the project?
- When will the tasks take place?
- How much scheduling flexibility (float) do we have? Float provides project managers with the ability to reschedule some tasks without delaying the overall project activity.
- What is the impact of a missed activity?
- How can a fixed due date be met?

After the critical path has been identified, a great deal of information becomes available:

- The earliest date each task can begin.
- The earliest date each task can finish.
- The latest date each task can be started.
- The latest date each task can be finished without negatively impacting the project.
- The amount of float time each task has between the time it can finish and the time it must start.

Reviewing the schedule

The project manager must ensure that planning is as rigorous as possible and that the schedule is reviewed for completeness, accuracy and achievability. Some of the areas that should be considered are given in the checklist below.

Scheduling checklist

1. The schedule is realistic and achievable
2. The schedule reflects and corresponds to the WBS
3. The schedule identifies all appropriate milestones
4. Sufficient milestones are identified to permit frequent evaluation and assessment of progress
5. Each activity leading to a milestone has an associated estimate of duration and resource requirement (i.e., milestone progress is measurable)
6. A critical path has been identified
7. Resource availability has been factored into the schedule
8. Any applicable personnel training needs have been factored into the schedule
9. The schedule has been reviewed

Once work starts, the project becomes exposed to threats. Some threats can be predicted and countermeasures can be planned but others will appear unexpectedly. Whenever problems arise, the plan and schedules must be revisited and modified to meet changed conditions. In particular, where a dependency is missed (or is likely to be missed), the project manager should consider carefully the knock-on effect on the rest of the project. Similarly, if an assumption turns out to be wrong, or a restriction can no longer be accommodated, the plan and schedules should be revised to reflect the necessary changes.

Managing schedule changes

Virtually all software projects undergo some change to the original plans due to unforeseen events, priority changes, mistaken assumptions, etc. The project schedules are interrelated such that changes to one feature of the schedule often causes either a direct or indirect change to another scheduled feature. The project manager and his team must manage the impact of these unforeseen events. Their goal is to identify and quantify the indirect impact of changes on specific tasks and carry that impact through the task relationships to the schedule. Once indirect impacts have been identified and addressed, any remaining direct impacts on the cost and schedule can be addressed.

Managing the impact of these changes is accomplished through the following steps: assessment of changes to specific tasks; incorporation of new, modified, and deleted tasks into the project schedule; determination of whether time-related tasks (e.g., management, financial reporting) need to be altered; and incorporation of the related cost changes into the cost plans.

Classifying schedule changes

It is assumed that all potential or realized changes can be judged as having one or more of the four primary effects listed below. The results of these effects may be cost or schedule deltas.

1. Changes in the number of tasks.
2. Changes in the relationships or dependencies between the tasks (critical path).
3. Changes in the resources allocated to the tasks (personnel, equipment, etc.).
4. Changes in the effort/timing of a task (effort and time frame).

These primary effects may in turn lead to other primary effects, or may lead directly to a cost or schedule change. Figure 4.6 shows the potential change paths that must be considered when evaluating the impact of a potential or realized change.

Table 4.6 provides some examples of causes of changes that can be mapped to a primary effect and eventually traced through to a final estimation of the cost and/or schedule impact.

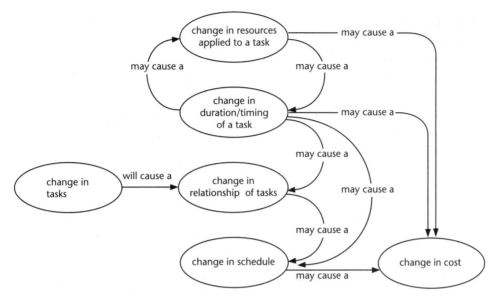

Figure 4.6 Change paths

Change control

It is essential to institute a formal procedure for change control (see also Configuration management) to ensure that only those changes are made which are absolutely necessary and properly approved, and that these are introduced in such a way that they cause the least possible disruption to the project as a whole. Once approved, changes will have the effect of adjusting the planned cost, programme or requirements.

Table 4.6 Examples of causes of changes	
Primary effect	**Some causes**
Change in the number of tasks	Forgotten tasks during the planning process
	Extraneous tasks included during the planning process
	Requirements changes that spawn new tasks or delete existing ones
	Customer requests (formal or informal) to add or delete tasks
	Further decomposition of existing tasks
	Combination of existing tasks
	Change in number of deliverables

Table 4.6 Continued

Change in the relationship of tasks (task dependencies that could affect critical path)	Change in the number of tasks Change in the effort/timing of a task Relationships missed/introduced in the planning process Requirements changes that introduce/delete dependencies Customer-introduced dependencies (product reviews for example)

Change in the effort/timing of a task	Change in the resources applied to a task
	Customer-introduced start/stop changes
	Underestimated effort for task
	   – Misunderstanding of a requirement
	   – Mis-estimate in effort (SLOC, difficulty, etc.)
	   – Mis-applied personnel/resources (skill-level)
	Requirements change resulting in different effort
	Actuals different from estimates
	Change in number of deliverables

Change in resources applied to a task	Change in the effort/timing of a task Loss of personnel/equipment Availability of personnel/equipment Change in cost of personnel/equipment Requirements change causing change in needed skills or equipment Defect or misapplication in customer-furnished resources
Change in schedule	Change in the effort/timing of a task Change in the relationship of tasks
Change in cost	Change in schedule Change in the resources applied to a task Change in the effort/timing of a task

Directing the project

The process of estimating the activities in a project provides an example of the relationship between the strategic and operational activities of a project. In all but a few cases, the estimated duration of project activities is based on the assumption that the staff employed will work at a given productivity rate (for example, a number of

function points per month). On making this estimation, the project manager naturally considers subjective factors, such as schedule pressures, workforce experience, and
workforce motivation. However, if in practice this informal analysis fails, all the effort
employed in the development of the work schedule will be wasted.

The overriding goal of the project manager and the team must be to achieve the
underlying business purpose of the system. However, reaching the successful completion
of a project means achieving numerous milestones and productivity targets along the
way. To this end, the team must have a clear understanding of each of these short-term
goals, as well as their impact on the project's long-term business goal. This thinking
supports the idea that all plans and their resulting schedules should have a strategic
perspective.

Managerial information needs for directing a project

The provision of information on a project has to be considered within the context of
the requirements of the project board, project manager and customer. In satisfying the
managerial information needs of these stakeholders the following points should be
considered:

1. The nature of the managerial needs. This includes such factors as:
   - Specification of the work
   - Assignment of responsibilities to the work within the organization
   - Work scheduling
   - Resource scheduling
   - Cost estimation/budgeting
   - Project monitoring
   - Evaluation of risk
   - Post project reviews
2. The factors to be explicitly considered. This includes such factors as:
   - Logic of the requirements
   - Cost of resources
   - Constraints on resource availability
   - Work resource requirements
3. The basic managerial decisions evaluated. This includes such factors as:
   - Cost and time trade-offs
   - Crashing activities
   - Scheduling resources among activities
   - Changes in logic of the project work structure
4. The impacts of uncertain events addressed. This includes such factors as:
   - Delays in completion of activities
   - Constraints in the schedule of activities
   - Resource constraints
   - Uncertainty in the duration of activities

5. The project estimations provided. This includes such factors as:
- Project duration
- Project cost
- Resource allocation

Team goals

In his book, *Doing it Now*, Edwin Bliss reflects on the fact that '...people who are really goal conscious don't spin their wheels. Their purpose is not to look and feel busy, but to achieve' (Finney, 1999). This is an important lesson for project managers to learn. Sometimes the best thing a project manager can do is to facilitate the setting of team goals and then get out of the way. In order to accomplish this, the team as a whole must commit to objectives within the following four goal categories:

1. Time goals
2. Quality goals
3. Approach goals
4. Technical goals

However, an important question to address is whether a team can work together over a long period of time (months, or even years) and yet still remain energized and enthusiastic. Part of the answer involves managing the way in which the team moves through the project team formation life cycle. This life cycle contains four basic stages as follows.

Stage 1: Individual identities
During the initial phases of the project, each team member must:
- Discover individual and team goals
- Understand accepted individual behaviour
- Establish a personal role on the team
- Determine personal level of responsibility and accountability

Stage 2: Cluster identities
During this next phase of the project, each team member concentrates on:
- Forming alliances with other team members
- Establishing lines of power and authority
- Challenging assignment approach and validity
- Maintaining decision-making independence
- Increasing/decreasing responsibility

Stage 3: Group identities
During the next phase, the members of the team begin to:
- Define acceptable group behaviour
- Create group standards
- Set and support group goals
- Form conflict resolution approaches

- Compete with other groups
- Share opinions and confidences
- Move from individual successes to group successes

Stage 4: Team identity

The greatest benefits are reached during this last phase, if the team can reach this point:

- Individual identity fuses with team identity
- Individuals strive to achieve team goals
- The team follows optimal problem solving and decision-making approaches
- Team clusters move from inner-group competitiveness to full team cooperation
- Everyone moves from individual and group successes to team success

The job of the project manager is to get the team members to successfully evolve through each successive phase of this life cycle. This means that a sharp awareness of the state of the team must be maintained. In addition, milestones and long-term goals must be continuously reviewed with the team as a whole. Progress must become the property of the group.

Controlling the project

We have discussed the need for a standard approach to system development to provide an effective mechanism for controlling projects under development. This approach must provide review points to enable project managers continually to monitor and assess progress, performance, and budget status and, where necessary, re-evaluate, reschedule, or even terminate development work.

Monitoring progress

A prerequisite to monitoring progress is to have an effective progress regime. This can lessen the time a project manager spends on supervisory control. This is normally achieved by setting up a routine method of making regular assessments of the progress of a project and to present the information in the forms suitable for use by all stakeholder groups. At a minimum, this should entail project tracking of progress against the master schedule.

Tracking projects

Project tracking involves tracking progress, comparing actual results to estimates, analysing impacts, and making adjustments. Its objectives are to complete the project within schedule and budget, and at the desired performance/technology level whilst utilizing the assigned resources effectively and efficiently. Project tracking can be accomplished using the following procedural steps:

1. Regularly-scheduled team meetings during which the project team will review the project activities. Additional meetings should be scheduled when a situation develops that needs attention (for example, significant problems with a deliverable or task, or an unforeseen risk occurs, etc.). If a third party is being used on the project, the third party should be represented. These reviews should cover the following topics, as appropriate:
   - technical, cost, staffing, and schedule performance, including per cent complete updates;
   - comparison of actual performance, as documented in biweekly updates, to the estimates in the plans;
   - risk management plans, risk status, and risk activities;
   - any changes that have occurred since the previous meeting. This includes, but is not limited to, changes in customer requirements, contractor requirements, status of configuration items, critical computer resources, size of work products, commitments of any affected group, etc.;
   - critical dependencies between groups that could impact schedule, cost or completion of the project;
   - conflicts and issues being resolved at a lower level.
2. A set of minutes of the meetings should be prepared for distribution to all affected groups and individuals. Significant issues and decisions should be documented. Action items from the meeting should be assigned and should be tracked to closure.
3. Corrective actions should be taken as necessary and documented to provide an audit trail and metrics for use by future projects. This may include changes to the scheduling and any related plans, assigning more resources, re-assessing risks, updating base lines, etc.
4. Periodic reviews of the project should be conducted with the team and the customer. Significant issues, action items, decisions, etc. that come out of these meeting should be documented, and tracked as necessary.
5. Updates to the project status reporting database should be carried by the project manager.

Project reporting systems

It is essential that project managers have a common reporting regime within the project, especially if the project manager is managing more than one project. Reports from project management systems that are not designed as part of an integrated project management environment become part of a flurry of paper that inundates the project manager rather than informing him or her of information that can be used to make useful decisions. It is not uncommon for managers to own a sheaf of reports on each project for which they are accountable, but still be unable to see how their projects are doing. Project managers who find themselves sinking in this morass of data should start by organizing themselves to operate with project management data in a 'management by exception' or 'variance analysis' mode. Figure 4.7 shows the

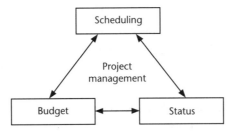

Figure 4.7 Primary information components

primary sources of information needed by a manager in order to maintain effective control of the project.

A properly integrated project management system (or project office) should be able to deliver reports of all or any combination of projects. This should allow managers to compare schedule and cost planned vs actual performance for one or more projects. By setting up acceptable thresholds, project managers can filter out a lot of project data that is pretty much on track.

An ability to descend into more detail for any project that exceeds these thresholds is also essential. In an integrated environment, project managers should be able to focus their attention instantly on the projects and tasks that are outside the acceptable limits.

Typical project reports include:

1. Project summary report
2. Critical task report
3. Critical milestone report
4. Tasks not yet started report
5. Completed tasks report
6. Tasks on hold report
7. Cash flow report
8. Budget status report
9. Tasks over budget report
10. Resources over budget report
11. Earned value report
12. Resource listing report
13. Task usage report
14. Resource usage report

Project administration

Many large system development projects typically employ the services of a project office. The project office is usually staffed by a team of skilled schedulers, estimators and project-related experts who act as brokers of information. From a project management perspective, the project office is the eyes and ears of the project manager, constantly available to report on the status of the project. A typical project office will cover every aspect of project transactions including recording changes to schedules and plans, maintaining project minutes, and so on. The contribution made by a project office can be summarized as follows:

• Source of key information for all involved in the project.
• Providing records of work done.
• Minimize risk of project oversight.
• Improve personal effectiveness of the project manager and the project team.

The project office is also an ideal place to centralize project management expertise and to establish whatever project management training might be required for the organization. As a source of training and useful data, standards can be introduced and offered as a path for improvement. In many organizations, the project office now delivers as part of its own fabric the practices and procedures that make project management possible.

Monitoring through management by walking about (MBWA)

Good project managers 'walk the job', known at a simplistic level as MBWA. To be effective in terms of project viability, however, this monitoring must adhere to certain rules. It must be sporadic, rather than a regular, anticipated occurrence. It must also be infrequent, otherwise it risks undermining the authority and trust vested in the management team. Furthermore, it must be an openly declared mechanism, of which everyone concerned is aware. After all, the intention is not to play 'big brother', employing secretive tactics and games of subterfuge. It is simply to demonstrate an interest in knowing what is going on at first hand.

If employed sensitively, cross-checks and audits should communicate a message of caring to those involved in the operations in question, without resulting in defensive behaviours from the intermediate level of management. Lastly, the monitoring channel should not be used as a whipping machine – misusing it to conduct lower level investigations from on high corrupts the integrity of the unit. It is unworkable at a practical level because of the complexity involved and implies a complete breakdown of trust through a significant cross-section of the organization.

Configuration management

A key management tool used in controlling software projects is configuration management (CM). Classical discussions about CM are given in numerous texts (for example, Berlick, 1992), but there is no universally accepted definition as to what constitutes a CM system. CM can be described as a discipline within software development that has the aim of controlling and managing projects in order to assist developers in synchronizing their work with each other. This is achieved by defining uniform methods and processes, having plans to follow and using tools that enable developers and project staff to attain a high level of productivity. In essence, CM is about maintaining control of the project's assets. The assets of a project are the products it develops and include:

1. System specifications
2. Software project plan
3. Software requirements specification
4. Executable or paper prototype
5. Preliminary user manual
6. Design specification (including preliminary design and detailed design)
7. Source code listing
8. Test plan and procedures
9. Test cases and recorded results
10. Operation and installation manuals
11. Executable programs
12. As-built user manual
13. Maintenance documents
14. Software problem reports
15. Maintenance requests
16. Engineering change orders
17. Standards and procedures for software engineering

Objectives of configuration management

From a management perspective, CM directs and controls the development of a product by the identification of the product components and control of their continuous changes. The goal is to document the composition and status of the defined product and its components. Put simply, the objectives of CM are to:

- Provide a centre of information about a project's products.
- Ensure that at any given time the status of each product is known.
- Ensure that only current versions of products are released for use.
- Safeguard all master copies of products.
- Provide information on the project status history, so that project audit trails can be carried out effectively.

Understanding the project manager's CM needs

As previously discussed in this chapter (see Change control), the goal for a project manager who is in charge of a software group is to ensure that the product is developed within time, cost and quality. In order to do this, the project manager will maintain close links with the team to ensure that changes are kept to a minimum during the project life cycle. To implement techniques for maintaining control over changes, the project manager should introduce mechanisms for making official requests for changes, for evaluating changes and for approving changes.

Elements

There are several elements which are the keys to solving the CM needs of the project manager. A number of these elements relate to the problem of preparation and the solving work-related issues. These elements make up what we term the CM solution.

- **Element 1: Planning**. This is deciding and resolving all issues that must be documented in the CM plan.
- **Element 2: Process**. This concerns describing the CM process and what level of control will be enforced when the CM process is implemented.
- **Element 3: People**. This is related to all the various roles, responsibilities and tasks that various people play during implementation of the CM process.
- **Element 4: Culture**. This concerns understanding the kind of culture that exists within the organization and finding a CM solution that matches that culture.
- **Element 5: Product**. This involves determining what products and parts of products will be placed under CM control, and what pieces actually make up the product.
- **Element 6: Automation**. This is deciding upon the requirements for the functionality of an automated CM system.
- **Element 7: Management**. This is resolving managerial decisions involving buying or building a CM and when to start using the CM system.

The following are the result of the above decisions and represent the keys to successful CM solution:

- **Element 8: The CM plan**. This is the actual plan that will be implemented to address the CM needs.
- **Element 9: The CM system**. This is the tool(s) chosen to assist in automating parts of the CM process.
- **Element 10: CM adoption strategy**. This is the strategy used to assist the organization (and its project managers) in adopting the CM process and the CM system.

It is generally accepted that a CM system needs to be part of an organization-wide process. This means that the CM plan needs to be in agreement with any other plans related to the corporate improvement effort.

The configuration management plan

Once the CM processes and procedures have been defined, the manager will be in a position to write a plan. Documenting the process should not be a arduous task, if the process is well-defined. A good plan can be written in 5–10 days. On the other hand, good procedures will generally take much longer. The only way to produce a good procedure is to document the steps that the manager believes must be executed. The manager should then attempt to execute these steps from the documentation alone. Often, even if a set of procedures have been fine tuned, managers will discover a better way to perform the task and will start the documentation process over again. This cyclic action is to be expected with procedures, but not with the plan. Since processes and procedures will be well-defined, it should be possible to write a good plan in one iteration, making only minor changes to it based on reviews by others on the project. The plan should be relatively stable, and there should already be buy-in from the other stakeholder groups that have to follow the CM process.

The goal in writing the plan should be to document the process well enough so that the plan will not need to be changed often, if at all. A secondary goal is to develop a plan that other groups on the project will understand and be willing to support.

Benefits of CM

The major benefits of a configuration can be summarized as follows:

1. At any point in the development life cycle, if a failure occurs, the current state of all project items can be regenerated from stored backups, base lines or safe copies of masters.
2. Design changes, corrections and enhancements can be made in a controlled manner.
3. CM can control the sharing of objects during the software development life cycle.
4. At any time, managers will know and are able to check the precise status of a deliverable internal item.
5. Whenever a product is delivered or released it can be supported by relevant and corresponding documentation.
6. After delivery, CM provides a starting point for controlled changes and future enhancements.
7. Operational issues can be related directly to the system components and their documentation.

Project handover and closure

Handover

Part of the project plan should include a strategy for handing the project over to the customer and the subsequent close down of the project. The project manager is responsible for agreeing the deliverables associated with the handover phase. The deliverables associated with this phase include:

- User documentation (including technical documentation)
- User training
- Development support during live transition
- Procedures for tracking user/system errors
- Help desk support

The project manager usually delegates responsibility for some of these deliverables to the project team. In cases where the production of some or all of the phases deliverables have been delegated, the project manager should still maintain overall responsibility for the production of quality deliverables.

Project closure

Project closure is perhaps the most important aspect of project delivery and requires the project manager to pay due diligence. Normally project closure requires input from various stake holder groups, particularly the project board. To ensure the orderly closure of the project, the final stage needs to have a clearly defined boundary. Figure 4.8 shows the process of project closure.

The key tasks associated with project closure include:

- Preparation of acceptance criteria.
- Preparation of project closure report (detailing any outstanding issues etc.).
- Preparation for the archiving project files.
- Preparation of acceptance letters to customer.
- Preparation of memo to project team thanking them for their hard work.
- Preparation for future system review.

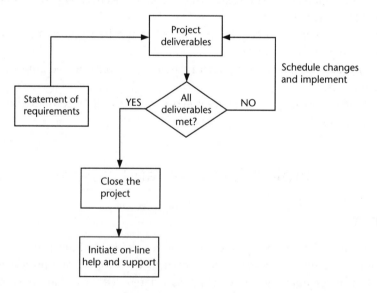

Figure 4.8 Project closure

It is necessary to make arrangements for a post-implementation review of the system. It is not sensible to hold such a review until the system has been operational for some time, say, six months. Wherever possible, however, the parameters for this review should be set by the project board.

Summary

▇ A project charter should be used to define and support all projects. The charter should include a vision statement, a mission and should identify customers/stakeholders.

▇ PRINCE is a methodology used to manage information systems. The method is widely used in the UK. PRINCE includes elements that deal with issues such as managing risk, organisation of teams, planning, scheduling and quality.

▇ Work breakdown structure (WBS) and product-based planning (PBP) are planning methods that are based around the deliverables (outcomes) generated by a project.

▇ A variety of methods can be used to allocate personnel and resources to a project. One model of strategies for resource allocation describes four basic approaches: monolithic, release or version, fast track, and hybrid.

▇ Scheduling can be carried out for the entire project or can make use of a rolling wave approach, where scheduling for each new phase of the project takes place at the end of the preceding phase.

▇ Identifying the critical path provides a wide range of information that can be used to improve scheduling.

▇ Changes to schedule plans need to be handled with care since their effects may disrupt the entire project. Managing change can be accomplished by examining the impact of individual changes in depth and through the implementation of formal procedures.

▇ The task of managing and controlling a project can be simplified by ensuring that team members (and others) share the same goals. This can be achieved by helping teams to develop an identity that is focused on the goals of the organization. The project team formation life cycle contains four basic stages: individual identities, cluster identities, group identities and team identity.

▇ Managers require access to accurate and timely information in order to control projects effectively. Project reporting systems help to establish a common reporting regime within the project. Project offices are a valuable resource since they allow centralized storage of project-related information.

■ Project managers should be visible to staff so that the day-to-day progress of a project can be monitored. However, 'management by walking about' should be handled sensitively, so that staff do not feel under pressure.

■ Configuration management can be described as a discipline that has the aim of controlling and managing projects in order to assist developers in synchronizing their work with each other. A CM plan is an invaluable tool for managing and controlling the assets that belong to a project.

Project checklists

Checklist 4.1 Data models and entity descriptions

The following guidelines provide a basic checklist for reviewing data models and entity descriptions.

Basic review of model

■ Ensure each entity has a singular noun as a name.

■ Ensure the diagram is well laid out. Topology guidelines include:
 – relationship lines as direct as possible, but retaining clarity;
 – master entities higher in the diagram than their details (so avoiding upward pointing relationship arrows);
 – minimum crossing lines.

■ The diagram should have no visible storage connotations, e.g.:
 – indexes and arrays should not be shown unless logically significant;
 – business relationships as opposed to physical access paths should be defined.

Review of business implications

Relationship review

■ Do the relationships in the model correctly portray business rules?
 – does the relationship between two entities actually exist (can an example be given)?
 – is the relationship correctly established (e.g. can a customer actually have multiple orders? Is it possible for one order to be jointly placed by more than one customer)?
 – have many-to-many relationships been established with the use of associate entities?

■ Are the relationships:
 – unambiguous?
 – correctly named?

– All present, e.g. is there more than one relationship between two given entities, or relationships between currently unlinked entities?

■ Are optional relationships being correctly used, i.e. can a detail exist without being linked to an occurrence of its master entity?

■ Where a mandatory relationship is shown, ensure that there are no instances in the business processing cycle where a detail entity could exist without its master entity being present.

■ Are the relationships redundant, i.e. can they be derived from other relationships in the model?

■ Are recursive relationships (bill structures) justified and accurate? (Are hierarchies, networks, or subtypes more appropriate?)

■ For each detail in the entity, check that the keys of each of its master entities have been included in the detail, as either foreign keys or as part of the compound key of the detail. Check there are no data items in an entity, which are key of another entity and not linked to it by a relationship.

■ Have the data, as opposed to the functional relationship, been modelled?

■ Ensure that the exclusivity relationship notation is being used correctly – see icon section of the methods handbook.

■ Has the model been oversimplified, e.g. use of 'bill' structures where hierarchies, networks or subtypes more appropriate?

Entity review
■ Are the entities too generic? Are relationships imprecise (often shown by many optional and exclusive relationships associated with one entity)?

■ Can entities be combined to simplify the model without losing meaning?

■ Do all data model entities reflect business entities, about which data must be stored? e.g.:

People	Employees
Places	Depots
Intersections	Assignments
Objects	Products
Organizations	Customers
Events	Sales orders

■ Does each entity have a unique key? Check that none of the items in the primary key is optional.

■ Has the key too many components – would an 'inverted' identifier be better?

■ Does the entity name accurately reflect the object it represents?

- Check that the data item name is not the same as the entity name except for operational masters where they should be the same.

- Do two entities have the same key?

- Are the date items in the key sufficient to uniquely identify a single occurrence within the entity? Are any data items in the key not required to uniquely identify a single occurrence?

- Where a data store contains more than one entity it should not have the same name as one of those entities.

- Are there too few or too many entities in a data store?

- Has the entity at least one non-key data item. If not, does it represent a true many-to-many relationship?

- Can at least three real world examples of each entity be identified?

Functional review

- The data model should be cross-checked against the functional documentation to ensure that the scope of the model is correct and consistent.

- Have the entities in the data model been cross-referenced to the data stores in the data flow diagram set? This will ensure that all the entities required by the DFD processing are present, and conversely, that all the entities are being processed.

- Do operational masters represent actual business needs?

Reviewing entity descriptions

The following points apply to the review of entity descriptions.

Basic review

- When the required system is being specified, are the data items for the entity present?

- Are the data items named according to standards?

- Have role names been used when required? Have they been used inappropriately?

- Have the system volumetrics been included, including rate of birth and death?

- Have descriptions been included for each relationship – are these consistent with entity volumes.

Business review

- Does the description:
  - clearly describe the entity (not its identification or other specific data item)?
  - explain what the entity is and its purpose in this system?
  - give an example of the entity?

– put the entity into context with its master entities?

– define the domain of occurrences (e.g. does 'customer' mean all active customers, active and past customers, potential customers, businesses actually buying goods or also those businesses' administrative offices)?

■ Has an adequate view of the future growth been taken into account when defining volumetrics?

■ Are any other objects mentioned in the description related to the entity or is the description inaccurate? Are any items mentioned in the descriptions included in the date items listed?

■ Have current restrictive business practices been retained in the model? For example, should one-to-many relationships be replaced by many-to-many relationships in order to provide flexibility?

■ Are key structures restrictive? For example, a sales location entity may have a key of state code and location number. This may have been originally created to meet a sorting need.

Data items

■ Are data items correctly named? Are they missing a qualifier, e.g. order number rather than order?

■ Are all data items described, including their length and format?

■ Does data item description cover all uses or only some roles?

■ Are all data items described included in entities except for calculated only items?

■ Do calculated only descriptions include details for calculation?

■ Does description clearly describe the item?

■ Does it
  – explain what it is and its purpose?
  – give an example?
  – cover all its uses (not just a few of its roles)?

■ Check for synonyms (the same data item given different names).

■ Check for homonyms (the same data item used to express different things, check entities used are in the same length and format.

Checklist 4.2 Design reviewing events

Introduction

The key activities in reviewing event descriptions are ensuring that all events have been identified and that the processing logic is correct. Detailed review points are provided below.

Basic review points

▨ Has the event description been completed properly?
- has the author been specified?
- is the event easily distinguished by its name?
- have the events been consistently linked to functions and/or DFD processes?
- have the events been consistently completed: an 'English' description in the brief description panel and a logical style in the detailed description panel?

Business review

▨ Have the events been completely identified?
- have all update events been identified; cross-check to the updating of data stores in the data flow diagrams?
- have all inquiry events been recorded (these create reports or provide online information)?
- have all the events due to external prompts been identified, i.e. those that occur when the system receives input?
- are all those events that are time-triggered recorded, e.g. 'print daily summary of orders taken'?

▨ During specification of the required system, as a minimum, all events should be identified.

▨ During logical design this event list should be amended as necessary, and each event's processing specified. Has this been done?

▨ Has all necessary logic been specified in the description for a programmer to be able to determine the best way of meeting the processing objectives. This would include the entries to be processed, data items to be manipulated, calculation formulae?

▨ Ensure that the events have been reviewed against the project quality objectives, e.g.:
- *Reliability*: is the logic correct and unambiguous?
- *Resource consumption*: has the logic been specified to aid *testability*, e.g. by modularity of logic and simplicity of decision making?
- *Maintainability*: has the logic been simply stated?
- *Integrity*: have the security, authorization and auditability requirements been addressed?
- *Adaptability*: has the logic been defined to isolate the system from external system malfunctions?

Checklist 4.3 Design review of dialogs and screens

Introduction

A frequent mistake made in using the dialog diagrams is that too much information is recorded in the diagrams. The diagrams should fulfil simple objectives.
1. Show menu option.
2. Show which transactions are in the on-line system, and where they are available in the menu structure.

3. Show which screens are used in a transaction and the flow available between screens.

These general points should be remembered when evaluating the dialog design. More detailed preview points are provided below.

Basic review

Ensure that:

■ The first IDS diagram (the 'root diagram') begins with a 'Start' symbol leading to the first menu (the main menu).

■ The hexagonal symbol has been used to represent a menu and the transaction symbol has been used to represent transaction, i.e. when data is input to be processed against the database (see example diagram below).

■ Each screen used in a transaction has been referenced in an exchange symbol.

■ Each icon is named to site standards.

■ Each diagram is easy to understand: has the 'Jump' facility been used to produce separate and more easily assimilable diagrams, rather than one large diagram?

■ All the transition arrows have been labelled with control values, except from the Start and Global symbols.

■ The control values are consistently named and to site-standard.

■ The screen formats are to be site-standard (see below).

■ All global symbols are on the initial 'root' IDS diagram (the loader facility will check this).

When a global value has been established, that the function supported by the Global is not repeated on other diagrams. If a work record is shown, it has both input and output flows.

Business review

■ Ensure that the design is complete.

■ Ensure that the design includes all online transactions including online inquiry facilities.

■ Check that for each transaction all necessary screens have been defined (in a TDS diagram).

■ For each field on a screen has the error checking, and the appropriate response been defined.

■ Ensure that the design has been reviewed against the project quality objectives, e.g. Usability:
  – does the design provide support for both novice and expert users?
  – use globals with transaction references to give ease of movement between transactions;

- the design maximizes menu navigation such that a particular group of users has all their transaction requirements in one menu;
- access to a particular transaction is provided from several menus where helpful;
- ease of record retrieval with multiple keys;
- help functions, both error explanation and functional assistance;
- check that each menu has a 'reasonable' number of options, e.g. between 4 and 12 options;
- is the dialog design compatible with the performance characteristics of the host software it will be implemented under?

▩ Ensure that the design has been reviewed against the project quality objectives, e.g. Integrity:
- if the ability has been provided to Add, Modify and Delete records from one screen, has the client been made fully aware of the possible consequences of this design?
- has the appropriate account of security access been included?
- have the audit needs been incorporated into the design?
- does the design include appropriate transaction authorization procedures?

▩ Ensure that the design has been reviewed against the project quality objectives, e.g. Maintainability:
- is the design consistent throughout?
- is the design simple?

▩ Ensure that the design has been reviewed against the project quality objectives, e.g. Adaptability:
- does the design allow use of a range of screen or keyboard configurations?

Checklist 4.4 Design review of normalization and composite logical data design

The review of the normalization should ensure that a system-wide selection of inputs was taken. This will ensure a broad-based date model for input to the business-need based creation of the composite logical data model.

Guidelines for reviewing normalization

▩ Was there sufficient variety of normalization sources, to ensure that normalization model has the same breadth as the LDS model?

▩ Were the relations optimized?

▩ Does each 'fully' normalized relation meet the 'Third Normal Form tests':
- given a value for the key is there only one possible value for each dependent item?
- is there any transitive dependency?

▩ Is a normalization report available for each input source, to check the normalization process and not just the final relations?

Guidelines for reviewing the composite logical data design

Basic review

Are both input models – the normalization and the LDS models – plus the entity and relation definitions available for inspection? If not, the review can proceed.

■ Have all repeated group relations been kept (their optimization should be a choice left for the DBA during physical design)?

■ If an entity was identified as an operational master in one model and as an entity in another, has it been retained as an entity?

■ If an operational master appears in one model and not the other, check the decision for its retention or omission. If a many-to-many relationship between two entities has been identified where a one-to-many relationship was previously recorded, how has this been resolved? Was the resolution on business principles? For example, in a car reservation system, a many-to-many relationship exists between rental locations and car types rented. However, only the one-to-many between the location and the car's type was retained. This was because most reservations are made with a known destination and the renter needs to know what car types are available.

■ Check that relations that have several key data items, and a few dependent items which are derivable from other data items, have been removed – the DBA should decide whether computer or DBMS processing overhead warrants their reintroduction.

■ This situation occurs, for example, when normalizing a complex report with many qualifying categorizations, such as total sales figures (the derivable item) for a given month by territory, area, region, product, etc.

■ Ensure that the entities in the composite data model have valid descriptions and data items assigned to them. (Guidelines for reviewing entity descriptions are given in the chapter on review of LDS data models.)

■ Where an entity occurs in both input models and is retained in the composite model, ensure that the data items from both sources are included in the entity definition for the composite model.

■ Ensure that the CLDD data model is reviewed against the project quality objectives as follows:

USABILITY

■ How difficult to use will optional relationships, exclusivity, bill of materials or many-to-many relationships be for novice users?

■ Does the design allow storage of incomplete data or 'error' (out of sequence) data with appropriate statuses, and operational master access paths?

■ Has adequate flexible record retrieval been accounted for, by the provision of operational masters?

■ Will the data structure have environmental impact, e.g. the degree of difficulty in gathering the data to maintain bills of materials?

■ Will the data model hinder independent user inquiries?

MAINTAINABILITY

■ Will complex relationships increase probability of programming error?

INTEGRITY

■ Has the need for encoded data been identified for security needs?

■ Has adequate password validation and storage been identified for auditability and security needs?

RESOURCE CONSUMPTION

■ How will the complexity of the data model impact the development and maintenance costs?

ADAPTABILITY

■ Has current business practice been built in to the model?

Checklist 4.5 Design review of entity life histories

Introduction

When reviewing an entity life history diagram a useful aspect to remember is that it is the life of one occurrence of the entity that is being reviewed. Also, only update events are examined in entity life histories.

One approach to reviewing entity life history is first to check the expected flow of events, and then consider what unusual activities occur.

The following is a list of review points to assist in reviewing entity life histories and error handling narrative.

Basic review points

Entity life histories

■ Does the entity life history diagram contain the one, and only one, data entity that is the subject of the diagram?

■ Is there at least one Insert, Modify, Read and Delete event?

■ Is there a diagram for each entity on the data model?

■ Is each event easily distinguished by its name?

■ Are the state variables present and are they correct: are the initial and final state variables set to null (a dash), has account been taken that an iterating event may occur zero times?

Error handling narratives

■ Has an error handling narrative been specified for each invalid predecessor event?

■ Have all state variable values, i.e. all events, been considered, not just those of lower numeric value, in defining the error handling?

Business review

■ Is the flow of events valid from the business standpoint?

■ Is the effect (Insert, Modify, Read or Delete) of the event correct for this entity?

■ Could an event that is displayed as occurring once in the life of this entity be iterative?

■ Are all iterations of an event the same? Frequently the last or first involve additional or separate processing.

■ Could an event be optional?

■ If an event does not occur, has an event been added to deal with the non-occurrence?

Review of events against quality objectives

Usability

Ensure that the system allows sufficient flexibility for the user. For example, consider two scenarios for adding new customers. In one case, the customer entity is added only by a specific addition transaction. In the second case, a new customer can also be added as part of a new sales order. Which situation will be allowed will depend upon the business: consider a stationery supplier versus a military hardware supplier's customers.

Integrity

Does the narrative cover all necessary action, including computer and manual processing? Are the following five questions addressed?

1. How does the system get to know about an entity occurrence?
2. Why does an entity occurrence leave the system?
3. Why will it change masters?
4. What causes a change to an entity's occurrences attributes?
5. What causes it to be linked to or become de-linked from optional master?

Checklist 4.6 Design review of program specifications

Reviewing program specifications has two aspects, the first to ensure that all programs have been specified and second to validate the integrity of individual program specifications.

Basic review

Check that all program specifications have been written.

■ For the batch environment check that a process outline has been created for each physical transaction.

■ For the online design check that a process outline has been written for each exchange.

■ Has an exchange sequence map been drawn to show the sequence of modules for the exchange?

■ Ensure that the program specifications are written or updated for the latest database design.

■ Have module operations been specified for the detail processing in the event?

■ Has a module sequence map been drawn where the detail processing is complex?

■ Ensure that all batch flow diagrams have been completed.

Business review

Verify the event description has been correctly translated into a program specification.

■ Has the logic in the event specification been correctly translated into the program specification?

■ There should be at least one module to process each entity in the event description. These modules may retrieve or update 'entities' – the entity reference should now be a database record.

■ Does the exchange/transaction sequence map include modules to input and output data to screen or files?

■ Have common modules been used where possible (use the module catalogue report to check)?

■ Are there modules in the specification that could be re-defined as 'common'?

■ Is the flow of operations shown by the module sequence map correct? Can it be improved, to make it simpler?

■ Is the sequence of modules optimal (dependent on both intrinsic logic and the DBMS in use)?

■ When an operation includes a calculation, are the data referenced and formulae correct?

■ When a data item is referenced is the data item name correct?

■ Where a data item exists with different roles or is in different records, has the data item been correctly qualified?

Check error processing

■ Has error handling been specified for all the error handling narratives for the event/entity combination being processed?

■ Have all other potential errors been dealt with (either in the code or generically as edit tables), for example
  – inter-field checking;
  – syntactical checks – the data is of correct format and type, and semantic checks – the data is a valid value?

◼ If an error message is to be displayed has the correct message been specified?

◼ Check that references to the menu structure and screen layouts conform to that previously specified.

◼ Check that all necessary batch run flows have been identified.

◼ Review the logic of a specific batch run flow:
  – has sorting been done at an optional point in the flow?
  – does the sorting utilize the most appropriate software?
  – are counts of data performed at the most economical point?

◼ Does the batch run flow include all functionality, e.g. reports, that it should? This can be checked by cross-referencing to the function list.

Review of quality objectives

Ensure that the program specifications are reviewed against the project quality objectives. This may include:

◼ *Usability*
  – Have the specifications been written to promote the various attributes of usability, e.g., comprehensive help facilities, part-key index record retrieval, etc.?

◼ *Maintainability*
  – Are the specifications consistently and correctly written?
  – Has the transaction auditing been included to aid maintenance?

◼ *Integrity*
  – Have the various aspects of design pertaining to integrity been included in the program specifications?
  – Have disaster recovery procedures been implemented?

◼ *Adaptability*
  – Have the specifications been written to promote adaptability, e.g., use of standard telecommunications protocol, interfaces designed for future flexibility, etc.?

Checklist 4.7 Design reviews

Introduction

Reviews can be divided into two categories, technical and management. A technical review is concerned with the technical quality of the system, whereas a management review evaluates progress, the resources plan and associated business case.

The reason for separating technical and management reviews is that the requirements of each type of review are fundamentally different, and the respective audiences will be concerned with very different issues.

This section provides a guide to the different types of review, which may be employed to ensure that quality objectives are met.

Degree of review formality

The degree of formality adopted during review will depend upon several factors. These include:

▥ The culture of the Information Service department.

▥ The quality objectives that have been set.

▥ The risks associated with developing the project.

▥ The project scale.

Whatever type of review is carried out, the following principles are recommended:

▥ Evolve an ongoing programme of reviews.

▥ Participation should be limited to those who are both affected by the project and able to contribute to the review sessions.

▥ Review meetings should be kept as small and as short as possible.

The introduction of formal, quality reviews into a project life cycle has been proved, time and again, to reduce significantly both development time and post-implementation maintenance. In addition, significant improvements in systems' quality have been achieved.

Table 4.7 outlines various types of review. Technical quality reviews are discussed in detail in this section. Management reviews are mentioned only for the purpose of comparison.

Working review

Nature of the review

▥ A working review is an informal check, usually carried out by a peer. This type of review should be done frequently, on an ad hoc basis. Asking someone to 'take a look at this, please' often initiated working reviews.

Table 4.7	**Types of review**	
	Technical	**Managerial**
Informal	**Working review** In progress work, e.g. team leader and author	**Team meeting** Review of progress against plan
Formal	**Individual review** By individuals, e.g. data administrator	
	Structured walkthroughs Development team Formal procedures Author-led	**Business review** Financial resource and business case Major deliverables, e.g. end of stage, prototype, etc.
	Inspection External inspectors Moderator-led 'Is the product self-explanatory?'	

▓ Though informal, the power of this type of review should not be underestimated. They often provide quality benefits by identifying obvious errors, questioning lines of thinking, bringing in new information and providing new perspectives. They also help to keep open lines of communication (which is often one of the biggest problems in system development).

▓ When properly performed, working reviews often help foster team spirit and mutual trust. Typical working reviews would include a programmer reviewing an analyst's dialog design, a data model reviewed by someone in an associated project and a functional description by a user.

Procedures

The nature of working reviews precludes formal procedures. There are, however, some ground rules that should be observed.

▓ Ensure that a request for someone to carry out a review is acknowledged and understood.

▓ Make sure that the person asked to carry out a review is competent to do so, and available to do the work in a timely fashion.

▓ Make it clear at the outset whether written or verbal communication of the result is required.

▓ Remember that written results do not fit with the concept of informality and may involve the reviewer in significant extra work, and possibly reluctance to criticize in black and white.

▓ If verbal communication is used, the person whose work is being reviewed should be available for questions and discussions during review.

▓ Follow up reviews at once. Left for a few days, crucial points are often forgotten, and the value of the review lost.

▓ Avoid acrimonious exchanges or heated discussions.

▓ A good reviewer is looking for why it is wrong, not why it is right.

▓ If your work is to be reviewed, it is best to subject it to a thorough review yourself, before passing it over. Make the reviewer work to find errors.

Individual review

Nature of the review

An individual review is one that is carried out by one or more people individually, without a meeting taking place. It is, however, a formal process where definite products are reviewed, and reviews are scheduled with expected times set for the delivery of results. Follow up action is taken and signed off. Examples of when individual reviews may be used include:

▓ Review of other people's relational analysis work.

▓ The presentation of business options by an analyst to his users may be attended by a member of the QA staff, who would review the content for its adherence to standards, and by a database administrator who would review technical feasibility.

▓ A user may be asked to review screen layouts of critical transactions.

▓ Individual reviews are carried out when the products to be reviewed are at a critical checkpoint. Meetings are not needed because the individual reviewers are expert in their own areas, and a consensus is not being sought.

Procedures

The following points are suggested as guidelines for individual reviews:

▓ The quality plan should show the project output to be reviewed and the type of reviewer needed. In some cases this may be a specific person.

▓ Reviews must be conducted on time, and each review should be scheduled with an expected delivery date set for the results.

▓ The reference and version number of the items for review should be stated, together with a brief description.

▓ Because this is a formal review, the results should be in written form.

▓ The purpose of the review should be clearly stated (different people may be reviewing different things).

▓ The reviewer's comments should be clear, unambiguous and objective. Each comment should be accompanied by a statement of acceptability, (e.g. passed review, not acceptable until corrected and re-reviewed or accepted subject to correction but without re-review).

▓ After a review, the reviewer should add their name, signature and review date to the review document.

Structured walkthroughs

The nature of structured walkthroughs

A structured walkthrough is a formal development team meeting, to review a product presented by its author. An important aspect of structured walkthroughs is that they allow the participants to review the work, but not to consider solutions. Solutions are sought and corrections made outside of a structured walkthrough meeting.

Roles at a structured walkthrough

In order to make a walkthrough effective; there are a number of roles that must be filled.

▓ *Coordinator*

– The coordinator is responsible for setting up the walkthrough, and ensuring that it is carried out properly. The team leader frequently fulfils the role.

▓ *Presenter*

– The presenter 'walks through' the product for the rest of the attendees. Usually the author of the product.

■ *Secretary*
   – The secretary takes notes at the meeting and produces the minutes after the meeting. This role cannot be combined with presenter or author.

■ *Reviewers*
   – All people at the meeting are responsible for reviewing the product.

Prior to the walkthrough
   – The product to be reviewed should be provided in sufficient time for it to be read by the reviewers prior to the meeting. If the reviewers have not done so the meeting should be postponed.

During the walkthrough
■ The coordinator must chair the meeting and remind everyone, when necessary, that fault logging and not solving problems is the objective.

■ The presenter should walk through the product, and the reviewers should raise perceived problems. The coordinator is responsible for obtaining consensus where there are differences of opinion. The reviewers should raise their issues as the presenter gets to the appropriate point. Although solutions are not discussed, the procedures for dealing with problems should be recorded as action points.

■ Reviewer attendance should be considered mandatory throughout the meeting, as this reinforces the view that the creation of an error-free product is a team effort.

■ The secretary must log the problems raised, and the agreed action to be taken. The action points should also state who is to take the action and what that action is. Actions will not provide answers, but they may include advice. Action points should also provide some guide to the importance of each problem.

■ At the end of a walkthrough the secretary should read through the notes, and those responsible for taking action should acknowledge their role.

■ A strict time limit should be placed upon the meeting, with break periods agreed in advance. The emphases in structured walkthroughs are on brevity, on the identification of all defects, and on obtaining censuses. Meetings should be short in order to maintain concentration; two hours is a suggested maximum. It is, however, more important to have a productive meeting than to have a short one.

After the walkthrough
■ When the meeting is finished, the secretary produces, and the coordinator distributes the minutes. They should be filed in a project review log for later reference.

■ Action should be taken by those responsible for correcting defects in the product.

Inspection reviews

The nature of inspection reviews

Inspection is a highly formalized review process with assigned roles, meetings and procedures. The method was originally developed by Michael Fagan at IBM. Although Fagan's inspection method is rigorous and formal, it has been shown that the process results in significant cost savings, by efficiently detecting and removing errors prior to coding. Whereas a walkthrough is a development team activity, an inspection involves participants who are not part of the team. In order to facilitate both productivity and commonality of approach, the inspection process should use standard review checklists, wherever possible. Examples are provided in later sections.

Inspection roles

■ Moderator
  – The moderator leads and organizes the inspection meetings, and must not be a member of the development team. Prime responsibilities include: deciding who should attend the meeting, creation of the defect list during the meeting and ensuring that corrections are made to the product following the meeting.

■ Secretary
  – The secretary records defects and the action to be taken. The secretary will prepare minutes of the meeting for distribution by the moderator.

■ Inspectors
  – Inspectors are the people who review the product.

■ Team members
  – Team members do not usually attend an inspection. This approach ensures that the documentation associated with the product is self-explanatory. However, a team member may be present to hear the opinions being expressed by inspectors, but not to defend the product or argue a case.

Prior to the inspection meeting

There are a number of precursors to inspection:

■ Inspection planning – the moderator decides who should inspect the product, and where and when the meeting should be held. Having chosen the inspectors, the product documentation is disseminated.

■ Overview – where necessary an overview meeting may be held for inspector operation.

■ Preparation – inspectors must familiarize themselves with the product before the meeting.

■ The inspectors should be provided with suitable checklists (frequently these are installed standard checklists) to guide the review.

The inspection meeting

The inspection meeting:

▒ Is lead by the moderator.

▒ Is attended by all inspectors – this is usually a small group of three to six people (beyond this size productivity will fall).

▒ Has a maximum of two hours' duration (as for all formal meetings).

▒ Discovers defects which are then noted by the secretary as minutes. All potential defects identified by the inspection are recorded, regardless of whether they are subsequently confirmed. Perceptions of errors are as important as detected real errors, because a product and its documentation should be self-explanatory.

▒ Does not include the analysis of problems, although brief suggestions may be recorded.

After the inspection meeting

▒ There are a number of post-inspection activities.

▒ Rework – the items on the defects list are assigned to the development team for action.

▒ Follow up – the moderator ensures that corrective action is carried out.

▒ Identify the causes of defects. It is useful to hold a further meeting to look at causes of defects.

Team review

The nature of the team review

Team meetings concentrate on progress against plans and re-planning activities. Team meetings are concerned with monitoring a project against a project plan, and allocating resources. It must be stressed that they are about management, and not about technical issues, which should be raised during other types of review. These meetings may also cover administrative tasks and social needs (such as the date of the next departmental ball game).

Procedures

A team meeting should be held every week, preferably at a fixed time (e.g., following timesheet completion).

1. It discusses resources against plan.
2. It is lead by the team leader.
3. It should be short, e.g. approximately 30–40 minutes.

Business review

Nature of the business review

A business review is a formal assessment of the business case for a project. These reviews should be carried out at the end of each stage, and on large and very visible projects, also at other critical decision points. A business review is non-technical, where the emphases are on business considerations such as the continuing justification for the project, costs against budget, resourcing and political issues.

Procedures

Business reviews should be scheduled in the project plan to occur at the end of each development stage, the meeting will be attended by senior client and information system managers.

The following should be available to the meeting in summary form:

■ Costs to date versus original budget, and revised budget.

■ Costs and budget for the last stage, with reasons for variance.

■ Re-assessment of project costs and resources required until completion, and any changes in estimated running costs.

■ A re-evaluation of the business case for the project, and any changes in the scope of the project.

■ Any outstanding issues that attendees could resolve.

■ The meeting has one key objective – to approve funding for the next stage.

Checklist 4.8 Technical architecture checklist

■ Is the overall programme organization clear, including a good architectural overview and justification?

■ Are modules well-defined including their functionality and interfaces to other modules?

■ Do neither too many nor too few modules cover all the functions that are listed in the requirements?

■ Are all major data structures described and justified?

■ Are major data structures hidden with accessing functions?

■ Is the database organization and content specified?

■ Are all key algorithms described and justified?

■ Are all major objects described and justified?

■ Is the user interface modularized so that changes in it will not affect the rest of the program?

■ Is a strategy for handling user input described?

■ Are key aspects of the user interface defined?

■ Are memory use estimates and a strategy for memory management described and justified?

■ Does the architecture set space and speed budgets for each module?

■ Is a strategy for handling strings described, and are character-string-storage estimates included?

■ Is a strategy for handling I/O described and justified?

■ Is a coherent error-handling strategy included?

■ Are error messages managed as a set to present a clean user interface?

■ Is a level of robustness specified?

■ Are necessary buy vs building decisions included?

■ Is the architecture designed to accommodate likely changes?

■ Is any part over- or under-architected?

■ Are the major system goals clearly stated?

■ Does the complete architecture hang together conceptually?

■ Is the top-level design independent of the machine and language that will be used to implement it?

■ Are motivations given for all major decisions?

■ Are you, as a programmer who will implement the system, comfortable with the architecture?

Checklist 4.9 Provision of service checklist

■ Has the service delivery strategy been approved?

■ Have service level agreements (SLA) been defined?

■ Have service schedules been defined?

■ Have service charges been agreed?

■ Have these service charges been communicated to all relevant parties?

■ Has a payment schedule been agreed and approved?

■ Has a timetable been agreed for delivery?

■ Has a service manager been appointed?

■ Has an agreed procedure been approved for SLA reviews?

■ Has an agreed procedure been agreed for variations to the service?

■ Has an agreed process and procedure been agreed for arbitration?

■ Has an agreed process and procedure been approved for termination of the service?

■ Have risks to provision of the service been identified and mitigated?

Bibliography

Berlick R., 1992, *Software Configuration Management*, Wiley Series in Software Engineering Practice, New York.

Finney R., 1999, *Critical Factors for Team Success*, White Paper, Tokyo Electron America, USA.

Lackman M., 1987, 'Controlling the Project Development Cycle' (Parts 1, 2, 3), in *Journal of MIS*, February 1987.

Lewis J., 1995, *Project Planning, Scheduling and Control*, Irwin Professional Publishing, USA.

Thomsett R., 1989, *Third Wave Project Management*, Yourdon Press.

Turner J. and Cochrane, 1993, 'Goals and methods matrix: Coping with projects with ill defined goals and/or methods of achieving them', *International Journal of Project Management*, Vol. IV, No. 2, May 1993.

Vandersluis C., 1995, 'Project Managers' Lack of Ability to Plan', *Computing*, May 1995, Canada.

Further reading

Dawson C., 2000, *Computing Projects: A student's guide*, Prentice-Hall, USA.

Marsh D., 1998, *The Project Manager's and Specialist Team Manager's Companion*, The Stationery Office.

Stevenson N. and Marmel E., 1998, *Microsoft Project Bible*, IDG Books Worldwide, USA.

Useful websites

http://www.techassoc.com/
This website provides information on project management scheduling tools such as Microsoft Project 2000. For example, Microsoft Project 2000 offers collaboration functionality, flexible analysis, new viewing features, and improved performance to provide a total project management solution that can grow with your organization.

http://www.artemispm.com/lang_en/default.asp
This website provides valuable information on project management tools. It also provides white papers on project management issues including case studies.

http://www.criticaltools.com
Web-based suite of integrated IT project management and collaboration tools that enable distributed teams to collaborate in real-time.

http://www.infoworld.com/testcenter/comparison/000131tcglossary.html
This website provides a glossary of information terms used in project management.

http://www.kay-uk.com/prince/princepm.htm
This is the website for the PRINCE Project Management Webring. PRINCE stands for **PR**ojects **IN** **C**ontrolled **E**nvironments and is a *de facto* standard method used widely by UK government and private sector projects, and also internationally. The PRINCE method is in the public domain and offers non-proprietorial best-practice guidance on project management.

Self-assessment exercises

1. What are the three main elements of a project charter?

2. What does PRINCE stand for?

3. Project planning using PRINCE 2 is task-based. True or false?

4. What is a PAT and what is its purpose?

5. Should a project board expect to see regular reports from a project manager concerning the progress of the project? Explain your answer.

6. What is the difference between a business risk and a project risk?

7. List at least three benefits of WBS and PBP.

8. Turner and Cochrane identified four types of project. What are the characteristics of these four types of project?

9. There are four basic system development (or project) strategies for resource allocation. What is the monolithic approach?

10. The project team formation life cycle contains four phases. Describe what occurs during the last phase, team identity.

11. In your own words, describe what is meant by configuration management (CM).

Case study

A methodology for a successful transition to client–server and beyond

Introduction

One of the greatest challenges facing IT professionals today is how to implement applications using new technology and maintain momentum in the client–server and web arenas without negatively impacting the application development staff's ability to stay on top of an overwhelming backlog of work and maintain legacy systems. Failure to take advantage of new technology is an unacceptable alternative.

With the support of the university administration and a few key customers, Administrative Computing Services at North Carolina State University was able to take an innovative approach to solving the problem. By creating a new application development team that operates as a self-directed work team, and employing major components of Rapid Application Development (RAD) methodology, we have quickly and successfully moved into the client–server arena and beyond. We have been able to maintain momentum there and are using evolving technology and developing and implementing both intranet and internet applications. We have completed three cycles with the new work team which resulted in the production installation of legacy data extract databases available to campus for ad hoc use and several client–server and web applications serving a varying number of customers.

In addition, we charged a Continuous Quality Improvement (CQI) team to explore the implementation of object oriented technology, web development tools, and other development methodologies. We have now begun the fourth cycle with the new development team and have been able to merge new knowledge and skill sets among the staff serving on the other support teams, which allows them new alternatives in serving their customers. The new charge shifts focus from medium-/long-term projects to short-term projects with a high impact on improving processing efficiency within campus departments. This shift in focus was, in part, brought about by budget cuts and staff shortages. Long range plans will include the development of executive information systems using object oriented technology and methods and distribution of more applications to the web. We are committed to continued advancement.

Developing the plan

North Carolina State University had a backlog of requests from the customer community and a small IS staff to respond to those requests. Our customers were becoming used to working in a Windows environment and expected their new applications to use GUI standards and 'leading-edge' tools. They demanded easier, less restrictive access to their data. Faced with the restraints of the existing backlog, the maintenance of legacy systems, and previously committed resources, we sought innovative solutions. To address these changes, we needed to assess the feasibility of changing the way we have traditionally operated without losing sight of the need to stay responsive in the existing environment.

Based on customer demands for high-quality applications, more user-friendly interfaces, and quicker turnaround, as well as a desire to follow new industry trends, we determined that client–server applications were the answer to our needs. A pilot team composed of application developers and systems support personnel was formed to evaluate hardware and software needed to operate in the client–server environment.

Over the period of a year, the pilot team, working with a small group of friendly, progressive customers, developed several small applications using a variety of tools. At the end of this evaluation period, the decision was made to use Sybase as a database engine and PowerBuilder as the primary development tool. We began researching alternatives to allow us to maintain the status quo while we moved forward into the client–server arena. The plan was to:

- identify the developers to do the work;
- choose an efficient development methodology;
- expand the existing toolset;
- identify projects that were candidates for this environment;
- sell the plan to the customers.

Implementing the plan

We recognized that we could not respond as quickly as necessary working within the framework of the existing application development teams. A result of the work done by the pilot team was the implementation of three client–server applications in three different customer areas. These applications were used to sell university administrators and campus customers on the benefits of moving into the client–server arena. University management became convinced client–server development was the direction we needed to go and committed to support the effort. Five new positions were created and assigned to the existing application development units. The new positions allowed us to establish a new applications development team. The team, called the Distributed Applications Resource Team (DART), developed applications and provided other customer resources using emerging technology. Each of the existing development units assigned one staff member to the DART team. The plan is to rotate the team members annually, providing a means for all staff members to participate and be trained in the new environment. The first group included one senior project leader, two senior programmer analysts, and two junior programmer analysts.

Our internal management decided that the DART team would operate as a self-directed work team. The team was staffed with developers having varied skill levels and experience who were participating as volunteers. By functioning without a supervisor, all DART team members would share equally in the success or failure of the project. It was necessary for team members to evaluate new concepts and work towards meeting team, rather than individual goals. The main criteria for choosing projects for the team were:

- the task should span a relatively short time period;
- they would have high visibility when implemented;
- they would alleviate some of the stress on the existing development units.

As we read about and discussed the experiences of other institutions and organizations and evaluated development methodologies, we concluded Rapid Application Development Methodology (RAD) had evolved into the methodology of choice for client–server development. RAD offered the flexibility needed to develop applications of varying size and complexity and was conducive to mixing with more traditional methods. RAD also promoted increased customer involvement in the process and demonstrated to the customer, first-hand, the commitments they would need to make the move successfully into the new environment.

Executing the plan

All members of the development units within the organization had received training in Sybase, SQL, and PowerBuilder. All members of the initial DART team had participated on one of the pilot teams and had some experience in relational databases and client–server development. To allow the DART team to become comfortable working in a new environment, the team's first assignment was to continue developing the legacy system extract databases that were begun by the pilot team. The team was able to get to know each other and to acclimatize themselves to the self-directed concept. This also assisted us in meeting the goals of the organization by providing easy access to legacy data for the customers which, in turn, alleviated some of the workload from the existing development units.

Once extract databases were established for financial, purchasing, student, and vendor data and the campus was provided with a user-friendly inquiry tool, the customers were no longer as dependent on IS support to access their data. This reduced the number of requests to the existing development teams. The extract databases were also highly visible in most areas of the campus community.

A division-wide application to track staff training was selected as the first client–server software package to be developed by the DART team using RAD methodology. The team began the process working with requirements from the primary customer. From the initial requirements document, we laid out the first draft of the database design and developed a high-level prototype for the main functions of the application. From this point through to production implementation of the application, the package was developed using RAD methodology. Joint Application Development (JAD) sessions were held to allow the developers to work through the prototype and to interact with customer representatives.

JAD sessions allowed developers to assess the customers' reactions to application elements and to change the prototype, as needed. Important knowledge about their preferences for the look and feel of the model was gained. The customers were able to see what the application was going to look like and how it would work before a single line of code was written. After the first two JAD sessions, components of the package were assigned within the DART team and coding began.

As programming of the major functions of each module was completed, the module was made available to the customer for testing. The customers and developers worked in a mode of iterative project development, one module at a time, and each module was installed into production following completion of testing by the customer. The application had been broken into logical pieces and each piece was delivered upon completion. This process allowed incremental installation of the application modules and allowed the customer to work with sections of the package as they became available. A key benefit of the process was that the customer could initially populate the database through the application which provided part of the training necessary for their staff. The end results of following this process were:

- the customer began using the application much earlier in the development process than was normal with traditional methodologies;
- the customer was actively involved in the development throughout the entire process (the deliverables required much less change than normal and the application was what the customer needed and wanted);
- delivery was made within a shorter time frame than would have been the case using a traditional approach.

This initial experience with RAD methodology reinforced our decision that RAD was appropriate for developing client–server applications. The process took longer than we had expected, but we felt the quality of the resulting product was significantly better than using traditional methods and that time was saved by not having to revisit code and enhance the product to be what the customer really wanted. Iterative prototyping was very helpful in giving the team a true feel for what the customer liked and for identifying needs and expectations. We felt that the process provided the customer with a 'feel' for the new technology, and it exposed them to new terminology. The process enabled us to make changes easily, encouraged brainstorming, and uncovered elements of the application that might have been missed. The customer was much more involved in the design process, reactions to the application were easier to gauge, and pitfalls of the design were exposed very early in the process. The JAD sessions were invaluable. They required a commitment from the customer to make available the resources necessary for the project to be successful. Consequently the DART team did not have to wait for customer availability to move forward with the project.

To use JAD successfully, the right people must be involved. Decision makers, as well as people who understand and use the process the application is accommodating, are required. We found the sessions to be much more successful when attainable goals were set before each one. Our experience showed it to be important for the developers to know the requirements and have a prototype before the first session. It was important that roles be assigned to each developer for each session so that everything that occurred was documented and nothing was missed. We learned to listen to everything that was said by each person involved. Iterative project development and incremental installation of the application provided many plusses to the process.

One of the biggest benefits was that this technique allowed for early discovery of problems. The DART team had the luxury of being able to deal with problems at a more leisurely pace than if many problems surfaced at once during system testing of the entire application. We were able to make logical adjustments to the design instead of applying stop-gap measures. This development method kept the customer actively involved throughout the process and provided working modules of the application as the project progressed. This involvement boosted staff morale within the customer environment and assisted in gaining customer confidence early in the process. It helped to eliminate surprises at final installation, provided a built-in method to expose the customer to the client–server environment, and resulted in a higher-quality application.

The increased involvement of the customer in the development process when using RAD methodology was also valuable from the developer's standpoint. Even reluctant customers were led into a hands-on involvement in the project from start to finish. Iterative development techniques provide them with a venue for discovering design problems, omissions, and mistakes very early in the cycle. They have more of a feeling of being in the driver's seat and have a sense of accomplishment and ownership of the application, take pride in the final product and feel a need to share 'their' application with their contemporaries.

The learning experience

Following this process was a real learning experience for the developers and the customers. It gave us a good insight for developing with RAD, operating with a self-directed work team, and keeping pace within the framework of developing technology. RAD does not allow for skimping in the design process. Detailed attention to the database design process is essential. The database will be the foundation from which a good application can be developed. It is critical to have a prototype available for the first JAD session. The prototype is the tool that gets the customer's attention and motivates their involvement. The development team should set reasonable goals for each JAD session so that the team and the customers leave the sessions with a feeling of success and accomplishment. Roles should be assigned to each development team member for each session so that nothing is missed. Examples are:

- one person to facilitate the session;
- one to track requirement and database changes;
- one to operate and change the prototype;
- one to keep minutes.

The DART team used laptops during sessions to perform their assignments. Roles should be rotated at each session. It is important that the right application and customer be selected for the first project. The customer needs to understand the commitment they have to make for the process to be successful. Care must be taken not to create unrealistic expectations of the time frame of the project. One of the most important factors in ensuring the success of a self-directed work team is to choose the right people to serve on the team. Members must be open to new ideas, be willing to cooperate in the self-directed environment, and be willing to commit to the concept. One of the members should be appointed to the role of integrator. This role can be rotated to alleviate the feeling that the integrator is a supervisor. The integrator's role is to:

- ensure adherence to standards;
- coordinate the pulling together of application modules (oversee system testing);
- serve as the customer contact;
- direct the flow of information within the project.

Client–server technology is evolving continually. It is important to use CASE tools when they are available to facilitate and help to document the development of the application. The project team should continue to explore new tools for design, development, creating online help, testing, and documentation. Development staff cannot be afraid to experiment and should never tell a customer that a request cannot be fulfilled without first exploring for a way to accomplish what they need.

The results

As a direct result of the efforts of the DART team, the commitment from management, the evolution of a new set of skills within our other development teams, and the excitement generated in the customer community by these new methods and deliverables, a wonderful new set of applications exists to support the administration and students of the university. Benefits include:

- all important university data is easily accessible to campus through user-friendly query tools;
- all manual processes are automated or being automated;
- campus is gaining access to applications regardless of platform;
- departments are able to bring up one set of windows to access and update data from mainframe, server databases, and imaging systems at once;
- students are able to gain access to information without having to stand in line;
- university administrators are able to make decisions based on statistics and trends they can instantly create and use;
- university employees throughout the state and the world have or will have instant access to data and tools they need to do their jobs.

Through more active participation in the development of applications, IS customers are recognizing the benefit of higher quality deliverables that are easier to use. There is a new pride of ownership for these applications within customer departments. Staff are anxious to share new knowledge and capabilities with peers. Along with this, a higher level of expectation from the IS staff has evolved. With the new methodologies for development and new skill sets, the IS staff is much better equipped to meet these expectations. Staff morale has improved. The new methods and technology have injected new enthusiasm into the work environment.

Continuing the process

The process we at North Carolina State University have followed to move into the client–server and web arenas has been very successful for us. One of the key benefits has been that management has had the flexibility to change direction when necessary. We can adapt to shifts in focus brought about by emerging technology or customer desires without negatively impacting progress.

The second generation of the DART team began by focusing on learning about data warehousing and moving towards developing a data warehouse for the university. In response to the impact of legislative budget cuts and mandates to downsize throughout the campus and to the desire of the University Financial Officers to improve processing efficiency within departments, the focus of the team shifted to taking on short-term projects to achieve this efficiency.

An emphasis has been placed on publicizing campus-wide applications as well as departmental applications that may be sharable. Campus departments are helping by funding both contract and student staff on a temporary basis to supplement the development team's productivity. At this point, the DART team is a dynamic, flexible group with no long-term commitments.

In addition, there is a group operating as a Continuing Quality Improvement (CQI) team to explore and evaluate new software, hardware, and ideas. The CQI team operates under the direction of the Administrative Computing Services Research and Development unit. Members consist of staff from all areas of the Financial Information Systems Division. They have evaluated object libraries, object oriented development tools, network operating systems, document management systems, and web development tools, and have recommended a future direction for applications development at North Carolina State University.

We have begun to use contract staff to fill holes in resource availability and skill sets. This has the multiple benefit of providing improved response to customer needs and an additional training alternative for existing staff. We moved much more quickly into development of intranet applications by using contract staff. The new charge of the DART team is to continue responding to the short-term needs for customer support, to explore and learn new technology, to transfer this new knowledge to other teams, and to maintain the ability to shift focus quickly in response to a rapidly changing environment. With the flexibility we have built into the process and with a willingness to embrace emerging technology and methods, we have set no limits on what we can achieve.

Conclusion

The authors feel that we are on the right track for providing our customers with 'leading edge' solutions to their problems. More than once, we have found ourselves working with 'bleeding edge' tools to achieve needed results. We have been able to assist other institutions in moving into the client–server arena and consider ourselves to be progressive in this area. The process we have followed in order to move in a new direction in applications development is one that has been highly successful for us and one that we are proud to share with our peers in hopes that we can help others to be equally as successful.

Questions

1. What are the benefits of using JAD in planning a project?
2. What difficulties would you expect a project manager to encounter in planning a client–server systems project?
3. Define the critical success factors in project planning.
4. Discuss what part JAD plays in planning the implementation of a project.
5. Explain why user involvement is important during the early phase of a project.
6. Explain why team involvement is important during the project life cycle.

Note

1. PRINCE is acknowledged as a registered trademark of the CCTA.

(This paper was presented at the CAUSE 1996 annual conference at North Carolina State University, and permission to reproduce the paper has been given by Sid Holmes and Ellen Teague.)

CHAPTER 5

Producing software estimates and managing project risk

Introduction

This chapter examines issues related to estimating cost and managing risk. These two topics are closely related since dealing with unforeseen difficulties inevitably leads to increased costs. In addition, factors that serve to increase costs have an impact on schedules and budgets, sometimes to the extent of causing the project to fail.

The first part of the chapter describes a general approach towards estimating the size and cost of a software development project. The material leads on to describe some of the specific techniques used to produce estimates for labour costs, project size, project complexity and the time needed to complete a given task. Two specific techniques are covered in depth: COCOMO and function point analysis. Both methods are discussed in terms of their strengths and weaknesses and appropriate examples are provided to highlight the points made.

The second part of the chapter begins by defining what is meant by risk. Approaches to identifying and classifying risks are discussed, as are some of the factors that contribute to risk. Approaches to managing risk are explained and the material puts forward a comprehensive strategy for dealing with unexpected problems. The chapter concludes by describing how risk registers can be used to track problems throughout the life of a project.

Learning objectives

Some of the topics covered include:

- Overview of the process of developing software estimates. The material also provides an overview of models used to develop estimates.
- Estimating costs using the COCOMO model.
- Estimating the size and complexity of software systems using function point analysis.
- Identifying risks at different points in the project life cycle.
- Analysing and classifying risk by probability of occurrence and the severity of consequences.
- Strategies for dealing with risk: risk avoidance, risk control, risk assumption and risk transference.
- Techniques for tracking risk, including risk registers.

At the end of this chapter, students will be able to:

- Explain the process of developing software estimates, referring to some of the techniques in common use.
- Apply the COCOMO model to develop estimates.
- Use function point analysis to estimate the size and complexity of software systems.
- Identify and classify risks likely to occur at each stage of a project.
- Explain common causes of risk and approaches to monitoring and resolving risks.

Establishing software life cycle estimates

In the previous chapter we discussed the importance of having project plans which include resources, staffing levels, schedules and key milestones. Historically, the costs and schedules for most software projects have been greatly underestimated. Although some of the reasons for this were discussed in Chapter 1, there are many other reasons that we might consider. For example:

- Costs and schedules are often pre-determined by an outside source.
- A real in-depth analysis of the software development process may not have been taken into consideration, or in many cases was not fully understood.

- There is a general lack of acceptance of the concept that developing software is an expensive business.

The benefits of a good estimation process are well documented (see Further reading). A good estimate consists of a description of the project's scope, the estimation technique used, and the accuracy of the estimate. The accuracy of the estimate plays an important part in planning since it can help managers to find the earliest and least expensive delivery date.

What are software estimates?

According to the Project Management Institute an estimate: '...is an assessment of the likely quantitative result. Usually applied to project costs and duration and should always include some indication of accuracy.'

Estimates for software development projects should include units of measurement that are used to characterize:

- *Products*. Examples: designs, source code, and test cases.
- *Processes*. Examples: the activities of analysis, design, and coding.
- *People*. Examples: the efficiency of an individual tester, or the productivity of an individual designer.

Establishment of an estimation process early in the project lifecycle is essential. Accomplishing this will result in greater accuracy and credibility of estimates and a clearer understanding of the factors that influence software development costs. The process should also provide methods for project personnel to identify and monitor cost and schedules including risk factors.

If used properly, software estimates will allow us to:

1. Quantitatively define success and failure, and the degree of success or failure, for product processes and people.
2. To quantify improvement, lack of improvement or degradation in our products, processes and people.
3. To make meaningful and useful managerial and technical decisions.
4. To identify trends.
5. To take quantified and meaningful estimates.

The software estimation process

Software estimation is a continual process that should be used throughout the life cycle of a project. The software estimation process generally consists of at least five procedures:

1. Estimate size
2. Estimate cost and effort
3. Estimate schedule

4. Inspect/approve
5. Track estimates

The software size, cost, and schedule estimation process begins with the definition of the project's functional requirements. Without defining the requirements, it is impossible to determine the cost schedule for the software project. Once the functional requirements are known, personnel can be assigned to develop the estimate. When estimates are developed two or more people should be involved. This is because estimates should not be developed in a vacuum. Project managers should never rely on any one person or method to develop software estimates.

The next stage in the process is to develop the size estimate. The traditional definition of size is Source Lines of Codes (SLOC). Other methods exist for calculating size, such as function points. It is advisable to use more than one method to calculate software estimates. Once the size has been determined, the next step is to calculate the effort, cost, and schedule of the project using the size estimate that was calculated previously. Effort is usually calculated in person-months, which can then be translated into cost by using the applicable labour rates. Software effort, cost and schedule are all interrelated and a change in one will effect the other two. As an example, a compressed schedule usually results in a higher effort and costs. Effort, cost, and schedule can be calculated either manually or by using a cost model. Whichever is used, it is recommended that more than one method is used. Project managers should not rely solely on one method or model.

After the size, cost, and schedule have been calculated, a risk assessment should be conducted (this is discussed in more detail later on). Risk associated with the project is likely to cause estimates to change. Risks should be documented, tracked and updated over the life of the project. After the estimation risks have been identified and any required changes have been made to the previous estimate, the estimate must then be validated. The purpose of validation is to ensure that the assumptions made for the estimate are accurate. This also extends to verifying the methods used to develop the size, cost and schedule estimate, including identified risks, to ensure that the estimate is reasonable and accurate. This also serves to confirm and record the official estimates for the project. Validation is usually undertaken by business or quality assurance managers.

Having described the overall process of developing estimates, we can now turn to the five procedures described a little earlier and examine each of these in more detail.

1. Estimate size

The purpose of developing the size estimate is to determine the magnitude of the effort. Size is the major input that the cost model uses to calculate the effort, cost and schedule of a software project. The required input is the functional software requirements. Some would argue that defining requirements early on in a project could be a difficult task (Goodman, 1992). However, without knowing the requirements, it is impossible to accurately estimate a project's cost and schedule. If requirements are not known, estimates can be used, providing this is made clear to all of those involved in the project. If an incremental development approach is being used (see Chapter 3), then estimates should be based on the requirements that have been defined for that increment.

As mentioned earlier, software product size is generally measured in Source Lines of Code (SLOC). The software should be developed using all new code or from combining new code with existing code. The estimate for the adaptation of existing code is as important as the estimate for new code. Adaptation of existing code often requires as much effort as if code had been developed new. Estimates of software product size should be based primarily on historical data, if available, and past experience. Experience would suggest that two individuals should undertake a top-down/bottom-up size estimate as follows:

- Develop a high order architecture (top-down) diagram of the system based on the requirements that define each computer-software-configured item to be developed.
- Develop a functional WBS based on the major functions within each configured item.
- Develop a manual estimate of SLOC or function points to the lowest level of detail possible (bottom-up) for each major function based on experience with a similar application and historic data.
- Develop a nominal or expected size estimate plus a standard deviation (that is, the lowest possible size and a highest possible size) to reflect the uncertainty of the nominal estimate (Fenton, 1991). The spread between the lowest and the highest estimates may be as much as 50 per cent in the early phases of a project. The range may be even wider if experience is scarce or there is high technical risk.

2. Estimate of cost and effort

The purpose of the exercise is to determine the cost and effort required to complete the software portion of the project. The key input is size estimate for the project using either SLOC or function points and the WBS. The estimate should include all labour activities charged directly to the task. These activities will normally include (but are not necessarily restricted to):

1. Labour charges for software requirements analysis, design, code, test, and rollout.
2. Documentation.
3. Configuration management.
4. Business or quality assurance.
5. Project management.

An estimate of cost should be developed early in the project life cycle, as soon as the general software requirements are defined. Cost is usually estimated in effort or person days/weeks, which can then be translated into cost-based labour rates. For example, a 20-month life cycle project at 17.8 person-days per month based on a rate of £600 per person-day is equal to £213,600 of cost.

Checklist 5.1 offers some practical guidance related to configuration management. A number of methods exist to estimate software cost. Some of the popular methods used within the software community are described below.

- **Algorithmic models**. This consists of one or more algorithms that produce an effort estimate as a function of a number of variables or cost drivers. This is the most prevalent method utilized by software estimation models.
- **Expert judgement**. This method relies on one or more people who are considered experts in some endeavour related to the problem, for example, the software application effort estimation. This is perhaps the most widely used method of manual estimation (Bouldin, 1989).
- **Analogy**. This is a comparison of the proposed project to completed projects of a similar nature whose costs are known. This method emphasizes the need for software costs of historical databases. The more data that is available, the more accurate the estimates will be.
- **Top-down**. This is an overall estimate for the project and is normally derived from global properties of the software product. This estimate will usually be based on previous projects and will include the costs of all the functions in a project, for example, integration documentation, software quality assurance and configuration management.
- **Bottom-up**. This method addresses each component of the software product separately. The estimated results are aggregated to produce an estimate for the overall job. These estimates often overlook many system-level costs such as integration, software quality assurance and configuration management.
- **Automated models**. There are a number of conceptualized models available which estimate cost and schedule from user inputs of size and environmental cost factors. Most of these are algorithmic models that use lines of code as the measure of size.
- **The COCOMO model**. The best known software costing model was developed by Dr Barry Boehm and is known as COCOMO (COnstructive COst MOdel). COCOMO is a hierarchy of costing models. The hierarchy is made up of three models:
  - *Model 1: Basic COCOMO*. Static single valued model that calculates software development effort and cost as a function of program size expressed in estimated lines of code.
  - *Model 2: Intermediate COCOMO*. Computes software development effort (and cost) as a function of program size and a set of 'cost drivers' that include subjective assessments of product, hardware, personnel and project attributes.
  - *Model 3: Advanced COCOMO*. Adds to the intermediate model an assessment of the cost driver's impact on each step (analysis, design, etc.) of the software engineering project.

The model allows for three classes of software projects:

– A. Organic mode projects:

- small project size, low complexity;
- small team size;
- familiar application type in familiar environment;
- non-rigid requirements.

– B. Semi-detached mode projects:

- intermediate size and complexity;
- mixed experience in team;
- some parts of project familiar, some not;
- not all requirements are rigid, though some may be.

– C. Embedded mode projects;

- tight hardware, software and operational constraints;
- high software validation costs;
- rigid constraints;
- often little experience with application area.

The basic COCOMO model

The basic COCOMO model is a static single valued model.

The equations used are of the form:

Effort E = constant1 * (KLOC) constant2
Development time D = constant3 * (E) constant4

where *effort* is in person-months and *development time* is in chronological months. *KLOC* is the estimate for the number of thousand deliverable lines of code.

The constants vary depending on the class of the project. The values proposed by Boehm for the constants used are:

Software project	Constant1	Constant2	Constant3	Constant4
Organic	2.4	1.05	2.5	0.38
Semi-detached	3.0	1.12	2.5	0.35
Embedded	3.6	1.20	2.5	0.32

These values can be manipulated to give the following equations:

Software project	Effort	Development time
Organic	$E = 2.4 * (KLOC) 1.05$	$D = 2.5 * E0.38$
Semi-detached	$E = 3.0 * (KLOC) 1.12$	$D = 2.5 * E0.35$
Embedded	$E = 3.6 * (KLOC) 1.2$	$D = 2.5 * E0.32$

Notes:

- The definition of a line of code is not critical as long as the definitions are the same for the historical data on which the constants are determined and the estimate used in the model.
- The values of the constants should be modified according to the historical data for a company. The values above were derived from historical data for Boehm's company.
- The estimate for the effort is meant to include an average value for lost time due to holidays, training and sick leave. These will also vary between organizations.
- For small values of KLOC, the model will be nearly linear.
- The COCOMO model assumes requirements will not change significantly during development.
- The model assumes the project will be well managed by both the customer and the developer.

Simple model: Example 1

For an organic mode software project with an estimated size of 32,000 deliverable lines of code:

Effort $E = 2.4 (32) 1.05 = 91$ person months
Development time $D = 2.5 (91) 0.38 = 14$ months

The number of personnel required to complete the development over this time scale is:

Personnel $N = E/D = 91/14 = 6.5$ people

Simple model: Example 2

For a large embedded mode software project consisting of an estimated 128,000 deliverable lines of code the values are:

Effort $E = 3.6 (128) 1.2 = 1216$ person months
Development time $D = 2.5 (1216) 0.32 = 24$ months
Personnel $N = E/D = 1216/24 = 51$ people

Comments on examples

In the first example (organic mode project), the productivity of programmers is predicted to be 352 LOC/person-months or about 16 LOC/day.

For the embedded mode project, the predicted programmer productivity is about 105 LOC/month or about 4 LOC/day.

These estimates are consistent with productivity estimates from other research.

The COCOMO model also gives a minimum project duration that is dependent on effort rather than the number of software engineers working on the project. This is consistent with the experience that adding staff to a project that is behind schedule will not help.

Note that the COCOMO model does not predict the result of using fewer staff over a longer period of time.

The intermediate COCOMO model

There are many factors in addition to project size which effect the resources required by a project.

The intermediate COCOMO model attempts to include some of these factors. The inputs to the intermediate COCOMO model are the basic COCOMO model effort and resource estimates.

A set of 'cost drivers' is then used to modify the basic COCOMO model estimates. In the model developed by Boehm for his company, there are 15 cost drivers, grouped into four major categories as follows.

Product attributes

1. Required software reliability. Rated from low (failure minor inconvenience), through nominal where failure would result in moderate recoverable losses, to very high where failure involves risk to human life.
2. Size of application database. Rated from low (size of Db in bytes) is less than 10 times the code size (in lines of code), through nominal ($10\times$ to $100\times$) to very high($>1000\times$).
3. Complexity of the project. Rated from very low to extra high. Low means simple I/O operations, simple data structures, mainly straight line code. Nominal means some I/O processing, multi-file I/O, use of library routines and some inter-module communication. Very high and extra high could mean re-entrant code, recursive code, complex file handling, parallel processing, complex data management, etc.

The multipliers for the product attributes are:

Product attribute cost driver	Very low	Low	Nominal	High	Very high	Extra high
Software reliability	0.75	0.88	1.0	1.15	1.4	–
Database size	–	0.94	1.0	1.08	1.16	–
Project complexity	0.7	0.85	1.0	1.15	1.3	1.65

Hardware attributes

1. Run-time performance constraints:
   – nominal to extra high;
   – nominal means less than 50 per cent of available execution time used;
   – extra high means >95 per cent of available execution time used.
2. Storage constraints:
   – nominal to extra high;
   – nominal means less than 50 per cent of storage is used;
   – extra high is >95 per cent of storage used.
3. Volatility of the virtual machine environment:
   – combination of h/w and s/w on which the s/w product is built;
   – low rating means this is changed at most once a year;

– nominal is once every six months;

– very high is once every two weeks.

4. Required turnaround time:

– low means interactive system development;

– high means turnaround of more than 12 hours.

The multipliers for the hardware attributes are:

Hardware attribute cost driver	Very low	Low	Nominal	High	Very high	Extra high
Run time	–	–	1.0	1.11	1.3	1.66
Storage constraints	–	–	1.0	1.06	1.21	1.56
Virtual machine	–	0.87	1.0	1.15	1.3	–
Turnaround time	–	0.87	1.0	1.07	1.15	–

Project attributes

1. Use of software tools:

– low value means only basic tools (e.g. compiler) available;

– nominal value means a more complete set of implementation, testing and debugging tools;

– high value implies tools to support all development phases.

2. Application of software engineering methods:

– low means no use of these methods;

– nominal means some use;

– very high means that these methods are in routine use.

3. Required development schedule:

– a measure of how well the required development schedule fits the nominal development schedule estimated using the basic COCOMO model;

– very low means an accelerated schedule, very high an extended schedule;

– both high and low values increase the effort required for the software development.

The multipliers for the project attributes are:

Project attribute cost driver	Very low	Low	Nominal	High	Very high	Extra high
Software tools	1.24	1.1	1.0	0.91	0.83	–
Software engineering methods	1.24	1.1	1.0	0.91	0.82	–
Required schedule	1.23	1.08	1.0	1.04	1.1	–

Personnel attributes

1. Analyst capability.
2. Software engineer capability.
3. Application experience.
4. Virtual machine experience.
5. Programming language experience.

The multipliers for the personnel attributes are:

Personnel attribute cost driver	Very low	Low	Nominal	High	Very high	Extra high
Analyst	1.46	1.19	1.0	0.86	0.71	–
Software engineer	1.42	1.17	1	0.86	0.7	–
Application experience	1.29	1.13	1.0	0.91	0.82	–
Virtual machine experience	1.21	1.1	1.0	0.95	–	–
Programming language experience	1.14	1.07	1.0	0.95	–	–

The values for the cost drivers are multiplied together to obtain an effort adjustment factor (EAF). The typical range is 0.9 to 1.4.

The basic COCOMO model equation for effort estimate is adjusted by this factor.

Effort = $ai * (KLOC)\ bi * EAF$

The effort estimate equation has coefficients:

Software project	ai	bi
Organic	3.2	1.05
Semi-detached	3.0	1.12
Embedded	2.8	1.20

The values for the multipliers are organization-specific and should be calibrated for each particular organization.

The advanced COCOMO model

The basic and intermediate COCOMO models consider the project as a single entity. Most large systems are made up of a number of sub-systems which are not homogeneous; some sub-systems may be considered organic, others intermediate, some embedded.

The advanced COCOMO model allows for estimates to be made for sub-systems and the estimates can then be combined for the project estimates.

Model tuning

After a period of use (or if historic data is already available) the factors in the COCOMO model can be adjusted using actual project metrics from completed projects.

A least squares approximation can be used to fit estimated to measured costs. This method gives a curve of 'best fit' by minimizing the square of the distances of the actual data points from a curve by varying the parameters of the curve. Calibration of the intermediate model is difficult due to the large number of cost drivers, not all of which are independent.

Cost models in project planning

The intermediate COCOMO model (and other models) may have (possibly large) errors, however these errors should be fairly consistent if we vary some of the model parameters. This allows useful comparisons of, for example, different development environments.

EXAMPLE

Suppose basic COCOMO model predicts 45 person-months of effort to develop an embedded application on a workstation.

Suppose the effort multipliers for the intermediate model all have nominal value (i.e., 1.0) except for the following:

Requires software reliability	1.15
Storage constraint	1.21
Execution time constraints	1.10
Software tools	1.10

The intermediate COCOMO model thus gives an estimate:

$pm = 45 * 1.15 * 1.21 * 1.10 * 1.10 = 76$ person-months

Assume the average cost per software engineer is £7000 per pm, the cost is:

$cost = 76 * 7000 = £532,000$

Suppose an upgrade of the workstation was available with twice the processor speed and twice the memory, which would reduce the storage and execution constraints to nominal. However, this would require additional hardware interfaces to be developed at a cost of £30,000 and would reduce the software tools attribute from low to very low (new value 1.24).

The predicted cost is now:

$cost = 45 * 1.24 * 1.15 * 7000 = £449,190$

With a predicted cost saving of about £90,000 for an expenditure of £30,000, even taking into account any errors in the model, it can be seen that it would be worthwhile to upgrade the hardware.

Suppose an upgraded software development environment is also proposed at a cost of £120,000. If this reduces the turnaround attribute, the virtual machine attribute and the software tools attribute, the new estimated cost might be:

cost = 45 * 0.91 * 0.87 * 1.10 * 1.15 * 7000 = £315,472

The predicted saving is around £134,000 for an expenditure of £120,000. If the development environment will be useful in other projects, then it would be a worthwhile investment. It might pay for itself in one project, but would certainly do so over a number of projects.

In using COCOMO, there are advantages and disadvantages. One of the advantages is its simplicity, since it only requires a small amount of data – the LOC – to determine the effort, from which a cost estimate can be reached. It is a static single-valued model.

The disadvantages of COCOMO are that it is an empirical estimation model. The empirical data that supports its models are derived from a limited sample of projects. This increases the likelihood of producing inaccurate results since the different models depend on inaccurate constants. However, with an increased number of previous projects to consider, the data is likely to improve and the results produced by COCOMO are likely to improve as well.

The two method principle

Research (Moller and Paulish, 1993) suggest that estimates should be always be developed by using at least two methods. Using two methods provides a means of cross-checking individual estimates and increases the credibility of the overall estimate. In addition, estimating should be carried out by at least two people. For very large projects, three or more people should be involved in the estimation process. Early on in the project, a manual estimate should be calculated. Manual estimates should be accomplished to give the estimators an understanding of the process and parameters that automated tools utilize. After a manual estimate is completed, a second estimate should be developed using an automated tool (this could be a macro-driven spreadsheet). The manual estimate should be done first so that the automated toll will not influence the second estimate.

The results of the two estimates should be compared, and reasons for any large variances should be resolved. How large a variation is dependent on the nature and type of project, and the current point in the project life cycle. As a project matures, the estimates should converge. All assumptions and inputs should be documented in the project directory.

3. Estimate schedule

The purpose of the schedule estimate is to determine the length of time needed to complete the project and determine when major milestones and reviews will occur. Before this process can take place, the functional WBS, size and cost estimates must have been completed. The schedule estimate can be produced manually or by using automated estimation models. A combination of both manual and automated methods is recommended. One or more software developers with experience of the specific application under development should use the size estimate and experience with similar projects to develop a schedule estimate as follows:

- The WBS should be expanded to delineate the order in which functional elements will be developed. The order of development will define which functions can be · developed in parallel as well as dependencies, which drive the schedule.
- A development schedule should be derived for each set of functions
  (see Chapter 4) that can be developed independently, that is, a schedule for each build of an incremental development.
- The schedule for each set of independent functions should be derived as the aggregate of the estimated time required for each major phase of the development: analysis, design, code and unit test, integration and test.
- The total project schedule should reflect the aggregate of the product development, including documentation and formal reviews.

The points outlined above are typical of manual estimates. Automated tools provide a schedule estimate along with the cost and effort estimate. Automated tools allow the user to tailor the schedule in order to observe the impact on cost. However, most automated tools allow only a small amount of flexibility in shortening schedules.

Automated tools

There are a number of automated estimation tools that are derived from the COCOMO model. As one might expect, many of these tools originate from the United States. Some examples of these tools are WICOMO (Wang Institute Cost Model), developed by the Wang institute, ESTIMATE Professional developed by SPC Inc. and DECPlan developed by Digital Equipment Corporation. These tools provide only an estimate of the cost, and they need some preliminary values of LOC. Once this information has been provided, 'what if?' analysis can be carried out.

Automated tool capabilities

Major functional capabilities that should be considered when selecting a software estimating tool such as DECPlan are listed below. Depending on the organization's needs, the level of significance of these capabilities may differ, and should be considered accordingly. In addition, the organization should analyse its own needs and identify additional desired capabilities specific to itself. The organization should then match available tools with overall needs (Young and Obertreis, 1996).

In general, the tool should have the following properties:

- *Allow easy adaptation to an organization's development environment.* This means the tool needs to be capable of being customized to fit the organization's development environment. Customization includes allowing the developer to define applicable inputs, as well as allowing modification of coefficients and exponents of the equations used by the tool. This feature will allow continuous improvement to the estimation capability of the tool since the organization's historical data and current project data will be included in the software estimate generated.

- *Be relatively easy to learn and use.* The tool should be well documented and should include reference material for the methodologies and equations used. Documentation should be at a level that is understandable. The tool should include help menus and examples sufficient to assist the support staff in answering questions and providing training. The amount of formal training required to use the tool should be relatively minimal, required inputs should be well defined, and visibility into internal equations and theories should be provided.

- *Provide early estimates.* The tool should be capable of generating estimates early and quickly in the life cycle process, when requirements and development environments are not fully defined. The tool should also allow task detail to be added incrementally as functions, activities, and other information becomes more completely defined. Since there are many unknowns early in the estimating process, the tool should reflect degrees of uncertainty based on the level of detail input (risk analysis). In general, the tool should provide sufficient information to allow initial project resource planning as well as reasonably early 'go/no go' decisions.

- *Be based on software life cycle phases and activities.* The tool should be capable of providing estimates for all phases and activities of the most commonly used software life cycle models. It should allow the organization to decompose and map software development tasks into those phases and activities, as well as support a project WBS. In addition, it should allow for 'what if' situations and include factors for design trade-off studies.

- *Allow for variations in application languages and application function.* It is very important that the tool provide estimates specific to the application of the software project since the associated estimating equations, cost drivers, and life cycle phases should be unique to each application area. General application categories include information systems (IS), simulation and modelling systems, real-time systems, accounting systems, and systems based on higher-order languages.

- *Provide accurate size estimates.* The size of a software development project is a major cost driver in most estimating tools, yet size is one of the most difficult input parameters to estimate accurately. The tool should include the capability to help estimate the size of the software development project, or at least help define a method for estimating the size.

- *Provide accurate schedule estimates.* As previously mentioned, schedule overruns are common and can be extremely costly. The software estimating tool should be able to provide schedule estimates accurately. The purpose of scheduling is not only to predict task completion given task sequence and available resources, but also to establish starting and ending dates for the associated work packages and life cycle phases.

- *Provide maintenance estimates separately.* The software estimating tool should be able to provide software maintenance estimates as a separate item. Software maintenance includes such activities as correcting errors, modifying the software to accommodate changes in requirements, or extending and enhancing software performance.

4. Inspect and approve estimate

The purpose of this stage is to improve the quality of the estimates produced and obtain senior management commitment. The objectives of the inspection and approval of the estimate are to:

1. Confirm the software architecture and functional WBS.
2. Verify the methods used for deriving the size, schedule and cost estimates.
3. Ensure that the assumptions and input data used to develop the estimates are correct.
4. Ensure that the estimate is reasonable and accurate given the input data.
5. Confirm and record formally the official estimates for the project.

A process consistent with the organization's policies and procedures should accomplish the inspection and approval stage. At a minimum, the inspection should be attended by the personnel that developed the estimate, at least one other software analyst/developer from the same project, the project manager and, ideally, one other person with experience of a similar project. The project manager will be the person who will sign-off the estimate.

5. Track estimates

The purpose here is to check the accuracy of the estimate over time and to develop some empirical data over time. The use of an automated tool is perhaps a prerequisite in this activity. Estimates should be tracked over time comparing planned to actual outcomes. Tracking estimates over time allows those personnel involved (including project managers) to see just how the project is shaping up and how accurate their planned estimates were. The key to tracking estimates is to have a consistent means by which to do it and a mechanism for storing the results to give accessibility. A directory containing estimation information does not have to be put in a standalone software estimation file. It can, for example, be included in the software development plan.

Function point analysis

In 1979 an IBM software engineer, Allen Albrecht (1983), developed a method of estimating the relative size and complexity of software systems based on two critical assumptions. They are:

1. The complexity and size of a software system are major determinants of the length of the development process.
2. The complexity and size of a software system can be derived by examining and counting the data complexity and volume.

In essence the size is determined by identifying the components of the system as seen by the end user: the inputs, outputs, inquiries, logical internal files, and interfaces. Figure 5.1 provides an overview of the structure of FPA.

Each of the components of this model are examined in more detail by the following sections.

Data functions

These concern internal and external logical data files.

- *Internal logical files*. These are logical data files that store information for an application that generates, uses, and maintains the data. Each entity type and each

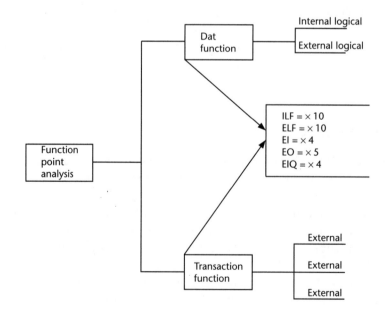

Figure 5.1 FPA structure overview

M:N relationship in an entity–relationship model is a logical file. Complexity is classified as follows:

(a) *Simple* – few data elements. No significant performance, validation, or recovery considerations.
(b) *Average* – neither simple nor complex.
(c) *Complex* – many data element types. Performance, validation, and recovery are significant considerations.

- *External logical files.* These are files which contain data or control information passed from, passed to, or shared by another application. To determine complexity, use logical internal file criteria.

Transaction functions

This element is concerned with external inputs – transaction data that come from keyboards, communication lines, tape, or other applications. In interactive systems, input screens are the major external inputs. Complexity is classified as follows:

(d) *Simple* – transaction contains few data element types and references few internal files. Human factors are not a major design consideration.
(e) *Average* – neither simple nor complex.
(f) *Complex* – transaction contains many data element types, uses many internal files, and/or human factors are a major design consideration.

External outputs are reports and messages that are sent to the user or another application. Reports may go to screens, printers, communication lines, or other applications. External outputs do not include responses to inquiries, output files, or reports that are required only because of the technology used. In general, the same criteria for complexity should be used as for external inputs. The following guidelines should be used for reports:

(g) *Simple* – one or two columns with simple data transformations.
(h) *Average* – multiple columns with subtotals; multiple data transformations.
(i) *Complex* – intricate data element transformations. Multiple and complex file references must be coordinated. There may be significant performance considerations.

External inquiries are queries from users or applications that result in a report to the user or application. External inquiries may read a database but do not add, change, or delete records. Each inquiry with different processing logic or a different input or output format is counted as a separate type. A generalized query facility is not an external inquiry – it consists of several external inputs, outputs, and inquiries. The complexity of an external inquiry is the greater of the input and output complexity as measured by the criteria for external inputs and outputs respectively.

Function points

Points are scored for each function identified in the proposed system, and these scores are then adjusted for the intrinsic complexity of each function. It is important to note that each business function is counted only once in order to avoid duplicated counting. After analysis of the system components and functions, a count is made of the number of each type of the preceding elements under a sub-classification of complexity, using categories of simple, average, or complex. These elements are then weighted by a relative complexity weight for each of the sub-classifications. All of these values are then scored and the total is expressed in unadjusted function points (UFPs).

Value adjustment factor

The unadjusted function point (UFP) count is multiplied by the second adjustment factor called the value adjustment factor (VAF). This factor considers the system's technical and operational characteristics and is calculated by answering 14 questions. The factors are:

- *Data communications.* The data and control information used in the application are sent or received over communication facilities.
- *Distributed data processing.* Distributed data or processing functions are a characteristic of the application within the application boundary.
- *Performance.* Application performance objectives, stated or approved by the user, in either response or throughput, influence (or will influence) the design, development, installation and support of the application.
- *Heavily used configuration.* A heavily used operational configuration, requiring special design considerations, is a characteristic of the application.
- *Transaction rate.* The transaction rate is high and influences the design, development, installation and support.
- *Online data entry.* Online data entry and control information functions are provided in the application.
- *End user efficiency.* The online functions provided emphasize a design for end-user efficiency.
- *Online update.* The application provides online update for the internal logical files.
- *Complex processing.* Complex processing is a characteristic of the application.
- *Reusability.* The application and the code in the application have been specifically designed, developed and supported to be usable in other applications.
- *Installation ease.* Conversion and installation ease are characteristics of the application. A conversion and installation plan and/or conversion tools were provided and tested during the system test phase.

- *Operational ease*. Operational ease is a characteristic of the application. Effective start-up, backup and recovery procedures were provided and tested during the system test phase.
- *Multiple sites*. The application has been specifically designed, developed and supported to be installed at multiple sites for multiple organizations.
- *Facilitate change*: The application has been specifically designed, developed and supported to facilitate change.

Each of these factors is scored based on their influence on the system being counted. The resulting score will increase or decrease the unadjusted function point (UFP) count by 35 per cent. This calculation provides us with the adjusted function point (AFP) count.

Approaches to counting function points

There are several approaches used to count function points. We believe that a structured JAD session conducted with people who are knowledgeable of the business functionality provided through the application is an efficient, accurate way of collecting the necessary data. The JAD approach allows the data analyst to develop a representation of the application from a functional perspective and educate the participants about function points. Function point counting can be accomplished with minimal documentation. However, the accuracy and efficiency of the counting improves with appropriate documentation. Examples of appropriate documentation are:

- design specifications;
- display designs;
- data requirements (internal and external);
- description of user interfaces.

Function point counts are calculated during the JAD and documented with both a diagram that depicts the application and worksheets that contain the details of each function discussed.

Wide Band Delphi Technique

In the Wide Band Delphi Technique, a number of separate estimates are obtained from individuals who might reasonably be expected to be sufficiently knowledgeable to provide one. These estimates are then circulated to all participants for review and discussion. Each estimator is then permitted to revise their personal estimate and the subsequent figures are averaged to provide a single value. The system assumes that the more competent estimators will be less influenced by the work of their colleagues. The suggested steps summarized below assumes group participation with participating members having a diversity of software related experience.

- Step 1 – The coordinator presents each expert with the project's specification and estimation proforma.
- Step 2 – The coordinator calls a group meeting in which the participants discuss issues and concerns related to size etc.
- Step 3 – Each participant fills out the proforma.
- Step 4 – The coordinator prepares a summary of the estimates on an iteration form and returns them to the participants.
- Step 5 – The coordinator calls a group meeting, primarily to discuss the most widely varied estimates.
- Step 6 – The participants review the summary and submit another anonymous estimate on the iteration form.
- Step 7 – Steps 4 through to 6 are repeated until a consensus of the lowest and highest possible estimates are reached.

PERT sizing

This method was originally used for estimating durations in the PERT system of network analysis. The method involves deriving three estimates: an expected size of the product, a lowest possible estimate, and a highest possible estimate. These three estimates are used to arrive at a PERT statistical estimate for the expected size of the product and a standard deviation.

Assuming that a beta distribution will apply to the estimating errors, the three figures are combined to give an overall estimate according to the formula:

E = overall product size = (lowest + 4 * (expected) + Highest) /6

Example single software module:

a = lowest possible size 10,000 single lines of code
b = expected size 12,000 single lines of code
c = highest possible size 15,000 single lines of code
E = 10 + 4(12) + 15/6 = 12,167 SLC

Standard deviation (SD):

SD = 15 − 10/6 = 0.833

This indicates that about 68 per cent of the time, the size will fall between 11,334 and 13,000. This approach assumes that the estimates are unbiased while, in fact, experience shows that estimates tend to cluster more towards the lower limit than towards the upper limit.

Using this approach it is possible to automate the process by calculating the minimum and maximum sizes as a percentage of the expected size. The appropriate percentages may be derived from look-up tables based on the adequacy of the size estimates, using the standard deviation figures.

Avoiding poor estimation syndrome

Evidence would suggest that even with good estimation policies/procedures, standards and functional experts, many organizations still fall into traps (Thamhain, 1992). All of the following have been identified as common causes of poor estimates and should be guarded against. They are:

- Unrealistic or poorly defined targets for estimate production.
- Lack of functional clarity.
- Down/up scoping by management.
- Misinterpretation of the statement of requirements (insufficient attention to detail).
- Omissions.
- Technical complexity underestimating the challenge.
- Uncooperative customer.
- Inaccurate WBS.
- Estimators not fully trained in the appropriate techniques.
- Risks not fully mitigated or understood.
- Failure to allow for cost increases (if the project is over a long time span).
- Failure to use forward pricing rates.
- No specific policy on how project resources will be estimated.
- No account taken of non-functional requirements.
- Lack of control in forecasting and justifying requirements.
- Inability to recognize potential project overruns (that is, no allowance for contingencies).
- Preliminary estimates adopted (no refinement made).
- No history recorded of past projects.
- Reliance on outdated information.

Managing risk in software projects

In an ideal world, projects could be planned on the basis that nothing will go wrong, and that nothing unpleasant will happen. In practice, it is recognized that this does not normally turn out to be the case, and that time spent predicting what might go wrong and planning to manage the situation, is time well spent.

Tom Gilb (1988) said: 'If you don't actively attack the risks, they will actively attack you.' Risk is a major killer of projects and as such it needs to be managed and controlled during the project life cycle. At the beginning of a project the project manager should endeavour to hold a risk workshop with the key stakeholder groups. As a project manager reporting to a project board, you will need to prepare yourself to answer questions related to project risk. Examples include:

- What are the biggest risks to this project?
- What would be the impact if these occurred?

- What are we doing to avoid the incidence of these risks?
- What are we doing to mitigate the negative impact, of these risks?
- What are our contingencies if we are unable to avoid these risks?

What is project risk?

Information systems projects are usually initiated in the context of change. Given this fact, the project tends to be unique and usually its objectives have to be achieved within given constraints. In addition, projects can be large, complex undertakings that deal with unusual or uncharted factors.

There are several definitions on what constitutes project risk. However, since this book is about information systems, we will use the definition offered by Gluch. According to David Gluch (1994) in *A Construct for Describing Software Development Risks*, a risk is a combination of an abnormal event or failure and the consequences of that event or failure to a system's operators, users, or environment. A risk can range from catastrophic (loss of entire system, loss of life or permanent disability) to negligible (no system damage, no injury).

The risk management cycle

Experience of managing several large projects teaches us that there are at least five phases within the risk management cycle and each phase needs to be addressed. These phases are:

1. Identify that a risk exists.
2. Analyse the severity of the risk.
3. Plan to combat the risk based on the risk's severity and likelihood of occurrence.
4. Mitigate the risk.
5. Track the risk. Once the risk has been mitigated to an acceptable severity level, the risk should be tracked to ensure the continued control of the risk. If at any time the risk seems to resurface, the risk management cycle should begin again, starting with the analysis phase.

Identify the risk

There are many ways of identifying project risk. One way of identifying risk in software projects is by use of a risk assessment questionnaire which should be completed at the outset of the project (and also at the end of each stage assessment if PRINCE is being used). This should provide an insight on the level of risk at any given point of time. One such risk questionnaire used in the development of software projects and developed by the Software Engineering Institute (SEI), in America is the Taxonomy-Based Risk Identification Questionnaire.

The Taxonomy-Based Questionnaire is structured into three main areas of software risk:

1. Product engineering.
2. Development environment.
3. Program constraints.

Each of these categories is subdivided further, narrowing the focus on particular aspects of risk. Almost all the questions below were taken from the product engineering section although some have been added to cater for the uniqueness of project management.

Requirements

Stability/completeness (assessed by evaluating the amount of information in the requirements).

- Are the requirements changing or yet to be determined? Consider the risk if requirements are being added, changed or are undetermined.
- Does the instructor have unwritten requirements/expectations? Consider the risk if some project requirements were given to you verbally.

Clarity (assessed by evaluating your comprehension of the requirements).

- Are you able to understand the requirements as written? Consider the risk if key requirements are vaguely stated (ambiguous).

Feasibility (assessed by evaluating the possible difficulties that might arise later in the project).

- Are there any requirements that are technically difficult to implement? Consider the risk if you are not sure how a requirement could be implemented in the development language.

Tracking (assessed by evaluating the ability to keep requirements visible during the project).

- Do you have a plan to track the requirements throughout the design, coding and testing phases? Consider the risk if requirements fall out of the process and are not handled in the correct phase.

Design

Functionality (assessed by evaluating the feature set and capabilities of the product).

- Are there any specified algorithms that may not (or only partially) satisfy the requirements? Consider the risk that the algorithms may be wrong, incomplete, or too complex.

Difficulty (assessed by evaluating the effort involved in producing the design).

- Does any of the design depend on unrealistic or optimistic assumptions? Consider the risk if requirements were too optimistic regarding design.

- Are there any requirements or functions that are difficult to design? Consider, for example, the risk that a complex tree search may require more effort to design.

Interfaces (assessed by evaluating the connections between components, or to the outside world).

- Are the internal and external interfaces well defined? Consider the risk of complex or numerous connections between components or systems.

Performance and quality (assessed by evaluating the functionality and quality of the product).

- Are there any problems with the expected performance, or quality, of the design? Consider the risk of inadequate response or turnaround time, or lack of functionality.

Testability (assessed by evaluating the effort required to sufficiently test the product).

- Is the software going to be easy to test? Consider the risks of high complexity and what that may do in testing the product.

Hardware constraints (assessed by evaluating the hardware of the target or development platform).

- Does the development or target hardware limit your ability to meet any requirements? Consider the risk of limitations on hardware speed, size, availability and functionality.

Software reuse (assessed by evaluating the extent to which software is reused in the product).

- Does reused or reengineered software exist? Consider whether there are more problems than designing original software.

Code and unit test

Feasibility (assessed by evaluating the relative ease necessary to perform code and test).

- Are any parts of the product implementation not completely defined by the design specification? Consider the risk of not being able to track the requirements to the design, and then to the code.
- Are the selected algorithms and designs easy to implement? Consider the risk of overly complex components, or components with poor internal interfaces.

Testing.

- Is there sufficient time to perform all of the unit testing that you specified? Consider the risk of not having enough time in the schedule for this activity.
- Will compromises be made regarding unit testing if there are schedule problems? Consider who will compromise, and on what components. Consider what may be missed.

Coding/implementation.

- Are the design specifications in sufficient detail to write the code? Consider the risk if the design is too high-level.
- Is the design changing while coding is being done? Consider the scope of the changes; large changes could cause wasted coding effort.
- Is the language suitable for producing the software of this program? Consider the risk of using a relational language to crunch numbers (extreme case).
- Does your team have enough experience with the development language, platform or tools? Consider the risk if your team is not well represented in these areas.
- Is there are risk that a key component or module will not be complete or on schedule? Consider the risk, for example, that a parsing component is incomplete in the late coding phase.
- Are you comfortable with your team's estimate on coding time and effort? Consider the risk if you grossly underestimated the effort required of you.
- Do you have a plan for configuration management of the code? Consider the risk if there is no revision control or there is uncontrolled code modification.

Integration and test

Environment (assessed by evaluating the hardware and software support facilities and test cases).

- Will there be sufficient hardware to do adequate integration and testing? Consider the risk of not being able to get computer time on campus near the end of the semester.
- Is there any problem with developing realistic scenarios and test data to demonstrate any requirements? Consider the risk of meeting the schedule, and testing coverage.

Product (assessed by evaluating the integration and testing of groups of components).

- Have acceptance criteria been agreed to for all requirements? Consider the risk of not knowing exactly what is expected.
- Has sufficient product integration been specified, and has adequate time been allocated for it? Consider the risk of meeting the schedule and getting sufficient testing coverage.

System (assessed by evaluating the integration between the product and target hardware).

- Has sufficient system integration and system integration time been specified? Consider the risk of meeting the schedule and getting sufficient testing coverage.

Maintainability (assessed by evaluating the effort required to locate and fix errors).

- Is the product design and documentation adequate for another class to maintain the code? Consider the risk if this is a requirement.

Specifications.

- Are the test specifications adequate to fully test the system? Consider the risk of poorly written requirements or specifications.

Communication, team compatibility and motivation

Communication (assessed by evaluating the ability of the team to exchange information).

- Is there a lack of good communication amongst your team? Consider the risk if class schedules conflict with team meetings.
- Is there a lack of good communication with your instructor about the project? Consider the risk to the quality of your work if you have incomplete information.

Compatibility of team (assessed by evaluating the ability of the team to work productively)

- Is your team familiar to you; have you worked together on a team project before? Consider the risk if the team is not comfortable working together, or has not done so before.
- Are tasks delegated in a fair manner amongst your team? Consider the risk if your team is not in agreement.

Motivation of team (assessed by evaluating the goals of the team).

- Is your team motivated to create a good product? Consider the risk to the project, if grades are the sole motivation.

Barry Boehm (1991) identifies a 'top 10' list of major software development areas where risk must be addressed. An audit by the authors of a number of large, medium and small software projects based on the questionnaire previously described identified a number of key risk areas. These items are offered in addition to Boehm's list and are numbered from 11–20. The order of these items is in relation to their probability of occurrence and their severity (or impact) to the project.

1. Skill shortfalls.
2. Unrealistic schedules and budgets.
3. Stability of external or off-the-shelf software.
4. Requirements mismatch.
5. User interface mismatch.
6. Architecture, performance, quality.
7. Requirement changes.
8. Legacy software.
9. Externally performed tasks.
10. Straining computer science capabilities.

These conclusions, based on risk assessments performed on 42 software projects since 1994, include:

11. Stability of development infrastructure.
12. Infrastructure limitations.
13. Procurement of infrastructure.
14. Multi-site software development.
15. Untested development methodologies.
16. Regulatory standards (for example health and safety).
17. Inadequate test strategy.
18. Development team involved in multiple projects or other activities.
19. Communication problems.
20. Availability of test sites or personnel.

Robert Charette (1989) explains that there are subtle environmental factors which are often overlooked when identifying sources of risk. They include:

- Software developments are very complex. The software problem has numerous elements with extremely complicated interrelationships.
- Problem element relationships can be multidimensional. The laws of proportionality do not govern changes in elements. It is well documented that adding more people to a project that is behind schedule, in many instances, will make it even later.
- Software problem elements are unstable and changeable. Although cost and schedule may be fixed, actual costs in labour and time to complete are difficult to project.
- The development process is dynamic. Conditions ceaselessly change; thus, project equilibrium is seldom achieved. The environment is never static – hardware malfunctions, personnel quit, and contractors do not deliver.
- People are an essential software development element and a major source of risk. Economic or technical problems are easy with which to deal. The higher-level complications, multidimensional ambiguities, and changing environment caused by conflicting human requirements, interaction, and desires are what cause problems. Software development is full of problems because it is a very human endeavour.

Additionally, there are other interrelated factors that contribute to software risk. These factors are:

- Communication about risk is one of the most difficult, yet important, practices you must establish in your project. People do not naturally want to talk about potential problems. Rather than confronting imaginary problems while they are still in the risk stage, they wind up having to deal with them after they become full-blown, real problems. Then there is a lot of communication! Effective risk planning only occurs when people are willing to talk about risks in a non-threatening, constructive environment.
- Software size can affect the accuracy and efficacy of estimates. Interdependence among software elements increases exponentially as size increases. With extremely

large software systems, handling complexity through decomposition becomes increasingly difficult because even decomposed elements may be unmanageable.

- Software architecture also affects software risk. Architectural structure is the ease with which functions can be modularized and the hierarchical nature of information to be processed. It is also development team structure, its relationship with the user and to one another, and the ease with which the human structure can develop the software architecture (Pressman, 1993).

Checklists 5.2, 5.3 and 5.4 provide practical guidance related to software metrics, making changes to code and commenting on code.

Analysing risk

The second step in the risk management cycle is to analyse those risks identified. This activity comprises three elements:

1. Probability of risk occurrence.
2. Severity of consequence if the event should occur.
3. Subjective judgement concerning the combination of the first two.

Figure 5.2 shows how risk can be classified according to the probability of a problem occurring and the severity of its effect.

Many specialized techniques have been developed to assist project managers undertaking risk analysis. Some have wide application, others are specific to particular kinds of risk (for example, British Standard 7799 Parts 1 & 2 – Code of Practice for Security Management). Table 5.1 summarizes some of the more common techniques in use.

There are also a number of software packages available to assist the project manager in risk analysis. Some packages are very general, enabling the project manager to build quantified risk assessments into standard spreadsheet models on their desktop PCs.

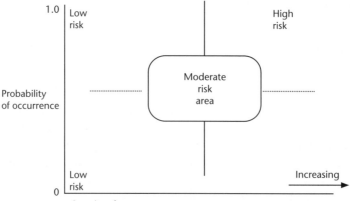

Figure 5.2 Classification of risk

Table 5.1   Risk management analysis techniques

Technique/Method	Application
Sensitivity analysis	Very wide application from economic appraisal and financial feasibility to operations and software maintenance models
Decision analysis	Choice amongst uncertain alternatives
Software engineering risk analysis	Wide application to proposals, projects and budget, through all stages in the life cycle of a project
Probability occurrence	Quantification of risk probabilities and consequence distributions
CRAMM[1]	Asserts that risk is dependent on the asset value, the threats and the vulnerabilities. The values of these parameters are assessed through interviews

Table 5.2   Impact/probability matrix

	Probability of occurrence				
Severity	Very high	High	Medium	Low	Very low
Catastrophic	High	High	Moderate	Moderate	Low
Critical	High	High	Moderate	Low	None
Marginal	Moderate	Moderate	Low	None	None
Negligible	Moderate	Low	Low	None	None

Such techniques enhance the role of the project manager by providing assistance in analysis and evaluation tasks, but they do not substitute for good judgement and management experience.

The last element in analysis is to determine the overall risk to the project. Using estimates on risk probabilities and impacts, the overall risk to the project should be gauged. In figuring out the overall risk, managers should consider how this risk may impact other risks on the project and make a note of them (risks are rarely standalone – interrelationships often exist). A matrix should be used to determine overall risk for each of effort, performance, and schedule. Table 5.2 provides an example of a matrix used to classify risk.

Plan for risks

After analysing risks, a plan should be formulated to address each risk. This planning process should cover the following stages:

- Specify why the risk is important.
- What information is needed to track the status of the risk?
- Who is responsible for the risk management activity?
- What resources are needed to perform the activity?

- A detailed plan of how the risk will be prevented and/or mitigated is created.
- Action planning can be used to mitigate the risk via an immediate response. The probability of the risk occurring, and/or the potential impact of the risk may be mitigated by dealing with the problem early in the project.
- Contingency planning can be used to monitor the risk and invoke a pre-determined response. A trigger should be set up, and if the trigger is reached, the contingency plan is put in effect.

Mitigating the risk

While you can never totally remove software risk, there are several different techniques that can be used to mitigate it. These techniques, of course, should be used in the structure of a software risk management process. This step identifies risk mitigation techniques and the basic software risk management process.

Risk mitigation techniques include:

- *Risk avoidance.* The risk of one alternative approach can be avoided by choosing another with lower risk. This conscious choice avoids the potentially higher risk. However, it really results in risk reduction, not complete risk elimination. While a conscious decision to ignore (or assume) a high risk may be a creditable option, an unconscious decision to avoid risk is not. Managers must assess, rate, and decide on the possible consequences of inaction. Managers must also decide if the benefits of acting on a risk merit the expense in time and money expended. Managers and developers should document all risk handling actions with supporting rationale. Managers should also employ risk management in concert with metrics and process improvement used to measure, track, and improve the project's progress and process.
- *Risk control.* Managers can control risk (the most common form of risk handling) by continually monitoring and correcting risky conditions. This involves the use of reviews, inspections, risk reduction milestones, development of fallback positions, and similar management techniques. Controlling risk involves developing a risk reduction plan, then tracking to that plan.
- *Risk assumption.* Managers can assume risk by making a conscious decision to accept the consequences should the event occur. Some amount of risk assumption always occurs in software acquisition projects. It is up to the manager to determine the appropriate level of risk that can be assumed in each situation as it presents itself.
- *Risk transference.* Managers can transfer risk when there is an opportunity to reduce risk by sharing it. This concept is frequently used with contractors where, for instance, contract type, performance incentives, and warranties are risk sharing contractual mechanisms. Although many of these techniques only share cost risk, risk transfer is often beneficial to the government and the developer.

The plan formulated in the previous step should be followed as closely as possible to mitigate the risk. If this approach does not work, the manager should return to the previous phase and make a new plan. If the plan does work, the manager should continue to analyse the risk to determine whether it has been reduced to an acceptable severity level.

As newly identified risks are brought to the project manager's attention either through weekly team meetings or third party communications, the project manager needs to determine whether to own the risk, delegate responsibility, or transfer the risk responsibility up the project organization chain. The project manager, if necessary, may transfer a risk(s) to external organizations, if that organization is best suited to handle the risk.

Tracking risk

Finally, an important function in the cycle is keeping track of those risks which pose the highest threat. Tracking involves identification of the project's highest-risk issues and tracking progress towards resolving those issues through subsequent progress reports. The major risk management benefits are similar to those of cost/schedule/performance tracking plus the added ones of identifying and maintaining a high-level risk consciousness. Tracking becomes critical because the one risk attribute whose influence is difficult to predict is 'time'. Generalizations about risk made early in the project can (and often do) decay with time. One reason for performing risk tracking is to keep a predictable, unpredictable, or unknown risk from becoming a known one. Tracking occurs after the decisions about mitigation strategies and tactics have been implemented to:

- Check if the consequences of our decisions are the same as envisioned.
- Identify opportunities for refinement in the area of risk mitigation.
- Help provide feedback for future decisions about controlling those new or current risks not responding to risk mitigation or whose nature has changed with time.

Risk tracking methods

The most effective way to track risk is measurement. The significant risk-reducing benefits achieved through a comprehensive measurement program cannot be stressed too much. Metrics data provide the means to compare risk elements with historical data, pinpoint risk drivers, and determine alternative risk reduction choices. Managers must aggressively track and control the risk drivers affecting their projects.

Cost/schedule/performance tracking involves using techniques such as work break structures, metrics, quality indicators, activity networks, and earned-value methods to determine and track project progress with respect to plans, schedules, and budgets. Cost/schedule/performance tracking is useful because potential schedule slippages, cost overruns, and performance shortfalls are identified early, and their impact on other interdependent system elements can be reduced. Other risk tracking methods are peer inspection's, reviews, audits, and meetings.

Checklist 5.7 provides some additional guidance on risk management.

Risk register

The easiest way to record risks is via a risk register (or log). Every project should have a risk register associated with it. This risk register should be created during the initial project start-up phase and reviewed at frequent intervals (say, once per month or at the end stage of a project), although the project manager may decide to undertake more frequent reviews, depending on the nature of the project. All information captured in the process should be recorded in the register. The register and the information it contains should be maintained by the project manager or a nominated member of the project support group.

When a risk register is formulated it should contain as a minimum the following information:

- risk register number;
- risk name;
- risk manager (who owns the risk);
- description of the risk;
- impact of the risk;
- risk assessment profile;
- how the risk will be mitigated.

This formalized process has a number of advantages:

1. It enables the time, cost, and technical risk analyses and the risk reduction and risk transfer planning to be undertaken and carried out, and a configuration controlled document to be created and maintained throughout the project life cycle.
2. It provides a central repository of knowledge around which risk management can be built.
3. It forms the basis of the required outputs from risk work, namely the risk analysis paper, the risk management plan and the risk mitigation plan.
4. It provides an audit trail, so that decisions made can be traced back to the assumptions, judgements and calculations on which they were based.
5. Finally, it forms an important interface with subsequent phases of the project, which take up the risk management plan.

Summary

■ The software estimation process involves five stages: estimating size, estimating cost and effort, estimate schedule, inspect/approve, track estimates.

■ Software product size is generally measured in Source Lines of Code (SLOC).

■ Cost is usually estimated in effort or person-days/weeks. This value can then be translated into cost based on labour rates.

■ Many methods are used to estimate software cost. These include: algorithmic models, expert judgement, analogy, top-down, bottom-up and automated models.

- COCOMO (COnstructive COst MOdel) is one of the most widely used costing models. However, since the constants used by the model are based on data from a relatively small number of projects, it is sometimes considered to be inaccurate.

- Function point analysis can be used to estimate the relative size and complexity of a software system. In turn, this allows the overall length of the development process to be estimated.

- Risk can be classified according to the probability of a problem occurring and the severity of its effect.

- The severity of a project risk can range from catastrophic (perhaps where life is lost) to negligible (perhaps where no damage or injury is sustained).

- A number of techniques can be used to identify project risks. The Software Engineering Institute's (SEI) Taxonomy-Based Risk Identification Questionnaire allows risks to be identified at each stage of a project.

- Various methods can be used to mitigate risk. These include: risk avoidance, risk control, risk assumption and risk transference.

- The most effective way to track risk is by measurement. A risk register is an important document that can be used to monitor risks and their impact on the project.

Project checklists

Checklist 5.1 Configuration management

General

- Is your software configuration management plan designed to help programmers and minimize overheads?

- Does your SCM approach avoid over-controlling the project?

- Do you group change requests, either through informal means such as a list of pending changes or a more formal approach such as a change control board?

- Do you formally estimate the effect of each proposed change?

- Do you view major changes as a warning that requirements analysis is not yet complete?

Tools

- Do you use version control software to facilitate configuration management?

- Do you use version control software to reduce coordination problems of working in teams?

- Do you use Make or other dependency control software to build programs efficiently and reliably?

Backup

▨ Do you backup all project materials periodically?

▨ Are project backups transferred to offsite storage periodically?

▨ Are all materials backed up including source code, documents, graphics, and important notes?

▨ Have you tested the backup recovery procedure?

Checklist 5.2 Software metrics

▨ Are software staffing profiles maintained of actual staffing versus planned staffing?

▨ Are productivity and effort measured and recorded for each phase of the project?

▨ Are profiles of software size maintained for each software configuration item?

▨ Are profiles of software complexity maintained for each software item?

▨ Are statistics on software design errors gathered?

▨ Are statistics on software code and test errors gathered?

▨ Are profiles maintained of actual versus planned software units designed, over time?

▨ Are profiles maintained of actual versus planned software units completing unit testing, over time?

▨ Are profiles maintained of actual versus planned software units integrated, over time?

▨ Are target computer memory utilization estimates and actuals tracked?

▨ Are target computer throughput utilization estimates and actuals tracked?

▨ Are design and code review coverages measured and recorded?

▨ Is test coverage measured and recorded for each module tested?

▨ Are software problem reports tracked to closure?

▨ Are the cost and effort needed to correct errors measured and recorded?

▨ Are any metrics defined and applied for measuring the quality of the software product?

▨ Are there any metrics to rate the quality of the software process?

▨ Are quality measures used to identify weak points of the product and the process and to verify quality criteria?

▨ Are measures used for initiating corrective actions, if a measurement value deteriorates or exceeds given boundaries?

Are measures used for introducing product and process improvements?

Are all data collected during the project recorded and evaluated?

Are process and product metrics (e.g. productivity and effort) used to plan following projects?

Are there any mechanisms to regularly review whether the defined metrics are still adequate and representative?

Do you plan for measurement activities?

Checklist 5.3 Code changes

Is the change part of a systematic change strategy?

Has the change been reviewed as thoroughly as initial development would be?

Has the software been regression tested to establish that the change has not degraded the software?

Does the change enhance the program's internal quality rather than degrading it?

Have you improved the system's modularity by breaking routines into smaller routines, when possible?

Have you reduced the use of global variables, when possible?

Have you improved the programming style – variable names, routine names, formatting, comments, and so on?

If changes cause you to look for ways to share code, have you considered putting the shared code at a higher level as well as considered putting it at a lower level?

Does this change make the next change easier?

Checklist 5.4 Commenting on code

General

Does the source listing contain most of the information about the program?

Can someone pick up the code and immediately start understanding it?

Do comments explain the code's intent or summarize it, rather than just repeating it?

Is the PDL-to-code process used to reduce commenting time?

Has tricky code been rewritten rather than commented?

Are comments up to date?

- Are comments clear and correct?

- Does the comment style allow comments to be easily modified?

Statements and paragraphs

- Does the code avoid endline comments?

- Do comments focus on why rather than how?

- Do comments prepare the reader's mind for what is to follow?

- Does every comment count? Have redundant, extraneous, or self-indulgent comments been removed or improved?

- Are surprises documented?

- Have abbreviations been replaced?

- Is the distinction between major and minor comments clear?

- Is code that works around an error or undocumented feature commented?

Data declarations

- Are units on data declarations commented?

- Is the range of values on numeric data commented?

- Are coded meanings commented?

- Are limitations on input data commented?

- Are flags documented to the bit level?

- Has each global variable been commented where it is declared?

- Has each global variable been documented each time it is used, either with a naming convention or a comment?

- Is each control statement commented?

- Are the ends of long or complex control structures commented?

- Are magic numbers documented or, preferably, replaced with named constants or variables?

Routines

- Is the purpose of each routine commented?

- Are other facts of each routine given in comments, when relevant, including input and output data, interface assumptions, limitations, error corrections, global effects, and sources of algorithms?

Files, modules, and programs

- Does the program have a four-to-five-page document that gives an overall view of how the program is organized?

- Is the purpose of each file described?

- Is the author's name and phone number in the listing?

Checklist 5.5 Evolutionary delivery

- Have you planned for several releases of the software before the full, final capabilities are present?

- Does the first release contain the germ of the program, the seed from which the rest of the program will be developed?

- Will the first release be made as early as possible to get the ball rolling?

- Is the first release usable, at least at some minimal level?

- Have you defined what each evolutionary stage will deliver as best as you can in the hazy dawn of the project?

- Does each release add significant capabilities?

- Is the process flexible enough to respond to user feedback? If not, is that the way you intend it to be?

- Is the architecture open enough to support a product that will be changed many times through several releases?

- Will each release be treated as a small project with its own coding and testing, and, in some cases, design and requirements analysis?

- Have you considered basing the process on modifications to an existing program?

- Do you use the results of each stage to improve your estimates and planning for the next stage?

Checklist 5.6 Risk management

Schedule creation

- Schedule, resources, and product definition have all been dictated by the customer or upper management and are not in balance.

- Schedule is optimistic, 'best case', rather than realistic, 'expected case'.

- Schedule omits necessary tasks.

- Schedule was based on the use of specific team members, but those team members were not available.

- Cannot build a product of the size specified in the time allocated.

- Product is larger than estimated (in lines of code, function points, or percentage of previous project's size).

- Effort is greater than estimated (per line of code, function point, module, etc.).

- Re-estimation in response to schedule slips is overly optimistic or ignores project history.

- Excessive schedule pressure reduces productivity.

- Target date is moved up with no corresponding adjustment to the product scope or available resources.

- A delay in one task causes cascading delays in dependent tasks.

- Unfamiliar areas of the product take more time than expected to design and implement.

Organization and management

- Project lacks an effective top management sponsor.

- Project languishes too long in fuzzy front end.

- Layoffs and cutbacks reduce team's capacity.

- Management or marketing insists on technical decisions that lengthen the schedule.

- Inefficient team structure reduces productivity.

- Management review/decision cycle is slower than expected.

- Budget cuts upset project plans.

- Management makes decisions that reduce the development team's motivation.

- Non-technical third party tasks take longer than expected (budget approval, equipment purchase approval, legal reviews, security clearances, etc.).

- Planning is too poor to support the desired development speed.

- Project plans are abandoned under pressure, resulting in chaotic, inefficient development.

- Management places more emphasis on heroics than accurate status reporting, which undercuts its ability to detect and correct problems.

Development environment

- Facilities are not available on time.

- Facilities are available but inadequate (e.g., no phones, network wiring, furniture, office supplies, etc.).

- Facilities are crowded, noisy, or disruptive.

- Development tools are not in place by the desired time.

- Development tools do not work as expected; developers need time to create workarounds or to switch to new tools.

- Development tools are not chosen based on their technical merits, and do not provide the planned productivity.

End users

- End user insists on new requirements.

- End user ultimately finds product to be unsatisfactory, requiring redesign and rework.

- End user does not buy into the project and consequently does not provide needed support.

- End user input is not solicited, so product ultimately fails to meet user expectations and must be reworked.

Customer

- Customer insists on new requirements.

- Customer review/decision cycles for plans, prototypes, and specifications are slower than expected.

- Customer will not participate in review cycles for plans, prototypes, and specifications or is incapable of doing so – resulting in unstable requirements and time/consuming changes.

- Customer communication time (e.g., time to answer requirements-clarification questions) is slower than expected.

- Customer insists on technical decisions that lengthen the schedule.

- Customer micro-manages the development process, resulting in slower progress than planned.

- Customer-furnished components are a poor match for the product under development, resulting in extra design and integration work.

- Customer-furnished components are of poor quality, resulting in extra testing, design, and integration work and in extra customer-relationship management.

- Customer-mandated support tools and environments are incompatible, have poor performance, or have inadequate functionality, resulting in reduced productivity.

- Customer will not accept the software as delivered even though it meets all specifications.

- Customer has expectations for development speed that developers cannot meet.

Contractors

▨ Contractor does not deliver components when promised.

▨ Contractor delivers components of unacceptably low quality, and time must be added to improve quality.

▨ Contractor does not buy into the project and consequently does not provide the level of performance needed.

Requirements

▨ Requirements have been base lined but continue to change.

▨ Requirements are poorly defined, and further definition expands the scope of the project.

▨ Additional requirements are added.

▨ Vaguely specified areas of the product are more time-consuming than expected.

Product

▨ Error-prone modules require more testing, design, and implementation work than expected.

▨ Unacceptably low quality requires more testing, design, and implementation work to correct than expected.

▨ Development of the wrong software functions requires redesign and implementation.

▨ Development of the wrong user interface results in redesign and implementation.

▨ Development of extra software functions that are not required (gold-plating) extends the schedule.

▨ Meeting product's size or speed constraints requires more time than expected, including time for redesign and re-implementation.

▨ Strict requirements for compatibility with existing system require more testing, design, and implementation than expected.

▨ Requirements for interfacing with other systems, other complex systems, or other systems that are not under the team's control result in unforeseen design, implementation, and testing.

▨ Pushing the computer science state-of-the-art in one or more areas lengthens the schedule unpredictably.

▨ Requirement to operate under multiple operating systems takes longer to satisfy than expected.

▨ Operation in an unfamiliar or unproved software environment causes unforeseen problems.

■ Operation in an unfamiliar or unproved hardware environment causes unforeseen problems.

■ Development of a kind of component that is brand new to the organization takes longer than expected.

■ Dependency on a technology that is still under development lengthens the schedule.

External environment

■ Product depends on government regulations, which change unexpectedly.

■ Product depends on draft technical standards, which change unexpectedly.

Personnel

■ Hiring takes longer than expected.

■ Task prerequisites (e.g., training, completion of other projects, acquisition of work permit) cannot be completed on time.

■ Poor relationships between developers and management slow decision making and follow through.

■ Team members do not buy into the project and consequently do not provide the level of performance needed.

■ Low motivation and morale reduce productivity.

■ Lack of needed specialization increases defects and rework.

■ Personnel need extra time to learn unfamiliar software tools or environment.

■ Personnel need extra time to learn unfamiliar hardware environment.

■ Personnel need extra time to learn unfamiliar programming language.

■ Contract personnel leave before project is complete.

■ Permanent employees leave before project is complete.

■ New development personnel are added late in the project, and additional training and communications overhead reduces existing team members' effectiveness.

■ Team members do not work together efficiently.

■ Conflicts between team members result in poor communication, poor designs, interface errors, and extra rework.

■ Problem team members are not removed from the team, damaging overall team motivation.

■ The personnel most qualified to work on the project are not available for the project.

- The personnel most qualified to work on the project are available for the project but are not used for political or other reasons.

- Personnel with critical skills needed for the project cannot be found.

- Key personnel are available only part time.

- Not enough personnel are available for the project.

- People's assignments do not match their strengths.

- Personnel work slower than expected.

- Sabotage by project management results in inefficient scheduling and ineffective planning.

- Sabotage by technical personnel results in lost work or poor quality and requires rework.

Design and implementation

- Overly simple design fails to address major issues and leads to redesign and re-implementation.

- Overly complicated design requires unnecessary and unproductive implementation overhead.

- Inappropriate design leads to redesign and re-implementation.

- Use of unfamiliar methodology results in extra training time and in rework to fix first-time misuses of the methodology.

- Product is implemented in a low level language (e.g. assembler), and productivity is lower than expected.

- Necessary functionality cannot be implemented using the selected code or class libraries; developers must switch to new libraries or custom-build the necessary functionality.

- Code or class libraries have poor quality, causing extra testing, defect correction, and rework.

- Schedule savings from productivity enhancing tools are overestimated.

- Components developed separately cannot be integrated easily, requiring redesign and rework.

Process

- Amount of paperwork results in slower progress than expected.

- Inaccurate progress tracking results in not knowing the project is behind schedule until late in the project.

▨ Upstream quality-assurance activities are shortchanged, resulting in time-consuming rework downstream.

▨ Inaccurate quality tracking results in not knowing about quality problems that affect the schedule until late in the project.

▨ Too little formality (lack of adherence to software policies and standards) results in mis-communications, quality problems, and rework.

▨ Too much formality (bureaucratic adherence to software policies and standards) results in unnecessary, time-consuming overhead.

▨ Management-level progress reporting takes more developer time than expected.

▨ Half-hearted risk management fails to detect major project risks.

▨ Software project risk management takes more time than expected.

Bibliography

Albrecht A., 1983, 'Measuring and Estimating' in *Application Development and Maintenance Guide 570 Conference Report*, No. DP 7234A, Guide International Inc., USA.

Boehm B., 1991, 'Software Risk Management: Principles and Practices', in *IEEE Software*, January 1991.

Bouldin B., 1989, 'What are You Measuring? and Why are You Measuring It?', in *Software Magazine*, Vol. 9, No. 10, pp. 30–39.

Charette R., 1989, *Software Engineering Risk Analysis and Management*, McGraw-Hill Book Company, New York.

Fenton N., 1991, *Software Metrics: A Rigorous Approach*, Chapman and Hall, New York.

Gilb T., 1988, *Principles of Software Engineering Management*, Addison-Wesley, USA.

Gluch D., 1994, *A Construct for Describing Software Development Risks*, Technical Report CMU/SEI-94-TR-14, Pittsburgh: Software Engineering Institute, Carnegie Mellon University.

Goodman P., 1992, 'Implementing Software Metrics Programmes: A Project Based Approach', in *Eurometrics Proceedings*, April 1992, pp. 120–127.

Moller K. and Paulish D., 1993, *Software Metrics: A Practitioner's Guide to Improved Product Development*, Chapman and Hall, UK.

Pressman, Roger S., 1993, 'Understanding Software Engineering Practices: Required at SEI Level 2 Process Maturity,' Software Engineering Training Series briefing presented to the Software Engineering Process Group in July 1993.

Thamhain H., 1992, *Resource Estimating for Technology Intensive Projects*, AACE.

Young D. and Obertreis R., 1996, *Report on Life Cycle Costing and Cost Estimation Software Tools for the RCMP Informatics Directorate*, Royal Canadian Mounted Police, Canada.

Further reading

Caper Jones T., 1998, *Estimating Software Costs*, McGraw-Hill Publishing, USA.
Kapur B., 2001, *Estimating Software Projects*, Longman Higher Education.
Roetzheim W., 1997, *Software Project Cost and Schedule Estimate*, Prentice-Hall, USA.

Useful websites

http://www.software-measurement.com
This website contains detailed information on software measurement techniques such as function point analysis.

http://www.dacs.dtic.mil/databases/url/key.hts?keycode = 4
This is a useful website for sites related to cost estimation tools and techniques. Contains lots of literature.

http://www.cigital.com/
Cigital is the leading authority on Software Risk Management for essential software. The website also contains all sorts of information relating to the management of software risk.

http://www.noweco.com/emse.htm
Engineering Management Services website. This is another useful site relating to software risk analysis software tools.

Self-assessment exercises

1. Provide a definition of the term *estimate*.

2. How is the size of a software development project traditionally measured?

3. A number of methods exist to estimate software cost. In brief, describe how a bottom-up model functions.

4. The advanced COCOMO model computes software development effort (and cost) as a function of program size and a set of 'cost drivers' that include subjective assessments of product, hardware, personnel and project attributes. True or false?

5. In the COCOMO model, what does KLOC represent?

6. Function point analysis describes complexity as being simple, average or complex. True or false?

7. In brief, explain how the Wide Band Delphi Technique works.

8. Provide a definition of risk.

9. Risk can be classified in terms of probability of occurrence and cost. True or false?

10. Explain an approach to risk mitigation by risk assumption.

Case study

Software risk management

Although risk characterizations are often completed for the benefit only of an organization's decision maker (that is a project manager or some other technical manager), it is important to recognize that various other parties use them when they exercise their rights to participate in the decision, either before or after the project manager acts. These interested and affected parties include customers, third party suppliers, industry groups, opinion leaders, and a variety of others. Acceptance of risk decisions by the broad spectrum of the interested and affected parties is usually critical to their implementation. Risk characterization processes and products should provide all the decision participants with the information they need to make informed choices, in the form in which they need it. A risk characterization that fails to address their questions is likely to be criticized as irrelevant or incompetent, regardless of how carefully it addresses the questions it selects for attention.

This major software provider to various government agencies whom we will call ACME was called upon to consider how to improve decisions about risks to safety critical software. The company concerned has responded with a series of studies that reflect the history of thinking about how managers can understand and cope with those risks. *Risk Assessment in the Company: Managing the Process* reported the results of a study that sought 'mechanisms that best foster a constructive partnership between providers and users' for informing contentious decisions about how risk is managed. The study aimed to raise the distinction between risk assessment and risk management and raising the issue of how best to keep these functions separate, yet coordinated.

Improving risk communication in the company focused on the relationship between producers and users of information about risks, addressing ways to improve communication 'in the service of technical understanding and better-informed individual and user choice'. More recently, it has sought ways to 'conduct a credible risk assessment of all the risks at all the sites where projects are being managed'. This case addresses a broad issue linking project risk and policy. The initial brief formulated the problem as follows:

> The way managers handle risk often breaks down at the stage of 'risk characterization', when the information in a risk assessment is translated into a form usable by a risk manager, individual decision makers, or the customer.

Oversimplifying the technical considerations or skewing the results through selectivity can lead to the inappropriate use of information in risk management decisions, but providing full information, if it does not address key concerns of the intended audience, can undermine that audience's trust in the risk analysis. This problem was of sufficiently broad interest that the study received support from the broader organization technical community. In some of the departments the interest and support came from several major internal units. Thus, the organization was asked to address concerns of entities as diverse as:

- business policy;
- business rules;
- business planning;
- supplier management;
- project management;
- software construction;
- standards and procedures.

To carry out this broad task, the organization convened a board of 12 members from a variety of specialisms including risk assessment, business planning, strategic management, technical management, project management and legal. Members were selected to ensure that the perspectives of all groups would be included, along with those of the technical community. Members were selected so as to assure a flexible view of the charge and to provide an overall balance to the board.

At its initial meetings the board heard from each of its sponsors and considered a detailed proposal from representatives of most of the sponsoring departments that presented a considerably broader reading of the charge, which appears to restrict 'risk characterization' to the translation of information already available from risk assessments. In particular, the proposal called on the board to consider the appropriateness of including in risk characterizations such considerations as:

- economic factors;
- equity issues;
- risk mitigation and tradeoffs;
- technical control feasibility;
- issues of social context (considerations not normally included in risk assessments).

The brief also called on the board for 'guidance... to improve the dialogue between risk assessors and project managers prior to and during the development of a comprehensive assessment so that all parties understand policy and management concerns. This request implicitly recognized the importance to risk characterization of communication before and during the process of conducting risk assessments, not only after they are complete. Some of the sponsors, particularly the non-technical community, also indicated that concerns about improving user participation, building trust, and similar issues were among those that had led them to support the study. As a result of discussion of these concerns with the sponsors' representatives, the board adopted a revised task statement that reflected a broader charge.

'Risk characterization' is a complex and often controversial activity that is both a product of analysis and dependent on the processes of defining and conducting analysis. The study board will assess opportunities to improve the characterization of risk so as to better inform decision making and resolution of controversies over risk. The study will address: technical issues such as the representation of uncertainty; issues relating to translating the outputs of conventional risk analysis into non-technical language; and social, behavioural, economic, and ethical aspects of risk that are relevant to the content or process of risk characterization.

This charge makes explicit that the board would consider both translation issues and those processes that determine whether project risk characterizations ultimately better inform decision making. The revised charge represents the first step in defining the board's view of its topic that is reflected in the use of the term 'understanding risk' in the title of this case.

The board held an informal meeting in March 1998 and 10 meetings between May 1998 and June 1999 to gather and consider information and to write its report. It engaged in discussions with sponsors' representatives and a variety of outside consultants and risk practitioners whose experiences with risk characterizations the board believed would be instructive. It sought knowledge from various sources, including experimental research on risk perception and methods of summarizing risk information; studies that evaluate the effects and outcomes of various ways of analysing and deliberating about risk; and the reflections of experienced practitioners of risk assessment, characterization, and decision making. The board discussed a wide range of risks, including risks to the whole software project life cycle. It discussed a wide range of uses for risk characterization, including informing regulatory decisions on approving software for safety-critical business use.

In summary given the variety of sponsors, risks, and decision situations, the board emphasized broad considerations about risk characterization rather than those that are specific to certain risks, decision types, or for example, government agencies. It developed consensus about how to think about and organize risk characterization efforts, without trying to offer detailed guidance for particular decision contexts. If its recommendations can be implemented with appropriate deliberation and judgement, the board suggested that more understandable, scientifically sound, and acceptable decisions will result.

Questions

1. Describe the importance of including stakeholder groups in carrying out a risk assessment.
2. Describe the process of undertaking a risk assessment.
3. Describe three risk mitigation techniques and how these may be applied to software projects.
4. How important is it to keep and maintain a risk register? Explain how a risk register should be maintained.

Note

1. UK Government's Risk Analysis and Management Method for Commercial Systems.

CHAPTER 6

Managing information systems quality

Introduction

No text on project management would be complete without a detailed discussion of issues related to quality. In the context of information systems projects, quality takes on a broad meaning that refers not only to the way in which organizations manage projects, but also to the software development process itself.

The chapter begins by defining the concept of quality. This material also explains concepts related to quality in the context of software development. The discussion emphasizes the fact that the different perspectives of those involved in a project will influence how quality is seen and measured. As an example, it is pointed out that the users of an application will be more interested in how easy the software is to use than in the underlying code. The basic characteristics of software quality are described in terms of ISO standards. Each of these qualities is then broken down further in order to clarify the explanations given.

The use of metrics as a means of providing a quantifiable view of quality is described and the material then moves on to look at common quality management frameworks. Three of these frameworks are examined in depth: ISO 9000, TickIT and the Capability Maturity Model. Each of these models is accompanied by detailed explanations, examples and an analysis of overall effectiveness. Throughout the discussion, a great deal of emphasis is placed upon continuous quality improvement and the importance of establishing procedures that will support all of an organization's activities.

Learning objectives

Some of the topics covered include:

- The meaning of quality.
- Characteristics used to determine/measure quality.
- Using metrics to quantify quality.
- Overview of ISO 9000, 9001 and 9002.
- Overview of TickIT.
- Overview of the Capability Maturity Model.

At the end of this chapter, students will be able to:

- Define the concept of software quality, referring to the major characteristics associated with software quality and the influence of context and individual perceptions.
- Explain the structure of ISO 9000, including how the auditing process works.
- Explain the structure of TickIT and its relevance to ISO standards.
- Explain the Capability Maturity Model with reference to the assessment process and the benefits of adopting such an approach.

The meaning of software quality

Hopefully, readers should have come to realize something that most experienced project managers have already learned: managers perform within a system that is always out of control to one extent or another. We might phrase this a little more accurately by saying that the performance of the project is very much influenced by variations in process. Project managers usually learn by discovery that the critical control points that would assure success have been pre-set by others. According to Professor Joseph Duran (1988), 90 per cent of all problems in organizations are systematic and beyond the positive influence of staff. Unfortunately, these problems also include issues related to quality. This means that one of the greatest challenges faced by project managers and software professionals alike is to get the process right first time. In turn, this means initiating a rigorous quality regime, which is both defined and measurable.

A widely used definition of quality has been supplied by the International Organisation for Standardisation (ISO8042, 1986): 'The totality of features and characteristics of a product or service that bear on its ability to satisfy specified or implied needs'. This view of quality has come to dominate the quality movement in many software companies. Software professionals generally acknowledge that the quality of a product (or software system) is very much influenced by the quality of the processes used to build it. This means in order to build high quality software systems, it is necessary to have high quality processes and people committed to quality.

It is also acknowledged (Gillies, 1996) that software quality has its own peculiarities. As an example, at a workshop a group of IT professionals were asked why software quality was different from other types of quality. It was suggested that each type of product made had its own quality demands but that computer software was particularly problematical for the following reasons:

- Software has no physical existence.
- The lack of knowledge of client needs at the start.
- The change of client needs over time.
- The rapid rate of change in both hardware and software.
- The high expectations of customers, particularly with respect to adaptability.

One of Joel Barker's (1992) observations on quality in his book, *Future Edge*, is that '...the beauty of the current quality movement is that system professionals are now motivated by their own values to do the best that they can do'. Barker's point is that people determine quality, not just procedures, tools or systems. After all, it is people that define the problems and specify the solutions. Many of the ideas to do with software quality can be traced back to the pioneering work of Joseph Juran and Edward Deming half a century ago (McManus, 2000). Today's quality movement could be described as a paradigm that comprises several concepts.

The first of these concepts relates to defining the software process to be improved. Defining the process means that all the activities to be performed have to be clearly stated, including the order in which they are to be performed and when they are considered complete. This is normally achieved by expressing exit criteria.

The second concept relates to using software processes – to improve a process it needs to be used on many projects. Improvement comes with experience. When the same process is used over different projects, it is always possible to find ways in which the process can be improved. Such improvements are usually small and relatively easy to implement. Over time, such small improvements lead to significant savings and have a positive financial benefit.

The third concept is that of metrics which should be collected to determine if changes incorporated into the process are really improvements. If so, there is a need to quantify the improvements noted. Measurement is a fundamental aspect of quality, reflected in the proverb: what gets measured gets managed; and what gets managed gets improved. Flood (1993) emphasizes the importance of this by commenting that: '...measurement is crucial in problem solving. Measurement specifications are the basic parameters by which intervention is guided. The choice of specification is therefore a crucial one'.

Most of the published literature cites a set of either four or five core metrics. The names and nature of these metrics varies. However, the data elements commonly identified within each of the mandated attributes are usually related as shown in Table 6.1. The measures in this table are not the only ones that can be used to describe software products and processes, but they represent a starting point and are practical measures that produce useful information. What is more, they are measures that the project manager should be able to define in ways that promote consistent use. The measures stated in Table 6.1 should be accompanied by checklists that an individual project manager can use to specify and obtain supporting data to address management issues that are important to the project organization.

Qualifying and quantifying software quality

According to Tom Van Vleck (see 'Software Engineering Proverbs' at http://www.multicians.org/thvv/tvv.html):

> We know as much about software quality problems as they knew about the Black Plague in the 1600s. We've seen the victims' agonies and helped burn the corpses. We don't

Table 6.1 Core metrics

Name of metric	Potential definitions	Characteristics addressed
Size	Counts of physical source lines of code (SLOC)	Size, progress, reuse, rework
	Function points or feature points	Size, progress, reuse, rework
Effort	Number of staff hours expended monthly	Effort, cost, rework, resource allocations
Software quality	Total number of errors opened/closed	Quality, readiness for delivery, improvement trends, rework
	Number of errors opened/ closed since last report	Quality, readiness for delivery, improvement trends, rework
	Type of error (testing, action item, document comment)	Quality, readiness for delivery, improvement trends, rework
	Classification and priority	Quality, readiness for delivery, improvement trends, rework
	Product in which error was found	Quality, readiness for delivery, improvement trends, rework
Rework	Number of open software change orders	
	Number of closed software change orders	
	Total number of software change orders	

know what causes it; we don't really know if there is only one disease. We just suffer –
and keep pouring our sewage into our water supply.

Although Van Vleck's statement is a little dramatic, it does underline the importance
of quantifying software quality. Apart from aesthetic appreciation of quality products,
our purpose in examining quality is not only to improve the software process but also
to facilitate decision making. One example of these decisions is in the choice of software tools, where there are several applications that might meet requirements. Another
example is the decision of whether to accept, and to pay for, a product that claims to
meet a particular need. Many project managers are often concerned with the issue of
quality versus price, that is, what quality is available for a given price, or how much
extra better quality would cost. Consequently, another example is in deciding what
investment tradeoffs are worth making in order to improve the quality of a given software system or product. In many cases, what we really want to do is predict what our
own level of satisfaction with the software will be, before we have had the chance to
exercise the software extensively in a particular context (Gentleman, 1996). This comes
up both when the software is unfamiliar to us, and when it is not yet complete.

Software quality is often defined in terms of fitness of the product for its purpose.
Different people however, have different purposes for the same software. A casual user
is probably more concerned about ease of learning and about robustness against misuse
rather than efficiency. On the other hand, a system integrator planning to incorporate
the software into some larger system might be more concerned about failure detection
and recovery than ease of installation. The point being made is that quality is many-
sided, and the importance of the different facets changes with the context, even for the
same person at different points in time. As an example, most users would agree that
they want secure software, that is, software free from defects, including viruses.
Users want applications that provide safe manipulation of data, meaning that the user
understands when data is changing due to the actions of the software. However,
the consequences of providing absolute software security may cause the product to
be deemed less attractive (i.e. usable) to one class of user versus another class of user.
The common 'are you sure you want to...' prompt is source of much derision for the
'sophisticated' user but the neophyte user can take great comfort from this extra little
bit of security. This may seem like a trivial point, but it is a simple example of how
quality standards should be judged within the context of the user population.

The way in which user perceptions influence quality is shown in Figure 6.1. The
illustration also shows some of the many other ways in which quality can be
influenced. According to Gentleman (1996) what matters is the importance placed on
quality between user and provider (the project team). Lists of attributes that quality
software must address have been known for some time (see, for example, Keller *et al.*,
1990), and many of these attributes seemingly address user needs. Some of the attributes identified include:

- How secure is it?
- How confident are users of its performance?

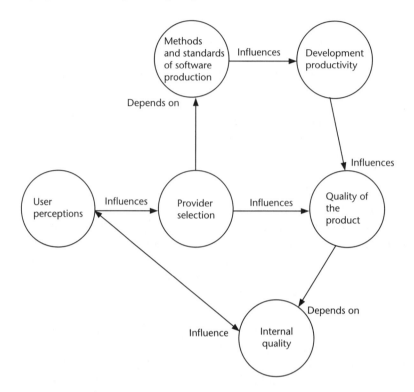

Figure 6.1 Software product quality influences

- Does it degrade smoothly under adverse conditions and is it easy to use?
- Does it conform to the requirements?
- Is it easy to maintain?
- Can its performance be verified easily?
- Can its performance be expanded easily?
- Is the data easy to change?
- Does it interface well with other systems?
- Is it portable?
- Is it easy to convert for use to another application?
- How well does it utilize resources?

Software Quality Characteristics

Many of the above attributes are explicit in various quality standards. As an example, the International Standard ISO/IEC 9126 (Software Quality Characteristics and Metrics), offers a model based on the work of Gilb and Boeham that lists six characteristics: functionality, reliability, efficiency, usability, portability and maintainability. This decomposition reflects the viewpoint of users and introduces the concept of quality in use: users are mainly interested in *using* the software product, and evaluate software mostly from the viewpoint of the performance and the service it provides, rather than on the basis of internal aspects or the development process. ISO/IEC 9126 suggests a further decomposition of each characteristic into a set of sub-characteristics. These sub-characteristics are a step closer to the quantitative, technical aspects of the software product. The way in which the major characteristics of ISO/IEC 9126 can be broken down further is described in the following sections.

1. Functionality

This is described as a set of attributes that bear on the existence of a set of functions and their specified properties. The functions are those that satisfy stated or implied needs.

- *Suitability*. Attributes of software that bear on the presence and appropriateness of a set of functions for specified tasks. Examples for appropriateness are task-oriented composition of functions from constituent sub-functions, capacities of tables.
- *Accuracy*. Attributes of software that bear on the provision of right or agreed results or effects (Sanders and Curran, 1994).
- *Interoperability*. Attributes of software that bear on its ability to interact with specified systems. Interoperability is used in place of compatibility in order to avoid possible ambiguity with replace-ability.
- *Compliance*. Attributes of software that make the software adhere to application-related standards or conventions or regulations in laws and similar prescriptions.
- *Security*. Attributes of software that bear on its ability to prevent unauthorized access, whether accidental or deliberate, to programs and data.

2. Reliability

This is described as a set of attributes that bear on the capability of software to maintain its level of performance under stated conditions for a stated period of time.

- *Maturity*. Attributes of software that bear on the frequency of failure by faults in the software.
- *Fault tolerance*. Attributes of software that bear on its ability to maintain a specified level of performance in cases of software faults or of infringement of its specified interface. The specified level of performance includes fail safe capability.
- *Recoverability*. Attributes of software that bear on the capability to re-establish its level of performance and recover the data directly affected in case of a failure and on the time and effort needed for it.

3. Usability

This is described as a set of attributes that bear on the effort needed for use and on the individual assessment of such use by a stated or implied set of users.

- *Understand-ability*. Attributes of software that bear on the users' effort for recognizing the logical concept and its applicability.
- *Learn-ability*. Attributes of software that bear on the users' effort for learning its application (for example operation control, input, output).
- *Operability*. Attributes of software that bear on the users' effort for operation and operation control.

4. Efficiency

This is described as a set of attributes that bear on the relationship between the level of performance of the software and the amount of resources used under stated conditions.

- *Time behaviour*. Attributes of software that bear on response and processing times and on throughput rates in performing its function.
- *Resource behaviour*. Attributes, of software that bear on the amount of resources used and the duration of such use in performing its function.

5. Maintainability

This is described as a set of attributes that bear on the effort needed to make specified modifications.

- *Analyse-ability*. Attributes of software that bear on the effort needed for diagnosis of deficiencies or causes of failures, or for identification of parts to be modified.
- *Change-ability*. Attributes of software that bear on the effort needed for modification fault removal or for environmental change.
- *Stability*. Attributes of software that bear on the risk of unexpected effect of modifications.
- *Testability*. Attributes of software that bear on the effort needed for validating the modified software. Note: values of this sub-characteristic may be altered by the modifications under consideration.

6. Portability

This is described as a set of attributes that bear on the ability of software to be transferred from one environment to another.

- *Adaptability*. Attributes of software that bear on the opportunity for its adaptation to different specified environments without applying other actions or means than those provided for this purpose for the software considered.
- *Install-ability*. Attributes of software that bear on the effort needed to install the software in a specified environment.
- *Conformance*. Attributes of software that make the software adhere to standards or conventions relating to portability.
- *Replace-ability*. Attributes of software that bear on opportunity and effort of using it in place of specified other software in the environment of that software.

Replace-ability may include attributes of both install-ability and adaptability. The concept has been introduced as a sub-characteristic of its own because of its importance.

Information system requirements are usually categorized as functional and non-functional. As discussed in Chapter 3, functional requirements address what the software can do, while non-functional requirements are concerned with the overall qualities of the system. The attributes discussed above are of a non-functional nature. In carrying out system development projects, a number of problems have been identified with non-functional requirements which the project manager should pay attention to (see, for example, Kontonya and Sommerville, 1998):

- Some non-functional requirements are related to a design solution that is unknown at the requirement stage.
- Some non-functional requirements are highly subjective, especially those associated with human engineering.
- Non-functional requirements have great diversity.
- Non-functional requirements and functional requirements are related methods that separate them out and make it difficult to see the correspondence between them.
- Non-functional requirements tend to conflict and therefore need to be treated as tradeoffs.

Many of the issues listed above can be seen in structured methods, such as SSADM, which places great emphasis on capturing functional requirements, supported by techniques such as data flow diagramming, data modelling, and a requirements catalogue. Although non-functional requirements are dealt with in SSADM there is no systematic approach to capturing them, no method support, and no mechanism for trading off conflicts between them.

Resource characteristics

The development of software products does not take place in a void and quality can not be supported without some measure of resource allocation. Gilb (1988) has highlighted four resource attributes that impact upon the quality and ongoing improvement of software development. These are time, people, money and tools.

1. Time resource is of two types: calendar time to deliver and the time taken by the system once developed to carry out a task.
2. People resources may be measured in terms of person-months. This, however, is a relatively broad-brush approach since people resources are often limited by skill shortages. In such cases, the availability of a skill becomes a critical attribute.
3. Money resources concern both development and maintenance costs. Financial budgets tend to limit what can be achieved in the software life cycle process.
4. Tool resources include all physical resources that are required to deliver the product and these are not limited to development tools.

It should be recognized that in any one application, it will be a small subset of attributes that will provide the critical constraints rather than all the factors considered here.

Metrics

Not all these software characteristics have equal weighting with respect to metrics. Watts (1987), for example, identified some 40 individual software metrics. Some 34 of these metrics are associated with the criteria of Maintainability (18), Reliability (12) and Usability (4). This uneven distribution of metrics seems arbitrary and calls into question the validity of any given metric. As an example, complexity is used as a handle on both reliability and maintainability, and 13 measures are described as based upon complexity.

Table 6.2 lists a variety of metrics that can be considered useful when examining aspects of quality.

Table 6.2   Some useful data metrics

Size
Total lines of code written
Total comment lines
Total declarations
Total blank lines

Productivity
Number of work hours spent on the project
Number of work hours spent on each routine
Number of times each routine is changed

Defect tracking
Severity of each defect
Location of each defect
Way in which each defect is corrected
Person responsible for each defect
Number of lines affected by the defect correction
Number of work hours spent correcting each defect
Amount of time required to find a defect
Amount of time required to fix a defect
Number of attempts made to correct each defect
Number of new errors resulting from each defect correction

Maintainability
Number of parameters passed to each routine
Number of routines called by each routine
Number of routines that call each routine

Table 6.2   Continued

Number of decision points in each routine
Control flow complexity of each routine
Lines of code in each routine
Lines of comments in each routine
Number of data-declarations in each routine
Number of go-tos in each routine
Number of input/output statements in each routine

Overall quality
Total number of defects
Number of defects in each routine
Average defects per thousand lines of code
Mean time between failures
Number of compiler-detected errors

Another ISO standard, ISO 9241-11, explains how quality in use can be measured in terms of user performance and satisfaction by the extent to which the intended goals of use are achieved. This standard includes the resources that have to be expended to achieve the stated and intended goals, and the extent to which the user finds the use of the product acceptable. Measures of user performance and satisfaction assess the quality in use of a product in the particular context of use provided by the rest of the working environment.

According to Bevan (1997), in order to specify or measure quality in use, it is necessary to decompose effectiveness, efficiency and satisfaction and the components of the context of use into sub-components with measurable and verifiable attributes. Measures of effectiveness relate the goals, or sub-goals, of the user to the accuracy and completeness with which the goals are achieved. In contrast, measures of efficiency relate the level of effectiveness achieved to the expenditure of resources. As discussed previously, relevant resources will include time, people, money and tools. Measures of satisfaction describe the comfort and acceptability of the use of the product.

A word of caution is required here. Care should be exercised in generalizing the results of any measurement of quality in use to another context, which may have significantly different types of users, tasks or environments. The specification of measurement of the quality in use of a particular product should identify:

- the characteristics of the users;
- the users' goals, the relevant context of use, (including the tasks and resources involved); and
- the measures of effectiveness, efficiency and satisfaction, which are chosen, as being relevant to the goals identified.

Quality management frameworks

An attempt to put metrics on a systematic level has been made by the European METKIT (Fenton, 1991) project. The use of metrics to measure criteria is part of an overall framework that includes quality control and assurance, quality models, reliability models, and performance evaluation. Over the years, a number of quality frameworks have been developed to enable organizations (including suppliers of software services) to measure and improve their product offerings to customers. At an organization level the most widely adopted are ISO 9000 (and TickIT at the individual project level) and the Capability Maturity Model (CMM).

The ISO 9000 framework

The International Organisation for Standardisation's (ISO) 9000 is a series of quality assurance standards with application for any business, whether in manufacturing, service, retail, or government, in producing a product or service. Popular in Europe, ISO 9000 is rapidly taking hold in the United States and around the globe. Some 60 countries, including the United States, Canada, Japan, and the members of the European Community have adopted ISO 9000 series standards. Table 6.3 lists the components of ISO 9000. As shown by the table, the ISO 9000 framework is a deep, vertical quality system. That means that it creates a system that tracks and controls a consistent set of factors involved in quality and service to the customer.

Table 6.3 Components of ISO 9000

Standard	Description
ISO 9000	*Quality management and quality assurance standards – Guidelines for selection and use* (1987)
ISO 9000–1	Revision of ISO 9000 (1991)
ISO 9000–2	*Guidelines for the application of ISO 9001, ISO 9002 and ISO 9003* (1991)
ISO 9000–3	*Guidelines for the application of ISO 9001 to the development, supply and maintenance of software* (1991)
ISO 9001	*Quality systems – Model for quality assurance in design/development, production, installation and servicing* (1987) A more detailed standard, which covers design, development, production, installation, and servicing, this applies to the software industry
ISO 9002	*Quality systems – Model for quality assurance in production and installation* (1987) Assesses the production and installation processes
ISO 9003	*Quality systems – Model for quality assurance in final inspection and test* (1987) Evaluates the final inspection and test phase
ISO 9004	*Quality management and quality system elements – Guidelines* (1987) Defines the 20 fundamental quality system concepts included in the three models

ISO 9001 is applicable in situations in which there is a substantial element of design. In situations in which design is predefined then ISO 9002 provides a focus on production. Where there is little or no production, then ISO 9003 is applicable. The ISO 9000 standard family requires that whatever process is chosen for development should be understood and documented and should be monitored to ensure it is actually used.

Organizations using this framework should have gone through a three-tier accreditation process that involves self-assessment, customer assessment and a third party assessment by an independent standards body. ISO 9000 is a powerful incentive for organizations to get their quality procedures right. Accreditation is a powerful evidence of this fact (see The ISO audit process).

From the information contained in Table 6.3, it is clear that ISO 9000 is intended to be generic so that it can serve a broad range of organizations. However, ISO 9001 is intended for applications where there is a significant design element. Since most software applications require significant design input, ISO 9001 is generally the standard applied within the software development industry. Figure 6.2 shows the overall scope of ISO 9001.

The 20 elements of ISO 9001

The 'Quality System Requirement' (Section 4) of ISO 9001 has 20 clauses which stipulate the conduct for a good quality management system. They are:

4.1 Management responsibility
4.2 Quality system
4.3 Contract review
4.4 Design control
4.5 Document control
4.6 Purchasing

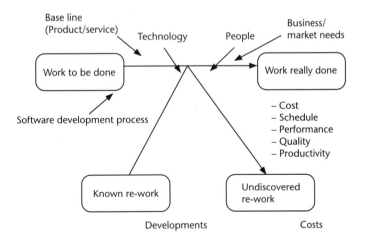

Figure 6.2 Abridge The Scope of ISO 9001

4.7 Purchaser supplied product
4.8 Product identification and tractability
4.9 Process control
4.10 Inspection and testing
4.11 Inspection, measuring and test equipment
4.12 Inspection and test status
4.13 Control of non-conforming product
4.14 Corrective action
4.15 Handling, storage, packaging and delivery
4.16 Quality records
4.17 Internal quality audits
4.18 Training
4.19 Servicing
4.20 Statistical techniques

The 20 elements together are deeply interrelated and satisfaction of all the elements creates an integrated, certifiable working quality system. Yet, a quality system that meets all the requirements in the standard does not guarantee a quality product, but should ensure that a product's quality level is repeatable. It is this repeatability that is at the heart and intent of ISO.

Crucial to the interpretation of these elements are a few key words. Probably the most important is 'shall'. In sections containing 'shall' the standard requires the company to address the issue but leaves the methodology to each individual company. Other, less restrictive phases include 'where practical', 'where appropriate', and 'other suitable means'. All these statements leave considerable leeway for the company to adapt the standards to fit the organization's current practices. The key management responsibilities are listed below.

- Establish a quality policy, including objectives for quality and the company's commitment to quality.
- Ensure the quality policy is understood, implemented, and maintained at all levels of the organization.
- Establish a quality infrastructure with appropriate responsibilities and authority.
- Identify the requisite verification resources and personnel.
- Appoint a management representative with executive responsibility to:
  – ensure that an ISO 9001-compliant methodology is established, implemented, and maintained; and
  – report to the company's management on the performance of the methodology.
- Establish a partnership with the customer to:
  – achieve continuous feedback;
  – ensure compliance of the software to the customer's agreed requirements specification; and
  – verify and accept test results.
- Conduct and document periodic reviews of the methodology.

Table 6.4 provides examples of the guidance provided by ISO 9001. Notice how the terms highlighted in the previous paragraph are used (e.g. 'shall').

Table 6.4 An example of the type of guidance provided by ISO 9001

ISO 9001:1994	**Clause 4.2 Quality systems** This clause covers the structure of the quality system of the organization and its documentation. It follows that a well-planned and managed quality system has to be defined and documented. This is dealt with by quality plans (e.g. which may include procedures, work instructions, as well as formal quality plans, etc.) and quality manual sub-clauses. The quality system should be documented in enough detail so that employees, suppliers and customers can understand it and that it can be audited (see Clause 4.17). **Clause 4.2.1 – General** This clause requires that the company has a quality manual as an essential part of the quality system. It also requires that the documented procedures are referenced from the manual. This means that a quality manual is now mandatory and must reference all the operating procedures either directly from the text or through a cross-reference matrix or table, etc. **Clause 4.2.2 – Quality system procedures** This clause requires that procedures are consistent with quality policy and that they are appropriate to the level of complexity of the processes involved and the skills and training required. The documented procedures must be relevant to the stated quality policy. **Clause 4.2.3 Quality planning** This clause states that the supplier *shall* define and document how the requirements for quality will be met. Quality planning shall be consistent with all other requirements of a supplier's quality system and shall be documented in a format to suit the supplier's method of operation.
Related ISO 9000–3:1997 guidance includes	Quality planning should address the following items, as appropriate: (a) quality requirements, expressed in measurable terms. where appropriate; (b) the life cycle model to be used for software development; (c) defined criteria for starting and ending each project phase; (d) identification of types of reviews, tests and other verification and validation activities to be carried out; (e) identification of configuration management procedures to be carried out.
Related ISO 9004–1 guidance includes	ISO 9004–1 guidelines suggest that: • You should control your products. Your quality system should control every phase of your product's life cycle. • You should control quality. Your quality system must monitor and control every aspect of quality. Any activity, function, or process that influences quality must be monitored and controlled.

Table 6.4 Continued

- You should provide the resources that your people will need to implement and maintain your quality system.
- You should use a quality manual. It should describe your quality system.
- Your quality manual should be used to guide the implementation and maintenance of your quality system.
- Your quality manual must also include a procedure that controls how the manual's contents will be revised and updated.
- Your quality system procedures and instructions should support, and be tied into, your quality manual.
- You should have quality plans. A plan should be developed for every product, process, project, or contract. It should define the:
  1. Quality objectives that must be achieved.
  2. Practices, processes, procedures, programmes, methods, resources, and equipment that will be used to achieve these objectives.
- You should encourage continuous quality improvement. Your quality system should create an environment that supports continuous quality improvement. An environment of continuous improvement is one that encourages everyone to improve the efficiency and effectiveness of all activities and processes for the benefit of both the organization and its customers.
- You should measure the financial effectiveness of your quality system and consider using one of the following methods:
  1. The quality–cost approach.
  2. The process–cost approach.
  3. The quality–loss approach.
  The quality–cost approach divides costs as follows:
  1. *Investments*, which are divided into:
     Prevention costs. This is money spent trying to prevent quality system failures and non-conformities.
     Appraisal costs. This is money spent on testing, inspection, and quality system reviews, evaluations, and audits.
  2. *Losses*, which are divided into:
     Internal failures. This is money spent dealing with products, that failed to meet quality requirements, before they are sold.
     External failures. This is money spent dealing with problematic products after they have been sold to customers.
  The process–cost approach selects a process, and then figures out what it costs to serve the needs of its customers. It divides costs as follows:
  1. *The cost of conformity.* This adds up all the money spent ensuring that the process continues to work properly.
  2. *The cost of non-conformity.* This adds up all the money that must be spent because the process fails to work properly.
  The quality–loss approach focuses on losses that are caused by poor quality. It divides losses as follows:
  1. *Tangible losses.* These are losses that result from re-work, repair, warranty work, and so on.
  2. *Intangible losses.* These are losses due to lost opportunities, systemic inefficiencies, and so on.

Table 6.4 Continued

	• You should prepare financial quality reports. These reports should be prepared and submitted to senior management, and should: 1. Discuss the effectiveness of your quality system. 2. Identify quality system weaknesses and problems. 3. Formulate quality and cost objectives.
ISO 9001: 1994	**Clause 4.16 Quality records** The requirements of this clause are that you must keep records, which prove that you have met all of the requirements of the standard. In some cases, this may include records from, or kept by, your subcontractors. Your procedures must ensure that the records are: • identified • readily retrievable • kept safe and free from damage or deterioration • retained for a defined period (this may vary for different types of record) • disposed of in a specified manner (thrown away, shredded, etc.) Where you agree with your customers to release records to them, you must identify who is responsible for the control of these actions. For your information, records include: • training records • drawings • specifications • inspection reports • goods-receiving notes • quality manual and procedures • policies • instructions • manuals • purchase orders • delivery notes • calibration records • sales orders • order acknowledgements • quotation forms • plans • etc.
Related ISO 9004–1 guidance includes	**You should develop a quality record keeping system.** Your system should control documents such as those listed above

The quality assurance process within ISO

ISO defines quality assurance (QA) as all those planned and systematic actions necessary to provide adequate confidence that an entity will fulfil requirements for quality. In its narrowest sense, QA is concerned with the production of consistent products (that is, software) that conforms to specification. The project manager's responsibility at the individual project level is to operate within the ISO framework and to take corrective and preventative action to ensure that the product meets the required specification. To this end the key project management tasks are listed below.

- Establish and maintain documented procedures for implementing corrective and preventive action. Procedures include:
  - the handling of customer complaints;
  - the investigation of non-conformities;
  - the sources of information used to detect, analyse, and eliminate potential non-conformities; and
  - the determination of action needed to deal with problems requiring corrective action.
- Analyze quality records and information to detect and eliminate deficiencies.
- Apply controls to ensure appropriate, effective, and timely corrective and preventive actions (problem tracking).

Some organizations establish independent QA teams to monitor and control their software processes. Such teams are usually made up of both functional and business experts. Some project managers see such teams as a direct threat and the ensuing conflict can end up destroying the ethos of QA. In such situations, QA becomes nothing more than a bureaucratic overhead. This aside, the benefit of incorporating QA is that it helps to eliminate or mitigate the non-value-added cost for software revisions, rework, and inconsistent project QA. This is achieved by opening up communication horizontally across traditional project boundaries by clarifying what to do and how to do it. Table 6.5 highlights key areas of non-conformance in software projects and software organizations.

The ISO audit process

The audit process is divided into two major activities. The first is the adequacy or desk audit and the second is the compliance audit. During the desk audit, auditors compare the company's documented system with the requirements of the standard. They are looking for the system to meet the fundamentals of the 20 ISO elements.

This initial audit produces an audit report, and as a result of this audit report – assuming all is well – the decision is made to proceed with the second part of the audit. During the compliance audit, auditors are on site talking to staff, asking questions about what they do and how they do it, what documents they have to use, what records they maintain, and who has all of this material. During the course of the audit, questions are asked of staff at all levels in the organization. The auditors will be following a pre-determined plan, an advance copy of which will be given to the area's management representative. Each auditor is accompanied by a guide whose job is to escort the individual from place to place, and to help the

Table 6.5   Areas of non-conformance

Non-conformities – macro level
1. Failure to audit the organizations quality management systems.
2. Failure by the organization to take quick and corrective action on quality issues.
3. Failure to establish procedures for planning and implementing internal quality.
4. Lack of management responsibility to carry through quality initiatives.
5. Lack of understanding of quality policy by project managers.
6. Lack of documentation to support the stated quality policy.
7. Unclear definition of how internal quality procedures will be adopted.
8. Unclear definition of how training will be conducted within the organization, department or project.
9. Project quality not tied into business drivers or key performance indicators.
10. Lack of adoption within the project rank and file.

Non-conformities – micro level (McCabe *et al.*, 1992)
1. Incomplete or erroneous errors
2. Deviation from requirements
3. Erroneous logic
4. Violation of programming standards
5. Erroneous computations
6. Documentation
7. Improper interruptions
8. Invalid testing
9. Wrong constant or data values

auditor identify the person they need to speak to about the issues they wish to examine.

Project managers should answer questions honestly, but should only answer what is asked. Lots of notes are taken during the audit – these are the audit findings. Most of what the auditor writes down will be about activities that they have found to be compliant with the standard and the documented system. Some will be things that are not right, and these may become audit non-conformances by the end of the process. Everything that is reported as a non-conformance will be supported by 'objective evidence'. In other words, the auditor has to be able to reference a clear requirement of either the standard or the management system which is not being followed in order to write a non-conformance. The guide signing off on them witnesses findings. At the end of the audit, the audit team will decide what they want to report and what they do not. This results in the audit report and findings which are issued to the company, together with the decision as to whether the system is regarded as acceptable or not.

Every area of the company can expect to receive non-conformances. The site being audited may contain many hundreds, even thousands, of people, documents, instruments needing to be calibrated, stock items and materials and so on. The auditors are likely to find a few things out of place in every facility and it does not matter if they do. A number of minor non-conformances will not impact the ability of any company to achieve certification. The auditors will assess the overall effectiveness of the system. The key issues which the auditors will be reviewing and seeking objective evidence of compliance for are:

- Are all the required elements of ISO 9001 in place?
- Is there clear evidence that staff know their role in operating the system?
- Are records generated as required and stored properly?
- Is the internal audit process robust and effective?
- Is there an adequate resource and effective corrective and preventive action programme in place?
- Is the management review process solid and operating effectively?

During the internal audit training, which all companies implementing ISO will need at some stage, the trainee auditors will learn more about what to look for and how to evaluate the significance of an individual finding. This information will be utilized in the operation of the internal audit programme and should help resolve a lot of these issues for the staff. The audit is nothing to fear: it is a collaborative, cooperative process...and you are the customer. Once the main audit is successfully completed, surveillance audits will take place on a regular basis, every six months or so. On a sample basis, auditors will revisit various parts of the company for short follow-up audits to ensure that the system remains fully operational. These surveillance audits will usually encompass a sample of activities. Typically, one or two elements of the ISO 9001 standard will be addressed in addition to the mainstream elements. There are three subjects, which typically get audited every time the auditors come around:

4.1.3 Management Review. The records of this process demonstrate that the system is being properly and effectively maintained.
4.1.4 Corrective and Preventive Action. This element demonstrates that the company is reacting to problems and identifies through either product, process or system review activities. A good corrective and preventive action process means that the system is being highly reactive and proactive to continuously improve.
4.17 Internal Audit.

The third item falls into the same category, but is exclusively system related. The internal audit activity, and the records it generates, tells the registrar if the system is operating successfully in between surveillance audits and is driving continuous improvement. Probably the biggest change that occurs as a result of the ISO 9001 implementation is the initiation of the internal management system audit process. This is one of the most powerful tools a company can use for driving continuous improvement – it also happens to be the one that costs the least. An effective internal audit process also enables management to measure its own effectiveness in controlling the operation of the company in the manner intended. Constant reviews of the workings of the management system reveal opportunities for improvement in the system, in the training of personnel, and in overall process control. Along with management review, the effective maintenance of the internal audit programme is a vital part of the system. Both activities should take place at regular intervals if management seriously intends to maintain the system. The internal audit process will be an ongoing activity, continually auditing different parts of the system and covering all areas of the organization on an established basis. Areas of the company where the audit findings are adverse should receive more frequent audits until such time as the audit results stabilize. Important activities should also be audited more frequently.

Acceptance

The primary purpose of applying the ISO 9000 framework is the confidence it will afford prospective clients, management, and development personnel that the organization's system for managing software quality is efficient, effective and measurable. According to Alan Gillies (1996), however, one of the biggest barriers to acceptance of ISO (particularly ISO 9001) amongst information technology practitioners is its generic nature and its origins as a manufacturing standard. Although ISO 9001 has been applied in many service industries, many information technology people still feel it is inappropriate and difficult to apply. The response to this from the standards bodies is to issue notes for guidance on the application of the standard to software development (an example of such guidance was given in Table 6.4). It should be stressed that these do not supersede the standard, but rather amplify its contents with the aim of explaining how the standard should be applied in a software context.

The TickIT system

In 1991 the British Standards Institute (BSI) introduced TickIT into the quality vocabulary. TickIT uses the checklist approach to gather detailed information on quality related processes. The aim of the TickIT system is to assist the take-up of ISO 9001 by the information technology sector and ensure that suppliers, purchasers and assessors have an overlapping understanding of the requirements in the IT sector. TickIT is a certification scheme developed to apply ISO 9000, but with the advantage of having been tuned to deal with special requirements of software development. Its main principles and objectives are:

- the interpretation of ISO 9001 for the information technology sector;
- the need to ensure continuing conformity for certified suppliers;
- the necessity to perform assessments with experienced and skilled assessors as witnessed by their ability to satisfy examiners;
- the benefit of accredited training and examination for entrants on the assessor register.

The TickIT Guide emphasizes the establishment of a 'delivery chain' from supplier to customer by means of a quality management system, which is documented, implemented and audited. *The TickIT Guide* includes the following information:

1. Purchaser's Guide.
2. Supplier's Guide.
3. Auditor's Guide.

The Supplier's Guide is aimed at software sector organizations requiring ISO 9001 certification and also includes guidance on the standard's application to support and service activities. *The TickIT Guide* provides background to the TickIT scheme, including its origins and objectives, how to implement a quality system and the expected structure and content relevant to software activities.

Independent assessment of an organization's quality system against ISO 9001 provides confirmation that it has achieved a base line level of performance for its quality-related processes and practices. In the UK, all recognized (accredited) certification bodies are required to perform an ISO 9001 assessment in the software sector under the TickIT scheme, which ensures the use of trained and experienced IT auditors and recognizes the guidance provided by ISO 9000–3 and *The TickIT Guide*.[1]

Maximizing the benefits from TickIT

In 1996, over 1000 IT and software organizations have achieved certification under the TickIT scheme.[2] Although generally viewed as a certification scheme, this is not its primary purpose. The main objectives are to stimulate information technology organizations to think about how they can benefit from a quality system and how quality performance may be achieved.

Certification is an end process which seeks to confirm that whatever the organization declares as necessary to their quality system is put into use and is effective. In doing so, certification assures that the appropriate parts of the quality system standard are addressed satisfactorily. The quality system provides a means of ensuring that quality is delivered. It determines how requirements are processed as input and how these are transformed into products and services. By its presence or absence, the quality system has a direct influence on the quality of product and service. Although, it is easy to measure the effectiveness of such programmes in terms of the number of firms achieving certification, it is sometimes less easy to quantify the overall effect upon software quality. ISO and TickIT share a common goal with quality. Each is driven by similar concerns and intuitively correlated.

The Capability Maturity Model (CMM)

No discussion on software quality is complete without a review of the Software Engineering's Institute's (SEI) Capability Maturity Model and its effect on both process and project management. The Software Engineering Institute, situated at

Carnegie Mellon University in Pittsburgh, PA, was established in 1984 to research issues associated with software development, quality and other items related to defence contracts. The SEI approach is based on an assessment process aimed at evaluating the capabilities of defence contractors providing software development services to the Department of Defense. Assessment data is then used to categorize an organization's software delivery practice in one of five levels (stages) that define process maturity and capability. These levels are known as the Capability Maturity Model.

Humphrey (1989), an IBM Software Engineer, established the process maturity framework on the quality principles of Deming and Crosby. This work became the basis for improving an organization's software process. Process improvement realized at each stage provides the basis for improvement possible at the next stage, which, in turn, becomes a guideline for continuous process improvement. The SEI has evolved the CMM to focus on product quality through a maturity framework that includes five basic steps. Like ISO 9000, these steps must have full management sanction and commitment to:

1. establish basic management control;
2. set quality standards;
3. define the process;
4. measure and evaluate;
5. institute continuous process improvement.

The CMM Model

The CMM is a five-level model that attempts to quantify a software organization's capability to constantly and predictably produce high-quality software products. The model is designed so that capabilities at lower stages provide progressively stronger foundations for higher stages. Each development stage or maturity level distinguishes an organization's software capability. For each maturity level there are associated key process areas (KPAs). The KPAs identify the requirements for achieving each maturity level. Level 1 does not include KPAs since it is the starting point. Table 6.6 shows the maturity levels and their associated KPAs.

Defining maturity

In essence, each of the maturity levels outlined in Table 6.6 is a well-defined step towards achieving a mature software process. Each maturity level provides a layer in the foundation for continuous process improvement. Each level comprises a set of goals that, when satisfied, will stabilize an important component of the software process. Achieving each level of the maturity framework establishes a different component in the software process, resulting in an increase in the process capability of the organization. What is important here is the organization's understanding of the level of commitment and focus required for achieving levels of maturity. This commitment must be supported and encouraged by both managers, and software professionals.

Table 6.6 CMM level framework

SEI CMM Definition	KPAs
1. Initial The processes are special and mostly defined. Success depends upon the individual effort	None
2. Repeatable Basic project management processes to track cost, schedule and functionality. Tools are in place to repeat success achieved on analogous programmes	1. Requirements management 2. Software project planning 3. Software project tracking and oversight 4. Software subcontract management 5. Software quality assurance 6. Software configuration management
3. Defined The software process is organization-wide and is employed by both management and engineering. The process is documented, standardized and integrated	7. Organisation process focused 8. Organization process definition 9. Training programme 10. Integrated software management 11. Software product engineering 12. Intergroup coordination 13. Peer reviews
4. Managed The detailed measures of the software process are collected, managed, quantified, understood and controlled	14. Quantitative process management 15. Software quality management
5. Optimized The software process continuously improves by quantified feedback from the process and testing new and creative ideas and technologies	16. Defect prevention 17. Technology change management 18. Process change management

Otherwise, the ability to realize process maturity goals will be sporadic at best and probably unattainable. Those characteristics identified with immature and mature organizations are summarized in Table 6.7.

Recent work undertaken by SEI[3] indicates that the potential for process improvement is significant and possible at any level of the CMM. The current state of maturity in the applications delivery area offers suppliers with an integrated process and project management solution an opportunity to provide both products and services to a growing number of organizations initiating software process improvement. A recent organization maturity profile is shown below in Table 6.8.

Table 6.7   Characteristics of mature vs immature organizations

Immature	Mature
Over budget	Proactive disciplined/consistent
Late delivery	Defined processes
Undefined processes	Defined roles
Reactive	Consistent monitoring
Crisis management	Predictive results
Poor quality	On time/within budget
Overworked/confused staff	Enabled staff
Unsatisfied customers	Satisfied customers
	Good communications
	Processes institutionalized
	Information systems viewed as strategic

The above statistics would indicate that 68 per cent of software organizations have immature software processes that are hardly followed. Project managers tend to focus on solving immediate crises, such that product functionality and quality are often compromised to meet a schedule. There are checkpoints built into the process between project initiation and project completion. In a defined organization level 3 project management has a good insight into the technical progress on all projects. Even within a project, management can monitor progress and verify that costs, schedules and functionality are on track and to plan. As with level 3, in a managed organization, management has a clear view of what goes on within the software development process. However, project management has the additional visibility of quantitative data and can benefit from analysis of quantitative measured results. At the optimized level, project management can not only monitor and measure what goes within various processes, but also supports an environment in which greater efficiencies are continually identified and implemented. Improvements may come incrementally through innovations or by applying new technologies or methods.

Key process areas

A KPA contains the goals that must be reached in order to improve a software process. A KPA is said to be satisfied when procedures are in place to reach the

Table 6.8   Levels of maturity

Maturity level	Process characteristic	Percentage of organizations
Initial	Chaotic	68.80
Repeatable	Disciplined	18.00
Defined	Constant	11.30
Managed	Predictable	1.50
Optimising	Continuously improving	0.40

corresponding goals. These key indicators offer an insight into whether the goals have been satisfied. When an organization collectively performs the activities defined by the KPAs, it can achieve goals considered important for enhancing process capability. A software organization can only claim to have reached a given maturity once all corresponding KPAs are satisfied.

A key process area for Level 2: repeatable software quality assurance (SQA)

The purpose of software quality assurance is to provide management with appropriate visibility into the process being used by the software project and of the products being built. Software quality assurance involves reviewing and auditing the software products and activities to verify that they comply with the applicable procedures and standards and providing the software project and other appropriate managers with the results of these reviews and audits. The software quality assurance group works with the software project during its early stages to establish plans, standards, and procedures that will add value to the software project and satisfy the constraints of the project and the organization's policies. By participating in establishing the plans, standards, and procedures, the software quality assurance group helps ensure they fit the project's needs and verifies that they will be usable for performing reviews and audits through-out the software life cycle. The software quality assurance group reviews project activities and audits software work products throughout the life cycle and provides management with visibility as to whether the software project is adhering to its estab-lished plans, standards, and procedures (Paulk, 1993).

Compliance issues are first addressed within the software project and resolved there if possible. For issues not resolvable within the software project, the software quality assurance group escalates the issue to an appropriate level of management for resolu-tion. This key process area covers the practices for the group performing the software quality assurance function. The practices identifying the specific activities and work products that the software quality assurance group reviews and/or audits are generally contained in the Verifying Implementation common feature of the other key process areas.

Goal 1 Software quality assurance activities are planned.

Goal 2 Adherence of software products and activities to the applicable standards, procedures, and requirements is verified objectively.

Goal 3 Affected groups and individuals are informed of software quality assurance activities and results.

Goal 4 Senior management addresses non-compliance issues that cannot be resolved within the software project.

Top level activities associated with software quality assurance (SQA)

Within CMM SQA the activities of preparing, reviewing and auditing the SQA plan are mandatory. Interactions on preparing a SQA plan are provided in Table 6.9. Once the SQA plan is complete, it should be attached to the software development plan (SDP).

Table 6.9 Key inputs and outputs

Key inputs	Process	Key outputs
Software Development Plan (see note)	Outline applicable software Development phases Identify major milestones and target completion dates	Software Development plan Audit reports
Key Milestones Software Metrics	Prepare SQA plan Undertake SQA reviews Issue SQA audit reports	

Original worksheets, revisions, estimates, and any other associated information needed should also be retained for reference.

Milestones should be used in the SQA plan to mark critical activities, required reviews, important points in the project, and completion dates. The information contained in the work breakdown structures should be used to assist in identifying precise and measurable milestones for the project. Table 6.9 shows an example of this approach.

Metrics:

Prepare Monthly SQA Report (track planned Vs actual number of SQA activities, for example: processes not followed, processes not documented, standards not followed etc;).

Prepare Weekly SQA Report.

From the SDP the SQA team identify which reviews will occur and the purpose for them. The team should distinguish what will be reviewed in each phase. The team will also identify how the products reviewed will be audited and who will attend the reviews. Deviations identified in the software activities and software products should be documented and handled according to the specified procedures. A SQA audit report is submitted when a phase is completed or when a problem is found. Audits should be undertaken at each level of the software cycle, for example at requirements, design, build, configuration management, unit testing and system integration testing phases.

CMM assessments

The CMM provides both internal and external assessments. Key indicators form the basis for the Software Engineering Institute's maturity questionnaire used to assess the capability of software organizations' internal processes. This assessment questionnaire contains 120 questions, where repeatable and defined levels contain about 40 questions each and managed and optimized levels contain about 20 questions each. Furthermore, a profile template is used which lists each KPA, such that they can be checked as not satisfied, partially satisfied, or fully satisfied. As stated earlier, an organization maturity level is set at the highest level at which it satisfies all KPAs. The following are the six phases of an assessment (Saiedian, Hossein and Kuzara, 1995):

1. In the selection phase, the organization is identified as an assessment candidate, and the qualified assessing organization conducts an executive-level briefing.
2. In the commitment phase, the organization commits to the full assessment process whereby a senior executive signs an assessment agreement.
3. In the preparation phase, the organization's assessment team receives training, and the on-site assessment process is fully planned. All assessment participants are identified and briefed. The maturity questionnaire is completed at this time by the organization.
4. In the assessment phase, the on-site assessment is typically conducted in a week. The assessment team then meets to formulate preliminary recommendations.
5. In the report phase, the entire assessment team helps prepare the final report and present it to the organization's assessment participants and senior management. The report includes team findings and recommendations for actions.
6. In the assessment follow-up phase, the assessed organization's team, with guidance from the independent assessment organization, formulates an action plan. After approximately 18 months, it is recommended that the organization have a reassessment in order to assess progress and sustain the software process improvement cycle.

In essence, CMM's capability evaluation has the same objective as ISO 9000's third party audits. Both have been developed to check the overall capability of a software organization to produce software in timely, repeatable fashion. The only difference is that in a CMM capability evaluation, a software organization is ranked according to the five levels, and in an ISO 9000 audit, a software organization is checked to see that it follows a given set of standards. Although some quality managers see the CMM as technically over-engineered, a CMM-compliant quality system is in many respects much more advanced than an ISO 9000-compliant system. ISO 9000 establishes a minimum quality programme for a software organization. The CMM establishes a continuous improvement focus. Whereas ISO 9000 deals with issues of quality control and quality assurance, the CMM talks about the maturity of the process. Table 6.10 maps the relationship between CMM and ISO 9001.

Table 6.10 Summary of mapping between ISO 9001 and CMM

ISO 9001	CMM relationship	CMM judgemental relationship
Management responsibility	Commitment to perform Software project planning Software project tracking Software quality assurance	Ability to perform Verifying implementation Software quality management
Quality system	Verifying implementation software project planning Software quality assurance Software product engineering	Organization process definitions

Table 6.10   Continued

Contract review	Requirements management Software project planning	Software subcontract management
Design control	Software project planning Software project tracking Software configuration management Software product engineering	Software quality management
Document control	Software configuration management	
Purchasing	Software subcontract management	
Control of consumer-supplied product		Software subcontract management
Product identification and tractability	Software configuration management Software product engineering	
Process control	Software project planning Software quality assurance Software quality engineering	Quantitative process management Technology change management
Inspection and testing	Software product engineering Peer reviews	
Control of inspection measuring, and test equipment	Software product engineering	
Inspection and test status	Software product engineering	
Control of non- conforming product	Software configuration management Software product engineering	
Corrective and preventative actions	Software quality assurance Software configuration management	Defect prevention
Handling, storage, packaging, preservation, and delivery		Software configuration management and software product engineering
Control of quality records	Software configuration management Software product engineering Peer reviews	

Table 6.10 Continued		
Internal quality audits	Verifying implementation Software quality assurance	
Training	Ability to perform training programme	
Servicing		
Statistical techniques	Measuring and analysis	Organization process definition; quantitative process management; software quality management

Reported benefits of CMM

The literature seems to indicate that, although an ISO 9001–3 compliant organization would not necessarily satisfy all the level 2 key process areas, it would satisfy most of the level 2 goals and many of the level 3 goals. Because there are practices in the CMM that are not addressed in ISO 9000, it is possible for a level 1 organization to receive 9001 registration. Similarly, there are areas not addressed in the CMM, for example a level 3 organization would have little difficulty obtaining ISO 9001 certification, and a level 2 organization would have significant advantages in obtaining certification.

In reviewing the literature, we could find no evidence of British software organizations who had achieved full level 3 status. Consequently, we have cited examples of CMM benefits reported in USA Journals.

Increased productivity vs decreased cost

Contractors have reported an increase in productivity due to the improvement of their software development process (Saiedian, Hossein and Kuzara, 1995). As an example, Dion (1994) states that: 'Raytheon yielded a twofold increase in its productivity and a ratio of 7.7-to-1 return on its improvement expenditures, for savings of $4.48 million during 1990 for a $0.58 million investment'. Various organizations have realized benefits from maturing from one level to the next. In some cases, productivity has increased from as little as 2.5 per cent to as much as 130 per cent: 'Published studies of software engineering improvements measured by the CMM indicate significant cost savings or profit return. This implies that software testing and maintenance costs were reduced, since the software better met verification and validation requirements.'[4] Some organizations showed savings of $2 million to $3.4 million in project dollars. Contractors have also experienced a decrease in rework, code problems, and re-testing costs.

Increased on-time deliveries

It is generally accepted that higher CMM levels lead to better quality software products and therefore a better company reputation. CMM compliance may also change the manner in which a company interacts with its customers because there are stringent requirements for maintaining a high maturity level. Highly rated organizations are more adept at handling quick demands by the customer. Fortunately, compliance leads to higher quality software at lower cost (Budlong and Peterson, 1996). Also compliance improves a company's reputation, which should be a very potent ingredient for winning and maintaining contracts.

Increased quality

Participating companies are looking at meeting their quality goals, meeting their requirements, building a maintainable product, and seeking better and improved quality as well as stabilizing schedule, meeting commitments, and accelerating or reducing schedule. Several software organizations have experienced a reduction in defects that ranged from as low as 10 per cent to as high as 80 per cent. One organization reported a 45 per cent decrease in its reduction error rate, while two more organizations' product error rates decreased from 2.0 to 0.11 per thousand source lines of code and from 0.72 to 0.13 per thousand non-commented source statements (Brodman and Johnson, 1996).

Summary

- The International Organisation for Standardisation defines quality as: 'The totality of features and characteristics of a product or service that bear on its ability to satisfy specified or implied needs'.

- The expectations of different stakeholders will influence the way in which quality is perceived. As an example, users will view quality differently to developers.

- The key elements of software quality can be described in terms of Functionality, Reliability, Efficiency, Usability, Portability and Maintainability.

- The ISO 9000 framework creates a system that tracks and controls a consistent set of factors involved in quality and service to the customer. The framework is based around an auditing process that takes into account a wide variety of factors, such as the handling of customer complaints and procedures for managing records.

- The TickIT scheme was developed by the British Standards Institute as a means of interpreting ISO 9001 for the information technology sector. The scheme uses a series of checklists in order to assist with the auditing process.

- The Capability Maturity Model gathers data that can be used to categorise an organization's software delivery practice in one of five levels (stages) that define process maturity and capability. This is an extremely popular model that has a number of benefits associated with it, such as increased productivity and increased quality.

Bibliography

Barker J., 1992, *Future Edge: Discovering the paradigms of success*, William Morrow and Company Inc., New York.

Bevan N., 1997, *Quality and Usability: A New Framework*, Tutein Nolthenius, Netherlands.

Brodman J. and Johnson D., 1996, 'Return on Investment from Software Process Improvement as Measured by U.S. Industry', in *CrossTalk*, April 1996, pp. 23–29.

Budlong F. and Peterson J., 1996, 'Software Metrics, Capability Evaluation Methodology and Implementation', in *CrossTalk*, January 1996, pp. 15–19.

Dion R., 1994, 'Process Improvement and the Corporate Balance Sheet', in *CrossTalk*, February 1994, pp. 7–15.

Duran J., 1988, *The Quality Control Handbook*, 4th edn, McGraw-Hill.

Fenton N., 1991, *Software Metrics: A rigorous approach*, Chapman and Hall.

Flood R.L., 1993, *Beyond TQM*, John Wiley and Sons, London.

Gentleman W., 1996, 'The Quality of Numerical Software: Assessment and Enhancement', in Boisvert R. (ed.), *The Proceedings of IFIP WG2.5 Working Conference 7*, Oxford UK, 7–12 July 1996, pp. 32–43.

Gilb T., 1988, *Principles of Software Engineering Management*, Addison-Wesley.

Gillies A. (ed.), 1996, *Case Studies in Software Engineering*, SUBSL.

Humphrey W., 1989, *Managing the Software Process*, Addison-Wesley Publishing Company.

ISO 9000–3 (2nd edn 12–15–1997) (Guidelines for the application of ISO 9001:1994 to the development, supply, installation and maintenance of computer software).

Juran J., 1988, *The Quality Control Handbook*, 4th edn, McGraw-Hill, USA.

Keller S. *et al.*, 1990, 'Specifying Software Requirements with Metrics', in Thayer and Dorfman (eds), *Tutorial System and Software Requirements Engineering*, IEEE, Computer Society Press.

Kontonya G. and Sommerville I., 1998, *Requirements Engineering, Process and Techniques*, John Wiley and Sons.

McCabe T. *et al.*, 1992, 'The Parato Principle Applied to Software Quality Assurance', in *Handbook of Software Quality Assurance*, Van Nostrand Reinhold Company Inc., New York.

McManus J., 2000, 'Quality Meets Process Improvement', in *Management Services Journal*, Issue 5 (May), pp. 14–16.

Paulk M., 1993, *Capability Maturity Model, Version 1.1*, Software Engineering Institute, Carnegie Mellon University, Pittsburgh, Pennsylvania.

Saiedian, Hossein and Kuzara, 1995, 'SEI Capability Maturity Model's Impact on Contractors', in *IEEE Computer*, January 1995, pp. 16–25.

Sanders J. and Curran E., 1994, *Software Quality, a Framework for Success in Software Development and Support*, Addison-Wesley.

SEI, 1996, 'Process Maturity Profile of the Software Community', in *Organisation Maturity Profile of the Software Community: 1996 update*.

The TickIT Guide (A Guide to Software Quality Management System Construction and Certification to ISO 9001, Rev. Issue 3.0).

Watts R., 1987, *Measuring Software Quality*, NCC, Blackwell.

Further reading

ANSI/IEEE Std 830-1984, *IEEE Guide for Software Requirements Specifications*, The Institute of Electrical and Electronics Engineers, Inc., 1984.

Bevan N., 1992, 'Quality and Usability: A new framework', in van Veenen-daal E. and McMullan J., (eds), 1997, *Achieving software product quality*, Tutein Nolthenius, Netherlands.

Cooper C. and Woolgar S., 'Software quality as community performance', in Mansell R. (ed.), 1994, *Management of Information and Communication Technologies*, Aslib.

Cringley R., 1992, *Accidental Empires*, Penguin.

Daly-Jones O., Thomas C. and Bevan N., 1997, *Handbook of User Centred Design*, National Physical Laboratory.

Useful websites

http://www.tickit.org/
This site provides you with the following information about TickIT: overview of TickIT, its objectives and how it operates, free quarterly journal which aims to keep readers up to date with certification issues, standards development and process improvement methods.

http://www.iso.ch/iso/en/ISOOnline.frontpage
Prime website for information relating to ISO software standards. The site contains lots of information and advice.

http://www.sei.cmu.edu/cmm/cmm.html
The Software Engineering Institute (SEI) runs this website. The SEI offers many ways for you to learn about the Capability Maturity Model for software and is a very useful source of information.

http://www.elsevier.nl/inca/publications/store/3/0/4/3/5/index.htt
The *International Journal of Project Management* offers wide-ranging and comprehensive coverage of all facets of project management.

Self-assessment exercises

1. How does the International Organisation for Standardisation define quality?

2. Six basic characteristics are associated with software quality. What are these characteristics?

3. Which ISO standard is applicable to situations where there is little or no production?

4. Which ISO standard is normally applied to the software development industry?

5. The ISO audit process is divided into two major parts. What are these parts?

6. By 1996, over 10,000 IT and software organizations had achieved certification under the TickIT scheme. True or false?

7. The Capability Maturity Model uses five levels of process maturity. List these levels in order of least mature to most mature.

8. Approximately 40 per cent of software organizations have immature software processes that are hardly followed. True or false?

9. As a result of adopting CMM, some organizations have experienced a reduction in defects of up to 80 per cent. True or false?

10. There are six phases in the CMM assessment process. Describe what takes place during the select and preparation phases.

11. During the course of an ISO compliance audit, questions are only asked of project managers, team members and customers. True or false?

12. As a result of adopting CMM, some organizations have reported productivity increases of up to 130 per cent. True or false?

Case study

Managing computer projects in the National Health Service (NHS)

This case study is chosen from the public sector, and is based on the report: *Managing Computer Projects in the National Health Service*. The report highlighted the need for higher standards of project management and quality assurance. Typical shortcomings identified in the report were:

- Inadequate training of staff including competency.
- Inadequate quality reviews.
- Inadequate quality assurance.
- Inadequate standards.
- Inadequate auditing.
- Inadequate planning.
- Inadequate and flawed contractual arrangements.

- Inadequate cost control.
- Inadequate feasibility studies.

In many of the projects examined there were no identified project manager, no quality assurance arrangements, poor specification of requirements, and no forward planning. In particular the report found that there had been a failure to involve key managers and users. In addition there was little attention paid to best practice and procedures such as ISO 9000. The principal recommendations of the report were:

- Introduce a more structured approach to project management (such as PRINCE).
- Improve training programmes for project managers and support staff.
- Improve the quality of project reviews and introduce more frequent check points.
- Increase the visibility of projects through NHS Information Management Centre (IMC) communication channels.

Approach to project management

Several NHS bodies had already undertaken work on project management and training, so the NHS IMC felt maximum use should be made of this existing material, and the various NHS groups concerned should be involved in any programme which promulgated a structured approach. In deciding how it should go about promoting such an approach, the NHS IMC had discussions with a major UK training company about adapting the company's CCTA PRINCE-approved project methodology. The objectives of the exercise were then to promote the need for project management within the NHS and cascade the relevant project management knowledge and skills down the organization. The aims of this programme were to provide comprehensive, balanced support and training for the following:

- Risk management.
- Project controls.
- Quality reviews.
- Quality assurance.
- Configuration management.

The approach developed to achieve these objectives was a series of structured workshops, promotional videos and an information tutorial pack (including case material). The workshops focused on the core principles of delivering projects under a quality umbrella, that is it concentrated on and provided coverage for all the relevant framework elements needed for compliance to the ISO 9000 series quality standards (as discussed in Chapter 6).

Training programmes

To support this new project management culture it was decided to develop a single overall competency model as a way of responding to the NHS's rapidly changing requirements. These models identified the skills required and how they would be provided and assessed. To achieve this overall programme the following goals were established:

- In line with ISO 9000-1, identify target development projects.
- Create project performance standards.
- Carry out skills assessment.
- Carry out training programme.
- Set goals and review.

To gauge whether the competency levels were realistic a questionnaire was used to assess all target project team members. This provided valuable feedback to determine which areas needed immediate attention and determine the speed and direction of project management implementation and provide a base line for ongoing measurement. The activity was coordinated by the NHS IMC and concentrated on the following elements of ISO 9001:

4.1 Management responsibility.
4.2 Quality system.
4.3 Contract review.
4.14 Corrective action.
4.16 Quality records.
4.17 Quality audits.
4.18 Training.

Quality audits

The basic principles of project management explained in the workshops included the importance of undertaking periodic quality audits (which have now become common elements of the new NHS project management culture). It was recognized that this was a good mechanism for protecting and building on the investment made in ISO 9000 and PRINCE. These project quality audits became mandatory (once every three months) and focused on What?, When?, Who?, Where?, Why? and How? Any lessons learned were fed back through IMC in the form of reports and were also used for future training programmes, new skills and on the job training.

Managing Computer Projects in the National Health Service, 1991, National Audit Report, National Audit Office, London, UK

Questions

1. Explain the importance of software metrics to project delivery.
2. Define five characteristics of software quality.
3. Explain how ISO 9000 can be applied to improve the success of project delivery.

4. Define the critical components of ISO 9000.
5. Explain the key differences between ISO 9000, CMM and TickIT.
6. Explain the importance of training to successful implementation of ISO 9000, CMM, and TickIT.

Notes

1. ISO 9000-3 (Second Edition 15 December 1997) (Guidelines for the application of ISO 9001:1994 to the development, supply, installation and maintenance of computer software).
2. *The TickIT Guide* (A Guide to Software Quality Management System Construction and Certification to ISO 9001, Rev. Issue 3.0).
3. SEI, 'Process Maturity Profile of the Software Community'. *Organisation Maturity Profile of the Software Community: 1996 update.*
4. Source: Esprit project 27699 – SITAR (Software Integration Testing Automatic Review), ESSI Process Improvement Experiment, GEC Marconi Avionics, Rochester, England, 1998.

INDEX